Ways of Being Free

COSTERUS NEW SERIES 194

Series Editors:
C.C. Barfoot, László Sándor Chardonnens
and Theo D'haen

Ways of Being Free

Authenticity and Community in Selected Works of Rushdie, Ondaatje, and Okri

Adnan Mahmutović

Amsterdam-New York, NY 2012

Contents

WAYS OF BEING FREE: INTRODUCTION

Postcolonial criticism in the Anglo-American academia has invested much value in the generation of Anglophone immigrant authors "writing back to the imperial centre", as Salman Rushdie put it.[1] In a conversation with Catherine Bush, Michael Ondaatje talks about such writers as "my generation", which "was the first of the real migrant tradition that you see in a number of writers of our time – Rushdie, Ishiguro, Ben Okri, Rohinton Mistry – writers leaving and not going back, but taking their country with them to a new place".[2] Such a "generation" exceeds definition through alignment along geographical, cultural, national, and religious boundaries. They form an alternate kind of community based in their shared anxiety about their postcolonial history in the contemporary world. Although they are uprooted, their anxieties still link them to their specific histories in which they struggle to articulate who they are as individuals and communities, and what they need to do in what Homi Bhabha called "the ambiguous history of the present".[3] Their writing back is also directed to the homes they left, the margins of the former empire as well as the political centre. This double writing back to the centre and the margin deflates both filiation and political affiliation, and constitutes these writers' way of being free.

From the "writing back" generation, which is otherwise dominated by the subcontinental writers, due to their strong connection to the former British empire, Rushdie, Ondaatje, and Okri have received an indelible exposure to critical attention, especially after their winning of the Man Booker Prize in the 1980s and 90s. Using the label of the "Third World Cosmopolitan", even Meenakshi Mukherjee foregrounds them as representatives of their generation who have enjoyed "favourable reception in the global centres of publication and

---

[1] Salman Rushdie, *Imaginary Homelands*, London: Penguin Books, 1991, 49.

[2] Catherine Bush, "Michael Ondaatje: An Interview", *Essays on Canadian Writing*, Toronto: ECW Press, 1994, 240.

[3] Homi K. Bhabha, *The Location of Culture*, London: Routledge Classics 2004, xix.

criticism".[4] Their novels – in particular *Midnight's Children* (1981), *The English Patient* (1993), and *The Famished Road* (1991) – have been praised as challenging and innovative contributions to critical negotiations of their postcolonial histories. These novels are clearly reactions to the turbulent historical pasts that the authors feel connected to, the pasts characterized by overwhelming ideological transformations and conflicts, the splitting and re-aggregating of identities, the struggle for independence and cultural preservation, and the dissolution of traditional communities in the wake of nation-building as well as inter-national wars. In Europe and the USA, they have been viewed as the insiders who not only have the right to represent and speak on the behalf of their native histories, but who can do it as outsiders that can observe things in a different light. A great deal of postcolonial criticism (Bhabha, Ashcroft, Griffiths, Tiffin, Brennan, and even Chakrabarty) has developed through negotiation with the literary and critical production of such postcolonial writers, in particular Rushdie, whose *Midnight's Children* holds the position of the paradigmatic postcolonial text. Rushdie is perceived as the epitome of a self-made man who defines himself against the grain. Like his character Saleem, he is a mock representative of an age.[5]

It is precisely because these authors have become functionally canonized icons of postcolonial literature that I want to go back and re-examine the whys and hows of their focus on history. Regardless of the epistemological and ontological issues that dominate critical discourse on these writers, they convey a sense of history that hurts, to

---

[4] Meenakshi Mukherjee, "The Home and the World: The Indian Novel in English in the Global Context", in *Anglistentag 1993 Eichstätt: Proceedings of the Conference of the German Association of University Teachers of English, XV*, eds Günther Blaicher and Brigitte Glaser, Tübingen: Niemeyer, 1994, 146.

[5] Clark Blaise claimed "*Midnight's Children* sounds like a continent finding its voice" (Clark Blaise, "A Novel of India's Coming of Age", *New York Times Book Review*, 19 April 1981, 19. Anita Desai said that Rushdie had "a voice that everyone present recognized instantly as being the voice of a new age: strong, original and demanding of attention" (See Anita Desai, "Introduction", in *Midnight's Children*, London: Everyman's Library, 1995, vii). Tariq Ali noted that while "Rushdie's novel will not reach the South Asian masses ... it will be read by an English speaking intelligentsia ... and, in that sense, it is extremely important" (Tariq Ali, "*Midnight's Children*", *New Left Review*, CXXXVI [November-December 1982], 91). Brennan praises Rushdie's criticism of nationalism and cynical vision of his origins (Timothy Brennan, *Salman Rushdie and the Third World: Myths of the Nation*, London: Macmillan, 1989).

use Frederic Jameson's qualification.[6] In the novels, history is not simply emptied of meaning, even though the nature and provenance of this meaning is in question or under negotiation. Rather there is an excess of meaning that inundates the characters, an excess that does not seem to be a rich source of intellectual inquiry for cultural eclectics, but a burden. Indeed, the writers' overarching concern with postcolonial histories arises from a deep desire to be freed from this complex burden, however it may be articulated.

Their histories have developed in a complex relation to the ideal of freedom, in particular political freedom from colonial authority and postcolonial political blocs and divisions of the world into three worlds. They were all, as Ondaatje says to Bush, a part of "that colonial tradition of sending your kids off to school in England", yet they have taken their home countries with them.[7] They use their education in the canons of the colonizer to counter the racist ideologies that deny their authenticity. Although they have been born after or escaped revolutions, they have received double legacies related to long histories and traditions of liberation (from colonialism, despotism, fascism, or patriarchy). Freedom becomes a strong common agenda that stands out despite the authors' differences. Rushdie, for instance, builds his entire narrative around the "midnight hour of freedom",[8] one of the most politically charged moments in South Asian history. Okri wrote his novel about postcolonial liberation to show that "the age demands that each man and woman become a light, a fire, a responsible heir to all the veins of freedom and courage that have enabled us all to get here".[9] Ondaatje broadens the scope of the history of freedom and conquest by creating a community of characters from four different continents, suggesting that freedom is a global issue despite the specificities of local histories in which liberation struggles take place.

Since "being-free" can mean many things, depending on the historical context of its experience and expression, and can in fact even be used to obscure forms of non-freedom, it becomes vital to analyse exactly what ways of being free these authors really explore,

---

[6] Fredric Jameson, *The Political Unconscious: Narrative as a Socially Symbolic Act*, London: Routledge, 1989, 102.
[7] Bush, "Michael Ondaatje: An Interview", 240.
[8] Rushdie, *Imaginary Homelands*, 26.
[9] Ben Okri, *A Way of Being Free*, London: Phoenix, 1997, 102.

or even advocate. In the novels, the desire for freedom takes different
turns, and yet there is a common undercurrent, which is marked by the
struggle of the characters to dismantle dogmatic beliefs, blindly
accepted ethical norms and ideologies. Various characters rework
their individualities in terms of communal action that arises as the
direct response to both authoritative and diffused power. Authoritative
power, as Michael Mann explains, "comprises definite commands and
conscious obedience", whereas diffused power "spreads in a more
spontaneous, unconscious, decentred way through a population,
resulting in similar social practices that embody power relations but
are not explicitly commanded".[10] In *Infinite Riches*, a sequel to *The
Famished Road*, Okri refers to this particularly salient dark other of
freedom as ideology:

> The air resounded with the clash of their myths and ideologies ....
> Their different kinds of music fought one another in their hidden
> ideologies and world-views .... They sang of death and power,
> conquest and courage.[11]

What all three novelists show is that the diffuse power is most
dangerous when embodied in social practices, which then appear to be
a matter of necessity and natural law, and when the betrayal of these
feels like a betrayal of oneself. When the central characters discover
that certain behaviour is a matter of a long tradition that has never
been examined, as Azaro does when he refutes the abiku cycles, they
appear as copies. Rushdie – who has famously been in conflict with
religion for decades – uses Islam as the paradigm of acquiescence and
submission. Ondaatje's characters too define themselves as anti-
religious (except for Kip). Okri, on the other hand, argues with Bel
Mooney about the import of devout scepticism, a "form of spirituality
[that] is different from religion. One has to do with an institution and
the other with the self's quest for the highest meaning that life can
offer."[12] For him, freedom is not incompatible with faith. Rather, faith
can serve to express the full richness and potential of historical reality,

---

[10] Michael Mann, *The Sources of Social Power*, Cambridge: Cambridge University
Press, 1986, I, 6.
[11] Ben Okri, *Infinite Riches*, London: Phoenix, 1998, 195-96.
[12] Bel Mooney, "Mixing It", *New Internationalist*, 370 (2004): http://www.newint.
org/features/2004/08/01/devout-scepticism/.

rather than being neutralized into a mere consciousness or pole of general normative relations.[13]

In response to variegated forms of oppression, their characters struggle for a creative engagement with inherited ways of being in the world and alternate ways of communal bonding. In *Mental Fight*, Okri writes about the need to "Open up history of horrors", to "turn around and face them / The bullies that our pasts have become",[14] and the need to clear out "the garbage / In our histories and our consciousness / ... / our grim ancient fears".[15]

These authors are not primarily concerned with the question of being rather than knowing, ontology rather than epistemology. I assume that they, like Frantz Fanon, begin with the question "Who am I in reality?"[16] But to ask what one is, is to ultimately examine how one is. Rushdie asks, what are

> ... the consequences, both *spiritual and practical*, of refusing to make any concessions to Western ideas and practices? What are the consequences of embracing those ideas and practices and turning away from the ones that came here with us? These questions are all a single, existential question: How are we to live in the world?[17]

---

[13] He does not attack religion wholesale, but systems of dogmas and power hierarchies: "Have all thoughts, possibilities, ideas, / Philosophies been exhausted? / Has Christianity found its fullest / Fruition in great cathedrals, charities, / Schisms, wars, orthodoxies, / And sundry creeds? / ... / Have Buddhism, Taoism, Hinduism, / Islam, Humanism and Existentialism / All the spiritual aspirations of the race / ... / Have they all been richly realised / Fully mined and made to serve / And ennoble and feed humankind? / I don't think so either" (Ben Okri, *Mental Fight: An Anti-Spell for the 21st Century*, London: Phoenix House, 1999, 27).

[14] *Ibid.*, 9.

[15] *Ibid.*, 8.

[16] Frantz Fanon, *The Wretched of the Earth*, tr. Richard Philcox, New York: Grove Press, 2004, 182.

[17] Rushdie, *Imaginary Homelands*, 18. Philip Tew suggests that one of Rushdie's "great strengths as a writer is to approach existential questions head on. It is, in a secular vein, to engage with what are often thought to be religious experiences but are perhaps equally well understood as existential experiences: anxiety, doubt, fear, conscience, death, figuring out who and what one should do, to which story one belongs, how one fits, or refuses to fit that shape and shaping: issues of truth and ethics" (Philip Tew and Rod Mengham, *British Fiction Today*, London: Continuum, 2006, 96).

The existential question of "how" is the question of freedom and action, that is, not just the ideas, but equally practices. Rushdie, as well as Ondaatje and Okri, show that a way of being free comes to the fore through active engagement, and as soon as one upholds certain principles that are too abstract, one fails to act. Action, as Okri shows when he dramatizes a number of fights between characters, is dependent on the specific contents of concrete situations, even when the lessons drawn from such fights tend to have abstract meaning as well. When the characters' worlds offer no opportunity for action, but rather only for acting out, individual reality or authenticity comes to be about asking what is to be done and doing it.

Authenticity: points of departure
Grappling with a subject as large, and with as much historical baggage, as authenticity appears to be akin to the proverbial endeavour of the five blind men to describe an elephant.

These authors appear to engage with at least two strong branches in the understanding of authenticity and freedom. The first is cultural essentialism, nativism, or what Rushdie calls communalism. The second is modern individualism, which dominates that which Charles Taylor labels the Western "culture of authenticity".[18] Taylor's phrase entails that the desire for personal freedom has a long history and that it has become a part of a generalized ethos, albeit too wide and vague. Stretching back to the European Romantics, and even to Socratic thought, the philosophical and political idea of authenticity reached its peak in the period around the Second World War with the projects of Sartre, Heidegger, Camus, and not least Fanon who has shown that colonial histories rework what seem to be exclusively Western discourses and concerns. Despite the specific differences between thinkers who were reluctant to be labelled existentialists, as well as the differences between the selected authors, common concerns emerge: the issue of existence in contrast to ideal essences; the idea that one is thrown into a world not of one's own choosing; the argument that one's essence is created through concrete action in this world; the focus on *angst* as that which arises when one's world breaks down, and which then reveals a factuality of freedom and even an obligation to take responsibility for one's actions.

---

[18] Charles Taylor, *The Ethics of Authenticity*, Cambridge, MA: Harvard University Press, 1992, 72.

An analysis of my selected novels yields resonances with existentialist thought, which cannot be overlooked by anyone who understands the influences of this heterogeneous movement on the post-Second World War culture. Existential thought, in particular that of Sartre, enters the postcolonial discourse by way of Fanon, whose discourse on political violence, national formation, national culture, uprooting from the past, the focus on action and the issue of community resonates in my selected fictions. When Ondaatje evokes the specific phrase "nervous condition", he practically acknowledges his Sartrean/Fanonian inspiration.[19] When Okri devotes an entire trilogy to exploring roads of freedom of "the wretched of the earth",[20] he is not only reacting negatively to the Road of destiny from the Igbo mythology, but also draws on Rousseau's "highway" motif from *Emile*, and Sartre's trilogy *Roads of Freedom*.[21] Rushdie's Saleem uses Heidegger's expression "being-in-the-world", and he practically ends his narrative by telling us he is descending into *Jahannum* like Dante, which turns out not to be some fire pit, but rather: "Hell is other people's fantasies."[22]

Sartre's and Camus' fictions dealt with estrangement and strangeness. These postcolonial narratives develop around characters who are indeed in conflict with the norms, habits and orthodoxies of their times, but moreover, they are practical aliens in their worlds. These characters present strangeness quite impossible to appropriate in any given system of thought, belief, or practice. This impossibility of full assimilation rockets their existential concerns much further. The worlds and characters in the novels have several levels of reality which disturb epistemological and even ontological paradigms that still hold sway in existential fiction. When Josna E. Rege argues that *Midnight's Children* follows a European paradigm of "bleak

---

[19] Jean-Paul Sartre, "Introduction", in Fanon, *The Wretched of the Earth*, liv.

[20] Okri, *Infinite Riches*,161.

[21] In *An African Elegy*, Okri writes: "The anguish from the arteries / Of the streets / Is spreading our hunger / From here to a new highway. / ... / Upon these times smash our lies. / Bare us to our naked highways. / Thundershine lights the fields: / We can reclaim our lives" (Ben Okri, *An African Elegy*, London: Jonathan Cape, 1992, 26).

[22] Salman Rushdie, *Midnight's Children*, 1981, London: Everyman's Library, 1995, 488 and 577.

existentialist novels",[23] the parallel is correct only to a certain point. If existential literatures, as well as philosophical and political thought, are responses and articulations of *angst* that arises from some particular histories, these postcolonial novels seem to show that the histories they are responding are at least as extreme as those of their European counterparts.

These and many more connections, similarities, or parallels are not cemented, fully categorized and structured. There are a number of intersections and some overlapping, as well as distinct differences. The similarities entail certain influences that are not binding, but serve as steppingstones. These postcolonial writers have taken from Europe some powerful notions and reworked them in their own ways, in relation to their own histories. To try to pry them apart is to ignore postcolonial hybridity, not only in Asia and Africa, but also in Europe itself. To call existentialism Western is to ignore that Fanon, Camus and to a certain extent Sartre emerged in relation to French colonial and postcolonial history, or Heidegger's eastern influences. Just as Sartre is right in claiming, "'All is lost unless ...' I, a European, am stealing my enemy's book and turning it into a way of healing Europe",[24] it is equally valid for these authors to use European thought as the indispensable-inadequate tool in reworking the experiences of political modernity in post-colonial states.[25] Finally to argue that postcolonial writers should not articulate their concerns in existential terms is to deny their drive to write back.

These writers are not simply or exclusively addressing those with whom they have racial, national, cultural or even political ties, but also all those who are connected to them through the history of colonialism. When Okri reminds "us" of "the veins of freedom",[26] the "us" seems broader than Nigerians or even Africans, including the

---

[23] Josna E. Rege, "Victim into Protagonist? *Midnight's Children* and the Post-Rushdie National Narratives of the Eighties", in *Critical Essays on Salman Rushdie*, ed. M. Keith Booker, New York: G.K. Hall, 1999, 189.

[24] Fanon, *The Wretched of the Earth*, xlix.

[25] As Michael R. Michau argues, it is not only the *zeitgeist* of existential philosophy that shaped Fanon, in fact, he "chose his conceptual tools for the same reason his European contemporaries chose theirs: because of the type of the problems that concerned them" (Michael R. Michau, "Fanon and a Radical Phenomenology of Responsibility", in *Department of Philosophy Graduate Student Colloquium*, Purdue University, February 2003, 4).

[26] Okri, *A Way of Being Free*, 102.

audiences that are most likely to encounter his discourse, in English or in translation. In "To an English Friend in Africa", he spurs this "friend" to be "grateful for the freedom / To see other dreams" and "not think [her] way superior".[27] He evokes recognizable Romantic discourse: "Learn to be what you are in the seed of your spirit / Learn to free yourself from all the things / That have moulded you / And which limit your secret and undiscovered road."[28] The familiar Romantic call for the liberation of one's true spirit, and the shedding of skins that are like old hand-me-down clothes – similar to Ondaatje's explorers' desire to "remove the clothing of [their] countries"[29] – is for Okri a seed, and not merely a Romantic dogma. He wants "us" to "transform our monsters",[30] and use old illusions to "free us from our smallness, / 'Our humiliated consciousness', as Camus said".[31]

Authenticity as a way of being free is articulated with respect to both social oppression and conceptions of what freedom means and how it is practised. To begin with, it is a common claim that the colonizers did not simply exploit natural resources and domestic labour, but also propounded their own culture as superior to the myriad of different local cultures that existed prior to colonization. The result was, as Bhabha has argued, a "'loss' of meaningfulness in cross-cultural interpretation", which then gave rise to "a hermeneutic project for the restoration of cultural 'essence' or authenticity".[32] Struggling against the colonial powers, the indigenous populations often took recourse to their original beliefs and practices as sources of empowerment. A demand to preserve the old traditions and communal models – as the bulwark against the remaining political and cultural imperialism – was indeed part and parcel of the emergence of new nations such as India and Nigeria. When the overtly authoritative power of the colonizer was replaced by a more diffuse form that worked under the veneer of freedom and independence, the most acute question was which aspects of the current social structures of the liberated peoples were unspoiled, pure, original – authentic. Despite

---

[27] Okri, *An African Elegy*, 82.

[28] *Ibid.*, 83.

[29] Michael Ondaatje, *The English Patient*, London: Picador, 1993, 139.

[30] Okri, *An African Elegy*, 9.

[31] *Ibid.*, 5.

[32] Bhabha, *The Location of Culture*, 179.

the value of communalism in the initial stages of liberation, as Fanon has argued, they are transitional and translational phases. Yet, such desires came to artificially sediment certain cultural values, entailing readymade decisions on the specific forms and contents of true ways of being.

Rushdie has found it necessary to address this issue even in his essays. He uses Gramsci's words to argue that "the old was [still] dying", but since the entirely new has not been born, "there arises a great diversity of morbid symptoms" which are due to nationalism's racist tendencies.[33] For instance, many Indo-Anglian writers evinced a desire to describe Indian culture in exclusive Hindu terms. They ignored "all minority communities", and used "a technique of alienation". They called the Muslims Mughals and "foreign invaders", deeming their culture "imperialist and inauthentic".[34] Similar "communalist forces" gained dominance in Pakistan. Rushdie's great worry became a cultural Puritanism advocated by "the goblins of sectarianism",[35] who argued that some ethnicities were no more Indian than the British invaders. The questions of legitimacy, belonging and authenticity topped the entire mountain of historical troubles and concerns.

Rushdie expresses how bizarre it is to be tied to different cultures, races, peoples and politics, and yet also to fall between them.[36] As Matt Kimmich shows, Rushdie's "authenticity as an Indian writer" has been questioned by both critics and Indian writers (for instance Richard Cronin and Feroza F. Jussawalla).[37] In some cases, as in the conflict between the Muslims and the Hindus, the bone of contention is religion, but it also became a matter of class when the Muslims became more prosperous (Saleem versus Shiva, rich Muslim versus poor Hindu). Class has been redefined in racist and ethnic terms. Rushdie proposes that the current "most dangerous pitfall" is "to confine ourselves within narrowly defined cultural frontiers" of given communities, and so enter a "form of internal exile, which in South

---

[33] Rushdie, *Imaginary Homelands*, 1.
[34] *Ibid.*, 2.
[35] *Ibid.*, 3.
[36] *Ibid.*, 15.
[37] Matt Kimmich, *Offspring Fictions: Salman Rushdie's Family Novels*, Amsterdam and New York: Rodopi, 2008, 5.

Africa is called the 'homeland'".[38] Rushdie articulates these "politics of religious hatred",[39] through Aadam Aziz:

> He was teaching them to hate, wife. He tells them to hate Hindus and Buddhists and Jains and Sikhs and who knows what other vegetarians.[40]

While the midnight's children generation is "too young to remember the Empire or the liberation struggle",[41] they are not cut off from the past. Rather, since they do not fully grasp the colonial past, they are even more under the sway of the communalist forces.

The political rhetoric of nativism, according to Vincent John Cheng, has spread throughout the globe and has become an important political force and problem in most "modern and contemporary cultures".[42] The "exclusionary urge" of nativism resulted "in both discursive and actual practices of 'ethnic cleansing'",[43] which is the type of consequences that figures strongly in *Midnight's Children*.

Fanon too maintained that the colonized peoples must resist the urge to prove their equality and justify their existence by pitting their "long historical past" against the colonizer, because "I am not a prisoner of History":

> I must not look for the meaning of my destiny in that direction. I must constantly remind myself that the real *leap* consists of introducing invention into life. In the world I am heading for, I am endlessly creating myself. I show solidarity with humanity provided I can go one step further .... And it is by going beyond the historical and instrumental given that I initiate my cycle of freedom.[44]

Like Fanon, the authors I study dramatize a certain will to disburden themselves of the past, but not simply in the sense of

---

[38] Rushdie, *Imaginary Homelands*, 19.

[39] *Ibid.*, 27.

[40] *Ibid.*, 50.

[41] *Ibid.*, 26.

[42] Vincent John Cheng, *Inauthentic: The Anxiety over Culture and Identity*, New Brunswick, NJ: Rutgers University Press, 2004, 3.

[43] *Ibid.*, 173.

[44] Frantz Fanon, *Black Skin, White Masks*, tr. Richard Philcox, New York: Grove Press, 2008, 204-205 (emphasis in the original).

complete abandonment or a form of postcolonial amnesia. As Okri argues with Jane Wilkinson:

> ... the facts of history alone are not enough to give an account of our consciousness and what we need to do with our age. We are in a very, very interesting age: we could go either way. We could go towards destruction still and we could go towards the greatest stage of creativity yet.[45]

Okri asks for creative remembering, which is a transformation of the past into new possibilities. For him, new spaces of existential and political struggle have been opened up, and they cannot be fully articulated and used if they are tied to old principles. In conversation with Pietro Deandrea, Okri pronounces, "Blessed are those who are overwhelmed, and who remember creatively".[46] All three novels give a sense that only through an active and creative engagement with the past is there a movement forward. There is a tension between the present and the past, the tension that pushes the protagonists on as much as it seems to pull them back. Unlike most characters, they do not seek to establish their individual autonomy and legitimize their communal belonging by referring to their ancestors.

Communalist desires are easily contrasted to the tendencies in contemporary Western cultures to valorize individualist self-sufficiency as the dominant way of being free. These desires are partly the result of a long history of liberation from old, traditional ways of being in Europe and the Americas (compare Rousseau's ideas of the natural man and *amour-propre*). The solitary European explorers from *The English Patient* elicit such response. As a reaction to inhospitable societies, there is an increase in isolation and self-centredness. From this point of view, community is a negative space permeated by that which Sartre called "bad faith".[47] Communalist authenticity then

---

[45] Jane Wilkinson, *Talking with African Writers: Interviews with African Poets, Playwrights and Novelists*, London: James Currey, 1992, 87.

[46] Pietro Deandrea, "An Interview with Ben Okri", *Africa, America, Asia, Australia*, XVI (1994), 21.

[47] Jean-Paul Sartre, *Being and Nothingness*, tr. Hazel E. Barnes, New York: Citadel Press, 2001, 532. Okri uses this phrase in *An African Elegy*, "Mythology reclaims the terrors; / The priests raise the dust: / ... / Our history has bred / Diseased raptors. / And our survivals have given / Rise to chimerical monsters. / The chalice of bad faith / Overflows" (Okri, *An African Elegy*, 23).

stands in opposition to this kind of focus on individual selfhood. At the same time, in both cases we find a similar understanding of selfhood as an essence.

There is no doubt that the novels I analyse present a certain negativity about community and maintain a focus on personal emancipation and a search for true selfhood. Both communal and Romantic essentialism are important stages but not the end goals in a process of self-creation through social action. Influenced by different threads in existentialist thought, these novelists try to de-essentialize the self, and argue in favour of existential processes of becoming and greater personal responsibility. To evoke Fanon again, instead of ending on "hypothesized results and conclusions", the goal is "an actual *change in my behavior* towards others. Similarly, my *responsibility* for others does not end; if I am to be seen as an authentic individual, I must always think of, and respond to, the Other".[48] With freedom comes great responsibility, to cut a phrase in a pop-cultural fashion.

Community

In the novels, both traditional and modern communities are viewed negatively as those social spaces that demand acquiescence and stymie personal development. Community can be understood as a gathering of social atoms around a common myth, cause, leader or race. In the novels, even such large formations as nations are thought in terms of communal ties. They are "imagined communities", in Benedict Anderson's famous phrase.[49] All the characters in the novels start with troubled communities they are born into and then become alienated from. The narration arises from broken down characters whose strong existential crises leads them to an exploration of freedom. For instance, while *Midnight's Children* seems to begin with the birth of the new nation state, the narration comes from an isolated subject who has but a weak connection to the development of Indian history. This structure puts the individual into an objectifying position from which he judges everything else. Everything circles around him. This holds true for Azaro, the otherworldly observer of humanity, as well as the multiple protagonists of Ondaatje's novel. It would seem

---

[48] Fanon, *The Wretched of the Earth*, 86 (emphases in the original).
[49] Benedict Anderson, *Imagined Communities: Reflections on the Origin and Spread of Nationalism*, London: Verso, 1983, 6.

that the narratives are constructed to espouse inner life and detachment from the public space. However, this is a transitional albeit important phase in the process of the creation of selfhood.

To begin with, the characters' anguish and self-consciousness is the result of the dissipation of the smaller, more intimate communities and families. Although I focus on the protagonists, the *angst* I speak about is personal but also shared. As Okri puts it, "The anguish from the arteries / Of the streets / Is spreading our hunger".[50] While in European historical contexts *angst* is presumably a private state of mind, in histories from these novels *angst* is also a communal. It can push those affected in at least two directions. The first is isolation and the quest for self-sufficiency. The second is a desire for restoration of original communality. The third option, which I will explore towards the end of this study, is a struggle for singular selfhood but through sharing and caring (beyond mechanical duty, habit and coercion). The characters come to form communities that reject traditional ties (myth, race, culture, ethnicity or the leader). While for philosophers like Heidegger and even Sartre communal everydayness may seem to elicit mostly inauthentic ways of being, in the novels this very sphere of existence is crucial. I take as my point of departure a basic assumption that community is the *a priori* of any singularity, and that beings always become in community, which I borrow from Jean-Luc Nancy.

The novels' focus on small practices and gestures against the background of gigantic historical movements highlights everyday life as the space in which characters reclaim and rework authenticity. (Mundane life thwarts the frameworks of heroism, or even super-heroism, as we can see when Saleem identifies with Clark Kent, instead of Superman, or when he turns mythical figures such as Ganesh and Shiva into mundane figures not unlike himself and his acquaintances.)

Agency and action

Agency is the capacity to make free choices. It ensures that humans do make decisions and act in the world. Whether or not there is an absolute free will is another issue. In the novels, authenticity presupposes both agency and the facticity of freedom, which is demonstrated in action, and which always partly suspends the power

---

[50] Okri, *An African Elegy*, 26.

structures that shape everyday lives. Sartre has famously argued that human agents are condemned to being free, condemned to make choices and become through their acts. Sartre attempted to convey Heidegger's idea that freedom is not human possession, but rather that freedom possesses man. The problem was that for Sartre to be condemned to freedom was nothing but being condemned to necessity. This is a desperate infusion to *homo metaphysicus*, as Nancy has argued, because Sartre's human "is not 'possessed' by freedom: he is forced by it into the 'free' knowledge of his infinite deprivation of freedom".[51] In the novels, the very desire for freedom (for instance, political freedom) implies a facticity of freedom. The primary issue for the characters is not whether or not freedom is a fact, but the "how" of freedom, the ways of being free.

Indeed, the intellectual threads of freedom have moved in many directions, some potentially harmful. In our theoretical quarrel with nativism, the idea of authenticity emerges as a historically crucial desire. Recently, authenticity has been revived as an important critical concept in different disciplines, for instance, the sociology of Margaret Archer, where it partly serves as a negotiation point in an analysis of human agency, then Anton Corey's elaboration of social selfhood, and David West's analyses of its value in a discourse on empowerment. While T. Storm Heter reclaims Sartre's ethics of engagement, Alessandro Ferrara re-examines and redefines it in what he deems the necessary rethinking of the project of modernity and an elaboration of values. K.A. Appiah takes John Stuart Mill's *On Liberty* as a point of departure in his articulation of the ethics of identity and authenticity in an attempt to surpass what he calls Romantic personalism and existential creativity.

The question is whether variegated existentialist thought is of any use after the criticism it has received over the years (for instance from Theodor W. Adorno)? Has the "myth of authenticity" not been deconstructed? Have we not moved on from the work of Fanon whose existentialist influences partly shaped his critique of "black civilization"?[52] While existentialism might have become less fashionable in academia, its influences on twentieth-century culture are undeniable. Postcolonial and postmodern criticism has incorporated

---

[51] Jean-Luc Nancy, *The Experience of Freedom*, tr. Bridget McDonald, Stanford, CA: Stanford University Press, 1993, 99.
[52] Fanon, *Black Skin, White Masks*, 17.

aspects of the existentialist thought, such as the deconstruction of essence.

Although it is only Ferrara who finds it important to address Adorno's critique, Adorno makes us cautious not to stop on the philosophical quagmire and jargon, that is, the drumbeating of the same terms to the point of appearing pure abstractions (and spirituality devoid of hope and comfort).[53] To reclaim and rework authenticity is not to repeat Heidegger's or any other rhetoric, but rather to engage with it insofar as it has bearings on the particular histories we deal with. There is an equal need to betray Sartre, Heidegger, etc. especially in the articulation of community.[54]

Indeed, since authenticity has been the subject of critical discourse from philosophical and social studies, to politics, I argue that literature has a major role to play. Historically, the articulation of authenticity finds its most fertile ground in literature, which has the ability to entice and dramatize, rather than objectify. Art can lay bare our inauthenticity and push us to overcome it, just as much as it can be used as ideological propaganda. Camus claimed that "writing in images rather than in reasoned arguments is revelatory of a certain thought that is common to them all [writers], convinced of the uselessness of any principle of explanation and sure of the educative message of perceptible appearance".[55] Similarly, Okri expresses a desire to lure readers into thinking "they are reading about something else when in fact they are reading about themselves", and about strong universal concerns.[56] Fiction in general seems crucial for the maintaining of the plasticity in the cultural domain.

---

[53] Theodor W. Adorno, *The Jargon of Authenticity*, London: Routledge Classics, 2003.

[54] Adorno's specific criticism of Heidegger has little bearing on my analysis. He exaggerates the role of the analysis of *das Man* (*ibid.*, 84). He assumes that *das Man* in the Nazi *Zeitgeist* is positive for Heidegger. However, National Socialism foregrounds the diffuse power that *das Man* is supposed to articulate: when everyone is "the one (*Man*)", the responsibility turns into a general irresponsibility for the atrocities committed. See Martin Heidegger, *Being and Time – A Translation of Sein und Zeit*, tr. Joan Stambaugh, New York: SUNY Press, 1996.

[55] Albert Camus, *The Myth of Sisyphus*, tr. Justine O'Brien, London: Hamish Hamilton, 1955, 82-83.

[56] Cited in David C.L. Lim, *The Infinite Longing for Home: Desire and the Nation in Selected Writings of Ben Okri and K.S. Maniam*, Amsterdam and New York: Rodopi, 2005, 61.

The difference between Camus and Okri is that for Camus in a good novel "the whole of the philosophy has passed into images".[57] For Okri literature is more than just philosophy: "Stories … are living things …. Their democracy is frightening, their ultimate non-allegiance is sobering …. Stories are subversive because they always remind us of our fallibility" and they "laugh at humanity's attempt to hide from its own clay".[58] Fictional form is suggestive and should re-dynamize the reader, rather than pacify him as a mere consumer of exotic history that is none of his real concern. It pulls the readers into experiencing the kinds of choices their characters are forced to make. The novels I have selected seem directed to shocking the reader into insights, but also splitting the insights into fragments and forcing him or her to take an active stance, participate (at least imaginatively) in making choices, aligning or dis-aligning with the premises in question.

Texts/authors: forms of alignment

As already stated, my choice of authors/texts comes from within certain cultural frameworks because the authors' popularity, the academic attention, the Booker, and even tendencies in contemporary publishing industry to perform what Graham Huggan calls "exoticist maneuvers".[59] Yet, exactly for this reason it becomes all the more important to re-examine these authors' responses to their history. Together, these novels tell something valuable about our shared myths and reality. In different ways, they transgress or migrate over historical limits, and use these as steppingstones into more general existential questions. The historical conflicts, the quarrel with nationalism and communalists' desires for origins are particularly evocative to me as an immigrant writer, who has experienced the dissolution of socialist Yugoslavia and the emergence of neo-nationalist camps that defined themselves strongly along ethnic and religious lines. Despite their specific tonalities, each novel speaks to me through similar concerns.

---

[57] Albert Camus, *Selected Essays and Notebooks*, tr. Philip Thody, Harmondsworth: Penguin, 1967, 167.

[58] Okri, *A Way of Being Free*, 44.

[59] Graham Huggan, "The Postcolonial Exotic: Salman Rushdie and the Booker of Bookers", *Transition*, LXIV (Autumn 1994), 26.

As Rushdie has argued, there seem to be greater similarities between these authors from different continents who have emigrated into the West, than between them and those who have remained working on their art in their countries of origin (Raja Rao, R.K. Narayan, Mulk Raj Anand, Chinua Achebe).[60] In fact, K.B. Rao has argued that Rushdie is "authentic when he writes about Bombay", but when he "writes about the rest of India, he is neither so forceful, nor so authentic".[61] He seems to argue that Rushdie has no true understanding of India and is therefore incapable of representing it. Here we enter the space of political empowerment and representation. For Rao it is irresponsible to describe or imagine one's country and a cultural identity in unsanctioned ways. For Rushdie it is the only responsible thing to do because displacement can bring about "a war over the nature of reality" in which "description is itself a political act".[62] The point is to introduce newness into reality rather than merely represent it. Rushdie, Ondaatje and Okri take their historical moments seriously, displaying awareness of the nearly impossible responsibility to act authentically (in the communalist sense). The object of their responsibility exceeds the traditional definitions of people, nation, race, class or even humanity in general. As migrants, as translated men who have crossed all manner of borders, they assume they should be able to discuss their work in connection to any other. This is in part what it means to write back, to deny legitimacy of the traditional forms of alignment and, as Rushdie put it, "to legitimately claim as our ancestry the Huguenots, the Irish, the Jews".[63]

This seems to be an inversion of Sartre's claim that any project undertaken by an individual, even those "belonging to Chinese, an Indian, or an African – can be understood by a European", and that this European can in fact, "reinvent within himself the project undertaken" by these others.[64] Arguing, "the past is a country from which we have all emigrated", Rushdie suggests an active and creative engagement with his heritage, which in this case is Nehruvian politics

---

[60] Rushdie, *Imaginary Homelands*, 20.

[61] K.B. Rao, "Asia and the Pacific: *Midnight's Children*", in *World Literature Today*, LVI/1 (Winter 1982), 181.

[62] Rushdie, *Imaginary Homelands*, 13.

[63] *Ibid.*, 20.

[64] Jean-Paul Sartre, *Existentialism Is a Humanism*, tr. Carol Macomber, New Haven, CT: Yale University Press, 2007, 42.

that gave his generation the meaning of midnight's children.[65] As Rushdie put it, his "identity is at once plural and partial" because he is not "willing to be excluded from any part of [his] heritage", and yet not ready to unwittingly accept every part of it either.[66] By creating plural communities and bonds (which are not ties), like their characters, Ondaatje, Okri and Rushdie seem to translate if not entirely transcend premises of historicism (historical unity, development in empty secular time, etc). Reacting to the historical traumas and anguish, they and their characters struggle for richer modes of existence, greater personal responsibility, and alternate ways of communal bonding. Their ways of being free are defined by a struggle to "open the universe a little more".[67]

---

[65] Tabish Khair characterizes Rushdie as a "bourgeois self-exile" (Tabish Khair, *Babu Fictions: Alienation in Contemporary Indian English Novels*, Oxford: Oxford University Press, 2001, 266), whose concern with plurality and cosmopolitanism is often a grand scale failure, because he is unable to choose between different heritages, nor to fully abandon them (*ibid.*, 267).

[66] Rushdie, *Imaginary Homelands*, 15. Indeed, Fanon prophesied a generation of anti-nationalist postcolonials as "psycho-affective mutilations: individuals without an anchorage, without borders, colorless, stateless, rootless, a body of angels .... Usually, unwilling or unable to choose, these intellectuals collect all the historical determinations which have conditioned them and place themselves in a thoroughly 'universal perspective'" (Fanon, *The Wretched of the Earth*, 156). They use a foreign aesthetic "steeped in humor and allegory" or even "anguish, malaise, death, and even nausea" (*ibid.*, 159).

[67] Rushdie, *Imaginary Homelands*, 21.

PART I

WAR IS EVERYTHING'S FATHER:
HISTORY AND DEATH AS CAUSES OF EXISTENTIAL ANGST

Introduction: Causes of Existential Angst

> When a people sense the end of a way, of
> an era, of a dream, they always sense it as
> the end of the world. Who can stop the
> end of the world?[1]

In *Midnight's Children*, *The English Patient*, and *The Famished
Road*, both violent history and death bring about identity crises and
existential *angst*. Overwhelming conflicts and changes within history,
as well as the deep awareness of life's finitude or mortality, rupture
the characters' lives and lead to an anguished concern with existence
and a desire for singular freedom.

The characters are situated in dissipating social realms that are also
being recreated, in particular under banners of nation states. By and
large their worlds can be characterized as the disbanding of traditional
communities, nation building, international war, religious and ethnic
conflicts, secularization, the uneven industrialization of developing
countries, neo-imperialist conquest, and exploitation of human and
natural resources. For them, it appears as if one world is dying and
another being born.[2] They cannot simply rely on or find refuge in
traditional cultural nodes, meanings, and practices to reproduce social
and personal stability. They no longer have access to rootedness and
meaningfulness, and "the naiveté of the first certainty" as Paul
Ricoeur put it.[3] But even if they did, they have come to believe that
such meanings and practices are forms of what Rushdie's Saleem calls
conformity and acquiescence, which is akin to Sartre's "bad faith".

They feel thrown or fallen into inhospitable world(s) in whose
making they have not participated, and which for the most part control
their development. They see that their social spheres are even more

---

[1] Ben Okri, *Starbook*, London: Rider, 2007.

[2] "World" is here used to mean a totality of different value and meaning systems. To
be in the world consists in having implicit access to its codes.

[3] Paul Ricoeur, *Interpretation Theory: Discourse and the Surplus of Meaning*, Fort
Worth: The Texas Christian University Press, 1976, 44.

shaped by authoritative and diffuse powers, which produce and maintain both physical and existential hunger, as, for instance, when the English patient feels strong anxiety when he realizes how he has become a tool in the politics of war. The different protagonists, Saleem, Hana, Kip, Almásy and Azaro seem lost on the ever-multiplying roads that seem to lead mostly to misery. The English patient finds being lost in the desert far more appealing than being alienated by war politics. They all suffer profound anguish over what they may become as well as what they have been. Experiencing nervous conditions and *angst*, the characters are forced to make decisions with heightened awareness of their singular choices and responsibilities. Yet, the choices are never obvious and unproblematic. *Angst*, as their fundamental insecurity, signals to them that something is not quite right with their worlds, and also that they may be deprived of freedom.[4]

Even the experience of life's finitude or mortality causes such profound disorientation and disruption of the characters' capacities to be, to make decisions and act. Okri connected such *angst* to the draining of death's meaning. Existential *angst* here entails very much Kierkegaard's despair,[5] and Sartre's nausea.[6] Okri seems to evoke Sartre when Azaro is "filling with unease and anxiety .... nausea and bile rising in my throat".[7] *Angst* is indeed negative, yet it also implies an opening to doubt, the kind of positive uncertainty that undermines oppressive social structures. As in Sartre's discourse, anxiety is also connected to the dizzying experience of freedom and responsibility, which both fascinates and repels the characters, as when Hana

---

[4] After Fanon, Bhabha reworked psycho-social effects of colonization, arguing that the very "subjects of study require the experience of anxiety to be incorporated into the analytic construction of the object of the critical attention", because "anxiety is the affective address of 'a world [that] reveals itself as caught up in the space between frames; a double frame, or one that is split'" (Bhabha, *The Location of Culture*, 306). Indeed, "the appeal to affects of disjunction, disorientation and doubling, particularly in the context of 'emergent' knowledges and practices cannot be envisaged without fear and trembling" (*ibid.*, 392). As Rushdie put it, the sense of falling between stools (Rushdie, *Imaginary Homelands*, 15) causes "deep, permanent, operatic anguish" (*ibid.*, 32).

[5] Søren Kierkegaard, *The Concept of Anxiety*, tr. Reider Thomte, Princeton, NJ: Princeton University Press, 1980.

[6] Jean-Paul Sartre, *Nausea*, tr. Lloyd Alexander, New York: New Directions Books, 2007.

[7] Ben Okri, *The Famished Road* (1991), London: Vintage, 2003, 523.

carelessly walks in the minefields and the mined villa, or when she steps forth to help Kip dismantle a bomb. Sartre's famous example is of an individual standing on a cliff who not only dreads falling off but is also anguished about the possibility of hurling himself off.

The factuality of freedom becomes obvious in that the individual sees a possibility that everything that is supposed to hold him back is not absolute and that in the last instance the choice is singular. There is a similar image in *The Famished Road*, when Azaro stands on the edge of a threatening forest pit dug open by industrial machinery. He does not simply fear falling, but the fact that he may decide the next moment to jump. Azaro discovers in anguish that he is free to honour his resolve to stay human or die in the pit with other ghosts and creatures. While everything pushes Azaro to take a fatal leap, the vertigo of freedom is experienced in the choice to hold back, to opt for life. In a sense, Okri puts a particular postcolonial spin on this recognizable motif, arguing that the history of colonialism and the postcolonial traumas exceed those of European history and actually drive individuals and communities to find peace and relief from suffering in the leap of certain death. Azaro's mother, for instance, twice attempts suicide. The way of being free, as is clear from Dad's continuous boxing fights and Azaro's ordeals, lies in opting for life (even in suffering), for standing against the impossible forces that seek to make each person submissive, obedient, exploitable, disposable, and finally, in fact, dead.

The characters struggle in anguish to create new possibilities, rather than merely choosing between the alternatives handed down to them. As a way of coping, many affected individuals/communities evince an immediate need to retrieve and re-establish their worlds (a need I characterized as communalism), or even a personal need to remain estranged. However, since they deem such retrieval both impossible and undesirable, the protagonists in these novels reclaim community as the space for individual freedom or authenticity. As Okri puts it, "Break this cycle / Break this madness / ... / Destroy this temple of living hell / Let us join our angers together / Forge a new joy for the age / Before our lives disintegrate. / Create / New breaks".[8] I will deal with these new breaks, freedom, action and community in

---

[8] Okri, *An African Elegy*, 45.

the second chapter. For now I will analyse the relationships between history and anguish, which are partly conditions for being free.

History: An Introduction

While Rushdie's and Okri's novels focus on the particular postcolonial histories of their native countries, Ondaatje's narrative is about the largest modern war, which implicates Europe, Asia and Africa. In all three novels, colonialism is implied as the historical burden, whose legacies keep affecting different countries that are moving towards some form of self-rule and freedom. Their freedom is shaped by European socio-political structures (especially in terms of governing). New imperialisms loom large, and the exploitation of human and natural resources seems unstoppable. Although the narratives are strongly driven to articulate historical changes in terms of shifts between eras (rather than generations), there is a sense of an idling of history, as if certain changes, such as those between paradigms, serve to maintain the continuous suffering and stifle freedom. Okri's Azaro best illustrates the violence in a transition from one world to another world, from one era to another era, and yet also how some old injustices remain.

In the novels, the historical changes are tied to the particular histories of the former colonies, but the given transformations appear to have larger, not to say global, proportions, even though they take place in different localities. The narrators often dramatize their histories in terms of a division between premodernity and modernity, which seems to be their colonial legacy of historicism. They often use adjectives such as "antiquated", "ancient", "traditional", or "mythical" to describe particular native beliefs and practices, and contrast them to modern ideas of the political, citizenship, state, the individual, public and private, democracy, and scientific rationality, as well as capitalism and industrialization. For Saleem, his generation of midnight's children

> ... can be seen as the last throw of everything antiquated and retrogressive in our myth-ridden nation, whose defeat was entirely desirable in the context of a modernizing, twentieth century economy; or as the true hope of freedom, which is now forever extinguished.[9]

---

[9] Salman Rushdie, *Midnight's Children* (1981), London: Everyman's Library, 1995, 255.

Like Azaro, Saleem feels the midnight's children's supernatural powers predict them on myths and legends, and yet they are the subjects of a secular nation state. Commenting on (post)colonial conditions, Sartre envisioned two incompatible worlds, which are also "two possessions".[10] In the novels, such double inheritance is much more ambiguous. It is a form of dispossession, as we can see in the takeover of Methwold's estate.

This preliminary bifurcation of antiquity and modernity, as it seems dramatized in the novels, emphasizes the fact that the characters are driven to make life-defining choices between conflicting ways of understanding and being in the world. Yet, those ways have are already been articulated for them. In the earlier quotation, Saleem does not say how he sees the children, but how they can be seen given different frameworks. The characters in all three novels seem both to straddle different eras and feel displaced into peculiar in-between zones, belonging everywhere and nowhere. There is a profusion of subject positions and identities, which, as Okri has argued, offer new possibilities. At the same time, to use Saleem's words, they cause individuals to become "knocked forever into that middle ground",[11] of non-belonging, isolation, and being-out-of-touch with the world, as Jonathan Rutherford put it.[12] This condition of fundamental displacement and uncertainty becomes a drive for individual freedom or authenticity and a reworking of communal existence.

Before I start with my specific analyses, I need to expand on the ways in which the novels plot both the national histories and singular lives as struggles to mediate between the teleology of progress and "the 'timeless' discourse of irrationality", to use Bhabha's words.[13] There is indeed no single unplugging from everything that may be deemed premodern and a fresh start of modern progress, which Rushdie shows by mocking the symbolic night of Independence, Okri through insistence on cycles, and Ondaatje through quick movements between time periods. Still, the historical changes in the novels are articulated in terms of the premodern/modern binary, which is

---

[10] Sartre, "Introduction", in Fanon, *The Wretched of the Earth*, liv.

[11] Rushdie, *Midnight's Children*, 12

[12] *Identity: Community, Culture, Difference*, ed. Jonathan Rutherford, London: Lawrence and Wishart, 1990, 24.

[13] Bhabha, *The Location of Culture*, 204.

constituted by an entire set of conflicts such as the local versus the national, rural versus urban, religion versus secularism, communalism versus individualism, handicraft versus technological mass production, orality versus (print) literacy. The reason the novels seem more thematically oriented to these conflicts, than to colonialism and postcolonialism, seems to point out the problem of equating colonialism with modernity. Indeed, colonialism opened up Asian and African localities to European influences, for instance in terms of government (secular democracy and nation states), as well as the humanist ideals of Enlightenment (civil rights, citizenship, individuality). Although colonialism preached these ideals, as Dipesh Chakrabarty has argued, it denied them in practice.[14]

Premodernity seems to be defined in terms of essential truths and traditional practices, and the mythical frameworks that predict characters on certain cosmic orders. Modernity is defined as the demise of such enchantments, and yet they keep haunting it. Rushdie has argued that he wrote *Midnight's Children* to foreground synchronic conflicts between peoples of different cultures, religions and political persuasions, which are at the same time marked by a diachronic transition from the era he calls the "Olympus" into the secular history devoid of myths and legends.[15] For Rushdie, the bizarre character of the midnight's children is the image of such conflicts.

As Okri writes, "In their native lands / Other Images were made / For new seasons / A new god / For a new / Age".[16] Okri ironically characterizes the Europe modelled modernity as the age of new gods, which arrived in Africa through the opening made by colonialism (see the poem "The Cross Is Gone", which evokes London).[17] It is clear from this discourse that modernity is seen as Western, but what is even more important is the fact that the binary premodern/modern is itself modern. The modern age in the West, as Hannah Arendt has argued, rises "with the natural sciences in the seventeenth century, reaching its political climax in the revolutions of the eighteenth, and unfolding its general implications after the Industrial Revolution of

---

[14] Dipesh Chakrabarty, *Provincializing Europe: Postcolonial Thought and Historical Difference*, Princeton, NJ: Princeton University Press, 2000, 4.
[15] Rushdie, *Imaginary Homelands*, 13.
[16] Okri, *An African Elegy*, 10.
[17] *Ibid.*, 15-20.

the nineteenth", but also in the twentieth century "through the chain of catastrophes touched off by the First World War".[18]

Furthermore, modernity seems to entail a change in the understanding of history as such. History changes from being the narrative that conveys the intrinsic meaning of myths about divine order, divinities and heroes, into history as man-made processes with no intrinsic meaning. For example, in *Midnight's Children* Saleem is born with mythical powers that would give him the status of a hero or even a deity in the past ages, and yet which have no meaning, purpose or historical significance in the modern nation of India. He feels a need to historicize himself in order to determine his meaning. I find this predicament aptly unpacked by Arendt:

> The modern concept of process pervading history and nature alike separates the modern age from the past more than any other single idea .... Invisible processes have engulfed every tangible thing, every individual entity that is visible to us, degrading them to functions of an over-all process.[19]

The characters in the novels seem to experience profound splits or gaps in their understandings of history. By contrast, as Ferrara has argued, "for a premodern social actor who acts in a 'traditional' way", knowing who one is "means to know one's station in social life, one's role, perhaps even one's personality".[20] For our protagonists, the question becomes a more individualized "Who am I, and who do I want to be?" This pertinent question makes the characters particularly disoriented and unsettled. They cannot go back to some pre-colonial, premodern identities, nor can they fully subscribe to the new gods. Bhabha has argued that such disorientations and indeed historical traumas arise from the *"aporetic coexistence,* within the cultural history of the *modern* imagined community, of both the dynastic, hierarchical, prefigurative 'medieval' traditions (the past), and the secular, homogenous, synchronous crosstime of modernity (the present)".[21] A choice between antiquity and modernity is a false choice. At one and the same time there is a split between these

---

[18] Hannah Arendt, *Between Past and Future*, London: Penguin Classics, 2006, 16.
[19] *Ibid.*, 63.
[20] Alessandro Ferrara, *Reflective Authenticity: Rethinking the Project of Modernity*, London: Routledge, 2002, 15.
[21] Bhabha, *The Location of Culture*, 358-59 (emphases in the original).

historicist abstractions and a mush of multiplying hybridities, which undermine "the teleological traditions of past and present, and the polarized historicist *sensibility* of the archaic and the modern".[22] The surge of both epistemological and ontological conflicts (within the history of postcolonial modernity, anti-modernity, and/or alternate modernities) causes deep nervous conditions and provokes profound desires for authenticity.

What is more, the novel's magical realist modes effectively show the confusion between the different sides of the assumed binary. For instance, although a Western secular reader would perhaps deem Azaro a creature from premodern myths, the narrative creates a sense of blurred boundaries so as to bring about epistemological confusion. As Wendy B. Faris has argued, magical realism, which labels the impossibility of final classifications and categorizations of historical phenomena, heightens our sense of the immensity of "existential anguish at an un-co-optable world".[23] Such *angst*, albeit personal, is also shared in the public space as a nervous condition, which in turn becomes the reason for an exploration of authentic singularity within changing communal spaces. The concern with authenticity, which for Marshall Berman is a European legacy, is also a response to the shared nervous conditions.[24]

Death: An Introduction

Like the shocking disorientation that comes with war and radical historical shifts, the experience of imminent death or rather the sudden sense of life's finitude can cause existential *angst*. Although death as such is the end of experience, as Jacob J. Golomb has argued, the

---

[22] *Ibid.*, 220 (emphasis in the original).

[23] Wendy B. Faris, *Ordinary Enchantments: Magical Realism and the Remystification of Narrative*, Nashville: Vanderbilt University Press, 2004, 8.

[24] Berman has argued that in Europe, the ideal of authenticity "articulated men's deepest responses to the modern world and their most intense hopes for a new life in it" (Marshall Berman, *The Politics of Authenticity: Radical Individualism and the Emergence of Modern Society*, London: Allen and Unwin, 1971, 311). However, new social structures (such as that of the bourgeoisie) turned out "just as destructive to human authenticity as the system it replaced" (*ibid.*, 313). The "constant alternation of enchantment and disenchantment, hope and despair, has made the search for authenticity almost unbearable; suffering souls in search of a way out of the anguish of themselves have formed a vast constituency for politicians of inauthenticity, for totalitarians both of the sword and of the veil, of the Right and of the Left – and, perhaps most insidious of all, for totalitarianism of the 'liberal' Center" (*ibid.*, 321).

"most acutely felt anxiety is that which arises in the face of imminent death".[25] In this context death signifies finitude, that is, the intimations of mortality in times when the hope of an afterlife has becomes radically questioned. As Okri has argued, death has become "drained of meaning".[26] The prospect of death makes characters undertake an anguished assessment of their existence.

Although death is a fact, it has been conventionally endowed with certain meanings tied to religion, the state, or love, all of which are supposed to ameliorate its impact.[27] Rushdie puts much emphasis on religious beliefs such as Islam, Christianity, Hinduism, and Buddhism. Ondaatje mostly focuses on modernized Christianity, and somewhat on the Sikh religion, while Okri is concerned with animism, barely touching upon the monotheistic faiths.

The Famished Road abides by different rules with respect to death, the spirit and the human world. It is a great deal more magical realist than the other two. Nominally, a different ontology should yield entirely different and incompatible dramatizations of death and preclude the existential discourse. The assumed reality of the spirit world in Okri's novel appears on the surface to stand against the other two. However, like the other two novels, it too dramatizes death as the cause of *angst*, which despite its overwhelmingly negative value appears to open the self to the factuality of freedom. Azaro, in order to fully experience humanity, abandons himself to the possibility of *angst* in the face of death. It is his love for his parents that pulls him out of his abiku self, that makes him open to their alterity (and his own alterity). This ecstatic movement happens several times in the novel, always in relation to death.

Heidegger has argued that death is one's "ownmost" possibility.[28] In all three novels, however, it is by way of the other's mortality that

---

[25] Jacob J. Golomb, *In Search of Authenticity: Existentialism from Kierkegaard to Camus*, Florence: Routledge, 1995, 107.

[26] Okri, *A Way of Being Free*, 56.

[27] Nancy offers a valuable insight that death for the state is not "the unmasterable excess of finitude, but the infinite fulfillment of immanent life". Rather, "an absolute circulation of meaning (of values, of ends, of History) fills or reabsorbs all finite negativity, draws from each finite singular destiny a surplus value of humanity or an infinite superhumanity" (Jean-Luc Nancy, *The Inoperative Community*, tr. Peter Connor, Minneapolis: University of Minnesota Press, 1991, 13).

[28] Heidegger made being-towards-death an ontological aspect of being-human. Death releases human beings from their social worlds and opens them to a true

the characters come to know their own finitude. There is a sharing of finitude, as between Hana, Kip, and the patient; as between Azaro and his human family; Saleem and the midnight's children. The characters come to understand that death cannot be easily appropriated by different collectivities, within their cultural paradigms. Death comes across as not theirs, not owned (by person or community). The characters, by narrating about their proximity to death, expose the limits of their social bonds, even when they do not manage to transcend them. They fend off, but also embrace their mortality through narration. As in Scheherazade's stories, which not only thematize but also delay death, these narratives are ways of coping with mortality, as well as the ultimate inability to cope with it.[29]

Indeed, to use Christopher Fynsk's words, "the very impossibility of representing its meaning suspends or breaches the possibility of self-presentation and exposes us to our finitude".[30] While the experience of finitude folds them back onto themselves, and emphasizes their singular concerns, the sharing of finitude in the novels seems to go against the long tradition that thinks authenticity in terms of isolated individuals.

---

understanding of Being. For Adorno "authenticity is death, and since only death is free, our freedom always costs us our lives" (Adorno, *The Jargon of Authenticity*, 125). Although Adorno is less sensitive to different levels of Heidegger's discourse, he shows that Heidegger fails to articulate the ways in which death also throws *Dasein* back into the facticity of life, and the way the intimations of mortality do not appear *ex nihilo*, but in the communal space where death is necessarily shared.

[29] For Giorgio Agamben, the awareness of finitude is connected to narrative. While animals perish, only human beings talk about death and give meaning to it. Giorgio Agamben, *Language and Death: The Place of Negativity*, tr. Karen E. Pinkus and Michael Hardt, Minneapolis: University of Minnesota Press, 1991.

[30] Christopher Fynsk, "Foreword", in Nancy, *Inoperative Community*, xvi.

CHAPTER 1

CHANGE AND CHANGELESSNESS
IN *MIDNIGHT'S CHILDREN*

Saleem Sinai is the son of a former colonizer and a poor Hindu woman, raised in the middle-class Muslim family and by their Christian ayah. Once his affiliations to the emerging Indian nation come to transcend his filial ties, he begins to see himself as the child "*of the time*: fathered, you understand, by history".[1] This history, which is politically and symbolically narrated with respect to the crucial midnight of 1947 Independence (the night of freedom), is the history of wars, colonialism, liberation struggle, the rising of national consciousness, nationalism, new faces of tyranny, ethnic conflicts and cleansing, exploitation, poverty. The midnight of Independence serves as a necessary meaningful sign of a break with the colonial past and a conscious step towards the creation of India as a modern, secular, democratic nation: "A moment comes, which comes but rarely in history, when we step out from the old to the new; when an age ends" (146).

Assuming that historicism made possible European dominion of the world, it seems infinitely ironic that the midnight sign of liberty is also an official, political sign of Indian immersion into the historicist time. The Independence midnight is politicized as a split between ages, but it also becomes a synchronic split between ethnicities. The diachronic partition, as it seems from Nehru's speech, is not only the transition from colonialism to postcolonialism, but also a step into modernity. Rushdie seems to have wanted to explore how Indian peoples could "build a new, 'modern' world out of an old, legend haunted civilization", which remains at "the heart of a newer one".[2] However, *Midnight's Children* shows how modernity still relies on myth, just as premodernity is not something that simply looms from

---

[1] Rushdie, *Midnight's Children*, 148 (emphasis in the original. All subsequent references to *Midnight's Children* are given in the text).
[2] Rushdie, *Imaginary Homelands*, 19.

the past. Rather, it is also co-constitutes the Indian nation. What is important is that in the new place new forms of authority and exploitation stymie freedom. The conflicts between modern and premodern paradigms within the present time haunt the characters' sense of agency, and their freedom "to be this or that or the other" (537).

Since no clear cut from the past is actualized, the post-midnight time is characterized by an aporetic existence in which conflicting worldviews struggle for dominion, produce immense existential confusion and *angst*. While the new leaders put much hope into the secularization of the country as the only way of keeping ethnic conflicts at bay, the new age will remain burdened by them. The freedom wars turn into ethnic wars, and for Saleem, "there is nothing like a war for the reinvention of lives" (518). This reinvention will be governed by strong authoritative power, which deprives characters of agency. As the consequence of his having fallen into this turbulent history and not having immediate knowledge of his purpose or meaning in the world that he feels is shaped without his true contribution, Saleem experiences deep *angst*. As Rushdie explains, all questions are funnelled into "a single, existential question: How are we to live in the world?"[3]

History and the war over meaning
Saleem, as the child of history, struggles with two different understandings of history. First, he perceives history as that oral narrative which preserves and immortalizes the meaningful deeds of heroes and deities. Second, as someone born into a secular nation state, he sees history as progress, and as something in which events and actions have no intrinsic meaning but are the result of simultaneous processes that take place in the empty homogenous time, and which seem impossible to grasp in their entirety. Saleem realizes that the specificity of the politically determined moment of his and India's birth, and his powers have no intrinsic meaning. He feels like "'the gander' ... the mythical bird, the hamsa or parahamsa, symbol of the ability to live in two worlds, the physical and the spiritual, the world of land-and-water and the world of air" (283). He cannot decide whether he and the children are "the last throw of everything

---

[3] *Ibid.*, 18.

antiquated and retrogressive in our myth-ridden nation, whose defeat was entirely desirable in the context of a modernizing, twentieth-century economy", or "the true hope of freedom, which is now forever extinguished" (255). While the gander embraces incompatible worlds into a synthesis, Saleem keeps falling in between them, while they also pull him apart. He says ironically:

> … thanks to the occult tyrannies of those blandly saluting clocks I had been mysteriously handcuffed to history, my destinies indissolubly chained to those of my country. For the next three decades, there was to be no escape. (7)

The problem is, this mystical handcuffing is also political and secular, and as such it has no essential, preordained meaning. If we read this claim as an ironic remark on the modern focus on history, the exchange between the historicist ideology and the faith in God (as in Aadam's case), then to be handcuffed to history means basically to live in a modern age. To claim that his bond to history is mystical actually highlights the fact that his modern understanding of history presupposes demystification. Unlike Okri's Azaro, for whom ghosts and mythical creatures are very real, Saleem is a dominantly historicist realist who is highly aware that he should not believe in "ancient insanities of India", "the fabulous antiquity" and "atavistic longings", which "plague honest folk", make them forget "the new myth of freedom" and push them to revert "to their old ways, their old regionalist loyalties and prejudices" (311). Even if he believed in Shiva, Ganesh, angels and demons, he still feels he must explain himself because his audiences probably do not share such beliefs.

Saleem's antiquated qualities are seen as potentially disruptive elements in what Rege aptly calls the secular-socialist nation, which "failed to deliver either material or spiritual results to a generation of believers".[4] Eventually, since he believes that in the ancient times certain figures were immortalized because their actions corresponded to their meaning or purpose, he seems to realize that his meaning is in fact vapid. While for him meaning is the same as purpose, that is, something to be corroborated in and through action, he has no idea what his actions should be. The entire narrative becomes one desperate attempt at finding his personal meaning. Meaning becomes

---

[4] Rege, "Victim into Protagonist?", 196.

an end in itself. His task is quite schizophrenic. He seeks to explain material causes in public history, that which Chakrabarty terms History1. At the same time, he wants to convey History2, which purports a plurality of lived, intimate histories with elements that defy integration into historicist frameworks.

At this point it might be fruitful to draw a parallel to Arendt's argument:

> [The] growing meaninglessness of the modern world is perhaps nowhere more clearly foreshadowed than in this identification of meaning and end. Meaning, which can never be the aim of action and yet, inevitably, will rise out of human deeds after the action itself has come to an end, was now pursued with the same machinery of intentions and of organized means as were the particular direct aims of concrete action.[5]

To understand this insight in the workings of the novel, we could even argue that it is Saleem's attitude to meaning that makes him modern. Yet, the state of affairs might not be as simple. Saleem argues,

> ... if everything is planned in advance, then we all have a meaning, and are spared the terror of knowing ourselves to be random, without a why; or else, of course, we might – as pessimists – give up right here and now, understanding the futility of thought decision action, since nothing we think makes any difference anyway; things will be as they will. Where, then, is optimism? In fate or in chaos? (97)

Action appears ineffective in chaos. Fate too is negative because it abolishes his historical agency, yet it is alluring because it entails that everything is meaningful: "I admit it: above all things, I fear absurdity" (7). Saleem's existential dilemma resonates with Sartre's idea that "never has *homo faber* [Man the Maker] better understood he has *made* history and never has he felt so powerless before history".[6] In fact, when Saleem says, "From ayah to Widow, I've been the sort of person *to whom things have been done*, but Saleem Sinai, perennial victim, persists in seeing himself as protagonist" (301, emphases in the original), he expresses a desire to affect history at the same time as

---

[5] Arendt, *Between Past and Future*, 78.
[6] Jean-Paul Sartre, *What Is Literature?*, tr. Bernard Frechtman, London: Methuen, 1950, 174.

he is shaped by it. While fate seems to guarantee that everything has an intrinsic meaning or purpose, it also entails that personal actions are predetermined.[7] What Saleem in turn denotes "chaos" does not entail lack of order, but rather the idea that these processes are incomprehensible, that they have no meaning, no true direction, that things are just happening.

The text here seems to parallel Arendt's argument that everything is a part of "a man-made process, the only all-comprehending process which owed its existence exclusively to the human race".[8] Indeed, Saleem acts, but at the same time he has no real force or even understanding of the historical processes he is a part of. His existence is mystical, transcendent, mythical, and yet also meaningless. Nehru, who seems to give a certain meaning to both India and Saleem, does not make it easier. When he writes, "your life ... will be, in a sense, the mirror of our own" (155), and thus makes Saleem into the allegory of the nation, Saleem at first has no idea what to do about it. Even if this truly is his meaning, it does not tell him anything about his actions. He starts by conceiving of his mind/body as the form that contains the multitudes in the manner in which his famous spittoon is a "receptacle of memories as well as spittle juice" (448).[9] While he ascribes the longing for form to India as if it was its intrinsic trait, we understand that this historicist desire is common to all nations. Even though it sounds like something mystical, it pertains to the modern myths of nationhood. In particular, following Nehru, Saleem tests the thesis that India as a modern democracy can hold the excessive diversity. What happens is that the politics of diversity and multiculturalism essentialize different groups and help create conflicts

---

[7] Saleem also wants to be "embroiled in Fate". According to Desai, outwitting *karma* is the peasant heritage in contrast to the "'great' tradition ... the possession of the learned and the scholarly (i.e. the Brahmins)" (Desai, "Introduction", in Rushdie, *Midnight's Children*, x).

[8] Arendt, *Between Past and Future*, 58.

[9] Erik L. Berlatsky points out Rushdie's wish to write what "Henry James would call the 'loose, baggy monsters' of fiction" which "derive, precisely, from an allegiance to history, and its multitude of events, not from a desire to deconstruct it" (Erik L. Berlatsky, *Fact, Fiction, and Fabrication: History, Narrative, and the Postmodern Real from Woolf to Rushdie*, diss, University of Maryland, 2003, 416). In addition, the vessel image could be a reference to Fanon: "National consciousness is nothing but a crude, empty fragile shell. The cracks in it explain how easy it is for young independent countries to switch back from nation to ethnic group and from state to tribe" (Fanon, *The Wretched of the Earth*, 97).

rather than allow for the proliferation of difference, to use Bhabha's argument.[10]

Saleem's endeavour to pertain to historicism is obvious when he claims he adjusts the narrative of his life to the national history, which "operates on a grander scale than any individual" and therefore takes "a good deal longer to stitch it back together and mop up the mess" (303). Although it is cracking like his body, he assumes there is the History that totalizes the heterogeneous crowds of the subcontinent. This totalization produces the sense of a metaphysical ground of history. In a sense, he barters God for history. Saleem's description of his predicament is peculiarly similar to Sartre's argument about: "*several* collectivities, *several* societies, and *one* history – realities, that is, which impose themselves on individuals; but at the same time it must be woven out of millions of individual actions".[11] This is how Saleem puts it:

> I no longer want to be anything except what who I am. Who what am I? My answer: I am the sum total of everything that went before me, of all I have been seen done, of anything done-to-me. I am anything that happens after I've gone which would not have happened if I had not come. I am everyone everything whose being-in-the-world affected was affected by mine.

The dispersed multitudes are arguably glued together by a web of history that he allegorizes. He is a singular that contains the universal. Eventually, Saleem falls into a Sartrean trap when arguing, "each 'I', every one of the now-six-hundred-million-plus of us, contains a similar multitude" (488). Here, a singular event contains the whole as well as it is a constitutive part of it. The problem is, as Robert Young explains, that singular elements cannot express or contain the whole because "the whole is only accessible as a concept", which is never immediately "*legible* in visible reality: like every concept this concept must be *produced, constructed*".[12] In some sense, Saleem is a concept

---

[10] Homi K. Bhabha, "Third Space: An Interview with Homi Bhabha", in *Identity: Community, Culture, Difference*, ed. Jonathan Rutherford, London: Lawrence and Wishart, 1990, 208.

[11] Jean-Paul Sartre, *Critique of Dialectical Reason, I: Theory of Practical Ensembles*, tr. Irene Clephane, London: New Left Books, 1976, 65 (emphases in the original).

[12] Robert Young, *White Mythologies*, London and New York: Routledge, 2004, 97 (emphases in the original).

that reflects a concept. Yet, although he shows this crux, he knows that such metonymy can be employed for real political gain (in the case of Indian leaders such as Indira Gandhi). Saleem gives himself the Herculean task of writing an all-embracing history and rejects any historiographic censure, which he terms *halal* history. Yet, in so far as history always betrays an aspiration to meaning, it cannot but be a performance of selectivity.

Eventually, Saleem detects discrepancies between his life and national history and says: "I am coming to the conclusion that privacy, the small individual lives of men are preferable to all this inflated macrocosmic activity" (554). What Saleem articulates here is a tension between different understandings of how history works. His desire to grasp the macrocosmic activity is clearly historicist. It is an attempt to see the woods rather than merely the trees. Chakrabarty calls this a Marxian legacy, and although he does not abandon the benefits of this analytic (the understanding of how global capital creates the world), he calls for a complementary understanding of history in terms of Heidegger's hermeneutic tradition which helps us contemplate "the diversity of life-worlds" and "affective histories".[13] When Saleem opts for the small lives, he seems to endorse affective histories, yet he does not abandon his historicist desires. Once affective histories infringe on the historicist unity, once the abstract vessel can no longer keep their plurality, he starts to crack:

> I shall now amplify, in the manner and with the proper solemnity of a man of science, my claim to a place at the centre of things. '…Your life, which will be, in a sense, the mirror of our own,' the Prime Minister wrote, obliging me scientifically to face the question: In what sense? How, in what terms, may the career of a single individual be said to impinge on the fate of a nation? I must answer in adverbs and hyphens: I was linked to history both literally and metaphorically, both actively and passively, in what our (admirably modern) scientists might term 'modes of connection' composed of dualistically-combined configurations of the two pairs of opposed adverbs given above. (302)

To assume an arguably scientific or analytic mind is for Saleem to constantly look at the world and look for internal connections and

---

[13] Chakrabarty, *Provincializing Europe*, 18.

unity. Yet, he realizes that all the different peoples and communities are predicated on a plurality of orders, especially mythical orders that must be demystified in the analytic model. While Chakrabarty shows us that different historical models (for instance, Marxian abstractions and Heideggerian intimacies) can be used in dialogue with each other in order to understand the complexities of alternate modernities of the postcolonial world(s), for Saleem there is only conflict and incompatibility, and yet his history cannot but be a hybrid of them. This conflict pushes him deeper and deeper into anguish. If Saleem can be said to truly allegorize the nation it is in the sense that he embodies the national *angst* or nervous condition produced by the conflicts that pull it apart while it is being formed.

Premodernity/modernity and existential crises
Since he conceives of his existence as being torn between mythical and scientific understandings of the world, which Neil ten Kortenaar rightly connects to Orientalist tendencies, Saleem tries to clarify the distinctions between different worldviews and forms of social existence through emblematic conflicts between Aadam/Naseem, Aadam/Tai, Narlikar/the-religious-masses, and even Saleem/Shiva (and yet not so much with respect to the colonizers such as the former landlord Methwold). Europeans are often secondary characters whose presence is strong mostly because of their absence, through innuendos, remnants of their ideologies, industries, statesmanship, etc.

To begin with, Saleem understands modernity in terms of secularism, the deflation of myth and community, the focus on individuality, innovation, novelty, and dynamism, whereas premodernity is strategically dramatized as metaphysical stasis, caricatured by Tai's changelessness. The metaphorical proto-genitor Aadam, a doctor educated in Europe for five years – which had "altered [his] vision" and had given him "travelled eyes" (11) – becomes to Saleem the emblem of the secular age.[14] Aadam is the first man in the family to abandon his religion. This altered vision makes his childhood place seem strange. For years after that first unhomely encounter with home "he would try and recall his childhood springs in

---

[14] To use Margaret Archer's words, he is Modernity's Man, a kind of "second Adam … intended to be a 'sovereign artificer' not only of himself but together with those like him, of his society" (Margaret S. Archer, *Being Human: The Problem of Agency*, Cambridge: Cambridge University Press, 2004, 64).

paradise, the way it was before travel and tussocks and army tanks messed up everything" (11).

For Saleem, Aadam becomes a victim of his nostalgic marriage to a traditional wife. Naseem refuses to have sex with Aadam the European way, seeing it as a modern innovation and aberration. Then, when Aadam banishes a religious tutor, she refuses him food because "Aziz's death by starvation would be a clear demonstration of the superiority of her idea of the world over his" (51). To refuse him food is in a sense to excommunicate him. The sharing of food is indeed the primal communitarian gesture that creates bonds. She may not approve of the tutor's hate speeches, but the mullah's outspoken religious stance is reason enough for her to choose him over Aadam, who burnt her *purdah* as a violent gesture against her religious conformism. Saleem parodies, as Kortenaar suggests, "the union of tradition and modernity"[15] in his grandparents. By making Reverend Mother increasingly grotesque, he shows clear preference for modernized Aadam. It is significant that Aadam abandons his religion during a prayer, when he attempted to reconnect with Islam and forget the influence of German anarchists. In Aadam's fortunate fall, God is replaced by modern history, the eternal for the finite, and the spiritual for the material.

The crucial existential implication is that the displacement of God from Aadam's heart leaves a hole that needs to be filled. In the third generation, Saleem inherits his grandfather's hole – anguished being-in-the-world. In a sense, Saleem posits the *topos* of the heart as that which must be occupied by something. If not God then History, which either becomes like God or rival to it. In comparison, Sartre argued that a hole "presents itself to me as the empty image of myself",[16] and that it is a fundamental human tendency to plug up holes. The hole is the lack of a self. When Saleem takes the allegory of the nation as his purpose, the nation is supposed to fill that hole or void in him, but it does not have a stable self either. What Saleem does not spell out, but which seems obvious, is that he actually allegorizes national *angst*, India's colonial and even a postcolonial nervous condition. His lack of meaning is also India's lack of intrinsic meaning or purpose. If the

---

[15] Neil ten Kortenaar, *Self, Nation, Text in Salman Rushdie's* Midnight's Children, Montreal: McGill-Queen's University Press, 2004, 27.

[16] Jean-Paul Sartre, *Existentialism and Human Emotions*, New York: Philosophical Library, 1957, 84.

opposite were the case, then there would be no need for political desire for an original culture and meaning.

The second set of foils consists of Aadam and Tai the boatman, emblems of opposed forces of urban and rural nationalism, which for Fanon evolve separate dialectics.[17] In 1915, when Aadam returns from Germany, the subcontinent is still colonized but not yet a modernized place: "the valley had hardly changed since the Mughal Empire" (10). Tai, "the living antithesis of Oskar-Ilse-Ingrid's belief in the inevitability of change" (15), stands for the preservation of cultural essences to such an extent that he becomes an illustrative caricature. Tai struggles to encapsulate himself in a time that is already dying, posing as a bulwark against the surging industrialization of the country. People fear him as well as hold him in awe, because he knows the country to the least detail and because he delivers poignant monologues (14). He represents "the old place [that] resented [Aziz's] educated stethoscoped return" (9), with a "big bag full of foreign machines" (20). Tai mistakenly believes a stethoscope to be a smelling device (23). He fears that instead of the nose, Aadam will use machines to tell him how to perceive his world. Describing Tai in these terms and pitting him against Aadam, Saleem seems to buy into the historicist judgment of the peasantry as "a shorthand for all the nonmodern, rural, non-secular relationships and life practices".[18] Here science and technology are deemed foreign and incompatible with the local modes of production. Obviously, Tai does not fear technology as mere objects, but the implied ideologies, and how these might affect his people.

Tai's aversion to the stethoscope might be another of Saleem's ironic exaggerations, but at the same time Saleem will come to share his fears with the rise of military and industrial technology that turns everything into just another, meaningless thing. While it is clear that Saleem has already opted for some Enlightenment ideals he learnt from Aadam and which for him constitute modernity, he still cannot make the full transition. The reason for this is his realization that modernity is not less mythological (white mythologies, as Young called them). Secondly, it seems to bring along the possibility of

---

[17] Fanon, *The Wretched of the Earth*, 71.
[18] Chakrabarty, *Provincializing Europe*, 11. Chakrabarty uses Guha's work to emphasize how resistance orchestrated by high-class West-educated figures overshadowed any peasant struggle, which was based in local religions.

meaninglessness and nihilism (allegorized by technology) that he simply cannot accept. He refutes Tai's changelessness, but he does not want Aadam's change to imply purposelessness of existence.[19] He finds it hard to opt for one set of beliefs and practices that he has been handed down without renouncing the truth-claim of any other. He finds it hard to distinguish between the idea that meaning is contingent and that there is no meaning. He becomes lonely in the bursting and growing Bombay, where all kinds of cultures meet, mix and repel. The multitudes and the threatening loss of meaning, which are for Rege "implicit in the crisis of the nation",[20] drive him to isolation, anonymity and *angst*.

Although he comes to endorse change, when he meets Shiva the Destroyer, Saleem sees himself in terms of Vishnu the Preserver (biographer). For him to change is to transform, whereas for Shiva it is to destroy. This is why Shiva embodies negative aspects of modernity, and becomes "a sort of a principle" of "all the vengefulness and violence and simultaneous-love-and-hate-of-things in the world" (379), and "the nuclear age" (517).[21] When Saleem pits both traditional Indian and Enlightenment ideals against this destructive force – "But ... free will ... hope ... the great soul, otherwise known as *mahatma*, of mankind ... and what of poetry, and art" – Shiva counters:

> ... there is only money-and-poverty .... All that importance-of-the-individual. All that possibility-of-humanity. Today, what people are is just another kind of thing. (324)

Just like the bourgeois Saleem, Shiva too has an existential crisis. His anguish and nihilist vision of the world leads him in another direction.

---

[19] In addition, the Tai/Aadam conflict corresponds to the one that characterizes centuries of Western philosophy, the oversimplified Parmenides/Heraclitus dialectic of being and becoming. Also see Stephen Barker's argument that although change "has to do with a strategic deviation from an identifiable convention or position", they are two sides of the same coin (*Signs of Change: Premodern→Modern→Postmodern*, ed. Stephen Barker, New York: SUNY Press, 1996, xv).

[20] Rege, "Victim into Protagonist?", 191.

[21] This might be an allusion to Oppenheimer's citing of Bhagavad-Gita in connection to the first nuclear attacks: "now I am become Death [Shiva], the destroyer of worlds" (J. Robert Oppenheimer: http://www.youtube.com/watch?v=n8H7Jibx-c0).

Saleem's existentialism, as we will see in the second chapter, leads to an exploration of individuality and community.

Technology and time

Although Saleem is not nostalgic for ancient traditions, he might appear so because of his fear of the negative aspects of technological development and exploitation of human beings under new regimes. He wants to outline what it is in modernity that causes him most pain. By characterizing Aadam's change as "stethoscoped return", Saleem shows that technology is perceived as the epitome of modernity, and yet it should not be so. The progress of modern science is not negative *per se* in Saleem's view, but the potential loss of meaning is. By deeming Shiva as the sign of "the nuclear age" (517) which denies the human worth, Saleem emphasizes that the nuclear age is not progress, but carries in itself the sense of myth, albeit a secularized one, just as the apocalypse in Ondaatje's novel too has a secular character. While technology, in the sense of Greek *techne*, signals human freedom and creativity (the myth of Prometheus), for Saleem and Shiva it turns everything into "just another kind of thing" (324). It signifies exploitation and commodification, rather than creativity. Man as such becomes conceived as the self-asserted shaper of existence, who conceives of everything as the raw material for his desires. Heidegger argued:

> ... the [uprising] producer who puts through, carries out, his own self and establishes this uprising as the absolute rule. The whole objective inventory in terms of which the world appears is given over, commended to, and thus subjected to the command of self-assertive production .... At bottom, the essence of life is supposed to yield itself to technical production.[22]

As for Saleem, he cannot accept the constant emptying of meaning, which he calls sterilization. He loves objects that brim with meaning. He elicits some Romantic tendencies in his entire "business of remarking [his] life" (8) under "guidance" of the perforated sheet and his spittoon. While the sheet is presented as Aadam's filial legacy, we also find out that Aadam does not hand it down. Rather, he hides it

---

[22] Martin Heidegger, *Poetry, Language, Thought*, tr. Albert Hofstadter, New York: Harper and Row, 1975, 109.

and Saleem discovers it by accident. It is Saleem who makes it the symbol of the fall of the progenitor. The suggested obligation is make-believe, and in a sense an example of Saleem's creativity. We can compare this gesture to Heidegger's claim that for our grandparents, "a 'house,' a 'well,' a familiar steeple, even their own clothes, their cloak *still* meant infinitely more, were infinitely more intimate – almost everything a vessel in which they found something human already there".[23]

Saleem performs such a gesture, but he removes the element of inheritance. He suggests that he and his family have been dominated by the meaning of the sheet, but the readers are given a hint that this is quite a ridiculous claim, which actually shows the facticity of his freedom and creativity. I will address such creativity, in the second chapter, as Saleem's authentic action.

The way Saleem dramatizes the conflict between Dr Narlikar and the religious masses lays bare his belief in the split between different meaning systems and his inability to either opt for any, synthesize them, or hybridize them. He says, the "technological miracle [tetrapods] had been transformed into Shiva-lingam ... the old priapic forces of ancient, procreative India had been unleashed upon the beauty of sterile twentieth-century concrete" (225). Although Saleem is aversive to the Shiva-lingam, he is equally repelled by the sterility of modern technological construction whose purpose is not only contingent but actually missing. The children's sterilization too emphasizes the implied power of inheritance, as well as the threat of meaninglessness that seems to be the offspring of the modern age.[24] This is why technology brings about his undoing. Knowing that the miraculous in the new age belongs to technology, he interprets his mystical ability in terms of the radio transmission (212). Two centuries earlier, he would interpret his ability in different terms. Although he argues that he needs no machine to gather voices and that his mind is not a radio, he feels he must use the scientific lingo that

---

[23] *Ibid.*, 110 (emphasis in the original). As Adorno argued, Heidegger succumbed to nostalgia for untainted low-technological peasant existence (Adorno, *The Jargon of Authenticity*, 43-47). The problem is not only that rural purity is an illusion, but also that it has been the ground of nationalism, and partly served as justification of ethnic cleansing.

[24] Saleem's obsession with sterility is a parallel to Camus' *The Outsider*, in which the protagonist lives, as Sartre put it, "magnificently sterile" life (Sartre, *Existentialism Is a Humanism*, 81).

may be more appealing and understandable to his contemporaries: "I seem to be stuck with this radio metaphor." To his audiences this metaphor is more accessible. It is more realist than magical. He begins "to act as a sort of network ... a forum in which they could talk to one another ... the parliament of [his] brain" (288). He uses the term for surveillance, "just think of me as a ... a big brother" (289, ellipsis in the original). Yet, his gift is also preternatural. Therefore, he anticipates his undoing in "telecommunications" (375). Saleem is burdened by the historicist split between the modern and premodern frameworks. He cannot entirely opt for any conflicting aspects, or even reconcile them in a stable synthesis, in part because the disparate elements enter all manner of relationships, exchange, barter, and produce alternate and counter modernities. The hybridity does not resolve the conflicts in stable syntheses but actually maintains them.

We have noted earlier that Saleem's existential confusion is related to historicist, empty, homogenous time, which seems to be his primary understanding of it:

> ... history, in my version, entered a new phase on August 15th, 1947 – but in another version, that inescapable date is no more than one fleeting instant in the Age of Darkness, Kali-Yuga, in which the cow of morality has been reduced to standing, teeteringly, on a single leg ... the age when property gives a man rank, when wealth is equalled with virtue, when passion becomes the sole bond between men and women, when falsehood brings success ... began on Friday 18th, 3102 B.C.; and will last a mere 432,000 years! Already feeling somewhat dwarfed, I should add nevertheless that the age of darkness is only the fourth phase of the present Maha-Yuga cycle which is, in total, ten times as long; and when you consider that it takes a thousand Maha-Yugas to make just one Day of Brahma, you'll see what I mean about proportion. (247)[25]

It is only in a time defined by historicist categories of unity and teleological development that the age receives its meaning. With respect to the Maha-Yuga, Independence has no grand significance. It does not mark the beginning of an age because it is but an instance in an extremely long age of darkness. Generally speaking, Bhabha calls this "the *despotic* time of the Orient that becomes a great problem for

---

[25] From the medieval Christian viewpoint, the world would be under creation at the time of the fourth Maha-Yuga.

the definition of modernity and its inscription of the history of the colonized from the perspective of the West".[26] If Saleem truly has a historicist conviction, it is no wonder he is confused: "no people whose word for 'yesterday' is the same as their word for 'tomorrow' can be said to have a firm grip on the time" (133).[27] This word is *kale*. Indeed, as Kortenaar maintains, Saleem ultimately understands that the modern nation-state relies on myth. Indeed, "Methwold's Englishmade clock does not measure empty time, but counts down the days and minutes until midnight, the witching hour … 'every nation' retains a strong component of the Messianic time supposedly left behind by modernity".[28]

This does not mean there is no change or no modernization. It does not mean we cannot distinguish between different hybridities and modernities because everything is hybrid or modernized. It only means that the change should not be oversimplified. For Saleem, the complexity of the hour of freedom shows that

> … time has been an unsteady affair, in my experience, not a thing to be relied upon. It could even be partitioned: the clocks in Pakistan would run half an hour ahead of their Indian counterparts … If they can change time like that, what's real any more? I ask you? What's true? (97)

Those who control clocks control people, "Mountbatten's ticktock … English-made, it beats with relentless accuracy" (133). There is double irony in this claim. The clock is not relentlessly accurate. Since

---

[26] Bhabha, *The Location of Culture*, 352-3 (emphasis in the original).

[27] Typical of pre-industrial peasant existence, Tai's time is time to sow, time to harvest, time to rest, etc. It is a time of recurrence, and implies an attunement to natural processes and their intervals as well as the cycles of *maya* (see Aruna Srivastava, "'The Empire Writes Back': Language and History in *Shame* and *Midnight's Children*", in *Past the Last Post: Theorizing Post-Colonialism and Post-Modernism*, eds Ian Adam and Helen Tiffin, Calgary: University of Calgary Press, 1990, 65-78). Cyclical time is constituted by a certain manner of historical existence, connected to a certain manner of production and not exclusively bound to the Orientalist vision of premodern India.

[28] Kortenaar, *Self, Nation, Text*, 23-24. Appadurai is of a similar opinion when he suggests that opposing "the most problematic legacies of grand Western social science major social forces have precursors, precedents, analogues, and sources in the past" that "have frustrated the aspirations of modernizers in very different societies to synchronize their historical watches" (Arjun Appadurai, *Modernity at Large: Cultural Dimensions of Globalization*, Minneapolis: University of Minnesota Press, 1996, 2-3).

time is not a constant, but rather "as variable and inconstant as Bombay's electric power supply" (133), the supposed English (scientific and technological) supremacy is undermined. The midnight hour is used to actually mark the moment when colonial powers officially allow for freedom of the Indian peoples, a freedom that is a double or even triple partition: between colonial and postcolonial eras, between premodern and modern ages, and also a synchronic split (or forking) between two major ethnicities. It is no accident that the large clock is like the all-seeing eye above the Methwold estate, from where Ahmed Sinai manages his enterprises. The possibility of counting time by means of a clock is suitable for escalating industrial mass production. Even Saleem ends up working on mass production of pickles, working against the clock. Chronometric technology makes capitalist mass production possible, and strongly downplays existential meaning. (If the clock marks Methwold's time, then it seems logical that it stops working.)

At one level, Saleem insists on historicist chronology, which gives the illusion that the whole operates by a uniform and therefore meaningful progression. However, this continuity is constructed out of what Chakrabarty calls discontinuous and affective histories of belonging and their specific temporalities. If the grand, national history is a compound of all the events and actions, of all the individual and local-communal histories, these elements cannot but disturb and complicate the progressive time-line. Only after we have read the entire story can we trace nodes that give the sense of a linearity, which amusingly enough is the imperative Saleem ascribes to his one-woman audience, Padma. The actual first reading gives the sense of stalled progression. Nothing ever simply unfolds and follows upon anything else without connecting and unfolding along other sidetracks. The problem is these sidetracks often make no sense in the grand narrative of the nation, like the fact that Ahmed hurt his toe on the night of Independence.

What does it then mean that thirty years after Independence, Saleem makes his "way back to the capital, conscious that an age, which had begun on the long-ago midnight, had come to a sort of an end" (562)? It means that the age only "sort of" ends, because despite modern technology and accuracy of time measurements, an age is an old concept. Any period of time can be an age, and in different societies ages come and go differently, that is, not according to the social simultaneity of historicist temporality. An age can be valued, and have meaning. It can be dark even when amusingly "contradicted by the available meteorological data". The midnight here has "excessively romantic" meaning (563). A transition between ages is a long and ambivalent process, and despite frequent ruptures there is no one single unplugging from the past, even within four generations (Aadam, Amina, Saleem, Aadam). The past pushes into the future, just as the future pushes against and into the past. The future-directed vector of time also contains several other vectors that point out of it, circle back in, etc. There are both continuities and ruptures, even though the specific epoch in which Saleem lives foregrounds discontinuities. The entire focus on time perception and its relation to technology serves to put a melodramatic emphasis on Saleem's existential conundrum and the nervous condition he shares with his nation. The standstill of the clock in a turbulently changing history is Saleem's way of expressing the aporia of his existence, the conflicts that rage but do not push forward. While he indeed opts for the modern idea of individual freedom, for Saleem authenticity becomes an opening of a critique of modernity as well, and an articulation of his way of being free.

CHAPTER 2

THE ROAD OF EXISTENTIAL STRUGGLE
IN *THE FAMISHED ROAD*

Okri's protagonist, the abiku spirit Azaro is born at one of the most precarious and chaotic times in the history of the African territory on the verge of becoming the modern, decolonized nation state of Nigeria: "Our road was changing. Nothing was what seemed any more."[1] Azaro further claims, "I knew we were in the divide between past and future. A new cycle had begun, an old one was being brought to a pitch" (256). This is the highest point of material and spiritual famine of the colonized peoples. Azaro, whose own transformation from spirit to human is partly an allegory of this historical transformation, suffers "anxiety", and "nausea" (523). The struggle out of his nervous condition comes to constitute Azaro's way of being free.

Writing from the aura of post-Independence disillusionment with nationalism, Okri dramatizes both material suffering, and what Ato Quayson calls "existential hunger" in pre-Independence Nigeria.[2] By having Azaro abandon the abiku cycles, Okri suggestively opposes a repetition of what Quayson calls "the cyclicality of political irresponsibility", because the country about to be born "has not done enough to transcend the trauma of unbending underdevelopment or the nausea of confusion in its unfocused attempts to escape it".[3] Brenda Cooper characterizes Nigeria as "the bizarre product of both new and old, tradition and burgeoning change", the latter being effectuated by "Western money, technology and education

---

[1] Ben Okri, *The Famished Road*, (1991), London: Vintage, 2003, 428 (all subsequent references to *The Famished Road* are given in the text).

[2] Ato Quayson, *Strategic Transformations in Nigerian Writing: Rev Samuel Johnson, Amos Tutuola, Wole Soyinka, Ben Okri*, Bloomington: Indiana University Press, 1997, 122.

[3] *Ibid.*, 132.

haphazardly and unevenly".[4] Okri dramatizes not only the conflicts between premodern and modern understandings of existence, but rather the ways in which these conflicts create the aporetic hybridity of them, and how the politicization of ghost, gods and myths produces even more terrifying oppressors of "the wretched of the earth".[5] Everyone except the power-mongering ideologues seems to lack agency to change the world. This is in particular true within the ghettos, which, as in *Midnight's Children*, are not integrated into the major social and economical shifts, but retain a form of liminal existence.

Edna Aizenberg suggests that Azaro's liminality does not render him "susceptible to fragmentation of identity bequeathed by colonialism" because his cyclical perception of time rises above the history of colonialism.[6] Azaro is not spared social ruptures. He is unable to articulate the changes except in terms of old/new. Not even cyclical time conception escapes the dynamic between before and after: "New spaces were being created ... which we couldn't name, and couldn't imagine, but could only hint at with unfinished gestures and dark uncompleted proverbs" (516). Azaro's predicament is indeed graver that of ordinary humans whose beliefs and practices are questioned. Rather his very ontology is in question:

> I ran through the yellow forests, through deluded generations, through time. I witnessed the destruction of great shrines, the death of mighty trees that housed centuries of insurgent as well as soothing memories, sacred texts, alchemical secrets of wizards and potent herbs. I saw the forests die. I saw the people grow smaller in being. I saw the death of their many roads and ways and philosophies .... I heard the great spirits of the land and forest talking of a temporary exile .... I saw the rising of new houses. I saw new bridges span the air. The old bridges invisible, travelled on by humans and spirits alike, remained intact and less frequented. As the freedom of space and friendship with the pied kingfisher and other birds became more limited with the new age,

---

[4] Brenda Cooper, "Out of the Centre of My Forehead, an Eye Opened: Ben Okri's *The Famished Road*", in *Magical Realism in West African Fiction: Seeing with a Third Eye*, ed. Brenda Cooper, London: Routledge, 1998, 67.

[5] Okri, *Infinite Riches*, 161.

[6] Edna Aizenberg, "'I Walked with a Zombie': The Pleasures and Perils of Postcolonial Hybridity", *World Literature Today: A Literary Quarterly of the University of Oklahoma*, LXXIII/3 (Summer 1999), 81.

something died in me. I fled deep into the salt-caves of rocklands. Hunters with new instruments of death followed. (524)

After thousands of years of reincarnations, Azaro experiences changes that entail the death of older ways of being and understanding the world, and the rise of something new. Although he is speaking about transformations (and escapes into exile), rather than abrupt shifts, the emphasis on dying serves to highlight the severity of the changes. Political shifts serve to increase rather than ameliorate or root out oppression and exploitation. In a sense, this transformation from the old to the new is also cyclical: ideologies change but the suffering recurs and even increases. While Azaro has a nostalgic yearning for some kind of pre-ideological mode of being when "human beings and animals understood one another, we were all free" (524), the very myth of the beginnings and the hungry road suggests that there never was such a general state of being. Shaken out of his musing, Azaro sees

> … the ghost forms of white men in helmets supervising the excavation of precious stones from the rich earth …. the ghost figures of young men and women, heads bowed, necks and ankles chained together, making their silent procession through the celebrations. They kept moving but stayed in the same place. Over them celebrants danced to the music of a new era that promised Independence. (521)

Azaro offers his agonizing vision of the future Independence, which is celebrated by the rich who can dance "with political erections" (522), benefiting from the changes, while the poor stomp in chains. Azaro says, "I saw a duiker gazing at me as if my freedom lay in freeing it from imminent death, from being sacrificed for the opening of the road of Madame Koto's destiny" (524). The symbolic duiker is about to be slaughtered by Koto for the sake of the Party of the Rich, the heirs of the colonial authority. Azaro traces his own existential death in the sacrifice of the animal.

Margaret Cezair-Thompson argues that *The Famished Road* is a far cry from the colonial/postcolonial concerns of other African writers, and that Azaro is not "burdened by a heightened awareness of history".[7] The trope "road" is predicated on an existential concern with history. The road of history stretches infinitely back into the past and with no end in sight: "there are never really any beginnings or endings" (559). Although the "road" motif seems to highlight the landscape, Okri uses it to suggest historical time. This myth of origins is also the myth of history, the roads of Man. Okri transforms the recognizable form of "In the beginning there was" (3), which he combines with the local myth of the volatile river that becomes a hungry road of history. This local myth is blown up into the master myth of the abiku trilogy. Anjali Roy suggests, "the road serves as a symbol of the enlightenment myth of progress viewed from a Yoruba perspective".[8] The mythical "King of the Road" (298), who swallowed passengers without offerings has transformed into the modern infrastructure that devours those who work on its creation. Like the mythical ones, the modern roads demand immense sacrifices. Yet, while the modernization of the country is supposed to bring about progress, Okri insists on the endless repetition of historical injustice: "I recognised the new incarnations of their recurrent clashes, the recurrence of ancient antagonisms, secret histories, festering dreams" (227). Therefore, a night of a riot can be "a night without memory" which keeps "replaying its corrosive recurrence on the road of our lives, on the road which was hungry for great transformations" (211). Like the primordial river, everything shape-shifts, yet nothing changes. This is why the famished road of history consists of cyclical transformations, which resemble "the condition of the spirit child" (558). Azaro's friend Ade prophesizes:

> There will be changes. Coups. Soldiers everywhere. Ugliness. Blindness. And then when people least expect it a great transformation is going to take place in the world .... A wonderful change is coming from far away and people will realise the great meaning of struggle and hope. There will be peace. Then people will forget. Then it will all start again, getting worse, getting better .... Our country is an abiku

---

[7] Margaret Cezair-Thompson, "Beyond the Postcolonial Novel: Ben Okri's *The Famished Road* and Its 'Abiku' Traveller", *The Journal of Commonwealth Literature*, XXXI/2 (January 1996), 36.

[8] Anjali Roy, "Post-modern or Post-colonial? Magic Realism in Ben Okri's *The Famished Road*", in *The Post-Colonial Condition of African Literature,* eds Daniel Gover, John Conteh-Morgan and Jane Bryce, Trenton: Africa World Press, 2000, 32.

> country. Like the spirit-child, it keeps coming and going. One day it
> will decide to remain. (547)

Madame Koto's bar becomes the emblematic site of the historical transformations. From a shabby bar serving old-fashioned wine and pepper soup, it becomes a place with electricity, gramophone, and a centre for political meetings. In Faris' words, this "mise-en-abime" is a stage "for encounters between modern inventions and ancient traditions", in fact, "a relentlessly hybrid place, which confounds our sense of space and time".[9] In the beginning, it is frequented by "mutant customers", ghosts transformed into humans, who keep "materialising, it seemed, form the night air" producing in Azaro "the purity of fear" (158). For Derek Wright the bar is "a ready made allegory of cultural transition",[10] a "zone of syncopated realities".[11] The spirits have become confused, not only trying to emulate humans, but pretending to be modern. Azaro fears and hates their borrowed humanity, perhaps because they reflect his own condition. Madame Koto "crossed the divide between past and future. She must have known that a new cycle had begun" (262). This is partly signalled when "the bar lost some of its fairyland quality" (249) and became a place where political agitators have party meetings. When he sees a gramophone, Azaro thinks he "stepped into another reality on the edge of the forest" (312). The turning disc "seemed a perfect instrument for the celebration of the dead" (314).

Azaro is not wrong when he deems it a product of a new god, because the dancing "full of hunger, yearnings" is in a sense a modern ritual that promotes worship and fetishism. Using the vocabulary that is more suggestive of the mythical universe for things and practices, Azaro both emphasizes the split between modernity and premodernity, and blurs the boundaries between the two. The magical realist vocabulary foregrounds both epistemological and ontological confusions and shared disorientations. The characters' "lives kept turning on the same axis of anguish" (322). Modernity fails to deliver on the promise of freedom and progress, and puts a new face to the cycles of oppression.

---

[9] Faris, *Ordinary Enchantments*, 99.
[10] Derek Wright, "Whither Nigerian Fiction? Into the Nineties", *The Journal of Modern African Studies*, XXXIII/2 (1995), 328.
[11] *Ibid.*, 327.

Azaro and the ghetto population come in conflict with Madame Koto, who acts as a forerunner of the new hybrid politics. They spread rumours of her involvement in "the most terrifying cults in the land", and even her "drinking [of] human blood" (428). To devalue her Party of the Rich, they interpret her as

> ... a fabulous and monstrous creation. It did not matter that some people insisted that it was her political enemies who put out all these stories. The stories distorted our perception of her reality. Slowly, they took her life over, made themselves real, and made her opaque in our eyes. (428)

The conflict culminates when Koto's bar lights up with electricity: "Illiterate crowds gathered in front of the bar to see this new wonder ... but they did not see the famed electricity" (427). Okri's descriptions are here, as Cooper puts it, "ironic inversions of reality, where the spirits are a routine part of the mundane everyday, and electric light and sound constitute the awesome and the unbelievable" modern miracle.[12] This miracle has a profoundly disturbing effect on the population. Figures in "white smocks" with "ostentatious Bibles" that look like "an instrument of vengeance" of their "self-anointed prophet" (429) come to protest. They all danced

> ... with righteous fervour and prayed with fearful certainty in front of the bar. They evoked visions of fire and brimstone, sulphur and torment and damnations. They prayed as if they were purging the land of a monstrous and incarnate evil. They sprinkled holy water over the ground and threw holy grains of sand towards the bar. (429-30)

Like "an army of divine vengeance" (430), they sang "a song of exorcism" as a "bitter attack against the scourge of Madame Koto's electricity". The head-priest delivers "a tremendous philippic on the apocalypse of science". He declares, "Let us stand as one to drive out this ABOMINATION" (431). He calls Koto "the GREAT WHORE OF THE APOCALYPSE". The question is why is she qualified as abominable. The man acts as if his Christian faith is still in the middle ages and not something already integrated and appropriated by the Western modernity and the machinery of colonialism. His faith seems to be at a

---

[12] Cooper, "Out of the Centre of My Forehead, an Eye Opened", 84.

different stage, more akin to that of the village herbalist. Although the sky opens by "an unbearably radiant being" and rain pours down and lightning strikes over and again, as if to disagree with his claims, the priest takes it as a positive sign and continues "railing against the prostitutes, science, theories of evolution, the enshrinement of reason against God, and evil women of Babylon" (432). As he does this, "a procession of cars" parks outside the bar, with no fear of the elements. Groups of fancily dressed people step out to join the party.

In order to cope with everything in ways familiar to them, in order to inscribe strange new things into their everyday existence, the people join a ritual of blessing Koto's car, the "crown" of their "amazement". Koto is the first "woman in the area to own a car" (433), "a pioneer" (434). A herbalist comes to anoint it, and even trace its "friends in the spirit world" (435). These gestures serve to alleviate the existential confusion that arises from the experience of change. Harry Garuba coins the phrase "prepossessing the future" to explain the way local animism is employed to provide a cultural "continuum rather than a chasm, thus giving an imposed subjective order to the chaos of history".[13] This gesture works as a temporary buffer that later caves in. The priest cries out:

> Too many roads! Things are CHANGING TOO FAST! No new WILL ....
> THEY ARE DESTROYING AFRICA! They are DESTROYING the WORLD and
> the HOME and the SHRINES and the GODS! (437)

Burnt out of the land, strange creatures keep emerging everywhere and the forest becomes "full of mirages from which [Azaro] could not escape" (282). Garuba sees animism as "a non-doctrinaire mould of constant awareness", an assimilative thought that admits of no binaries but is rather open to inclusion, even the inclusion of Marxist materialist thought.[14] However, Okri does no such thing. He describes Nigeria, and Africa in general, as the quarry of infinite riches, which are squandered by spiritually sterile elites (both indigenous and colonial) who have switched to the worship of new imperialist gods. Indeed, the upcoming industrialization of Nigeria, the building of infrastructure, roads and houses, is the Governor-General's dream of a

---

[13] Harry Garuba, "Explorations in Animist Materialism: Notes on Reading/Writing African Literature, Culture, and Society", *Public Culture*, XV/2 (Spring 2003), 270.
[14] *Ibid.*, 276.

"beautiful road" on which "all Africa's wealth ... would be transported to his land" (204).[15] The "famished road", both in its mythical and modern form, keeps the sense of the exploitation of African soil. Ancient forests, brimming with the country's spirituality, are mowed down, "a new world was being created amidst the old" (132). Azaro's Dad becomes one of the major figures who demand real changes that will reduce people's suffering: "There are many nations, civilisations, ideas, half discoveries, revolutions, loves, art forms, experiments and historical events that are of this condition and do not know it" (558). Dad claims that the new age is characterized by the silence of the gods and ancestors under the weight of modernity imported from "the Western world, our history and achievements rigged out of existence" (564).

The idea of cyclical transformations is a critique of the inability of Nigerians to carry through an authentic revolution, and unfetter themselves from the burden of both pre-colonial and colonial past, their inability to give birth to themselves. Dad explains:

> We have entered a new age. We must be prepared. There are strange bombs in the world. Great powers in space are fighting to control our destiny. Machines and poisons and selfish dreams will eat us up .... Our gods are silent. Our ancestors are silent .... We must take interest in politics. (571)

While Dad seems nostalgic for the lost past, he does not argue for an action towards its recovery, but a revolutionary engagement with the complex, conflicting, and confusing hybrid world.

Quayson uses the example of the spirit/human polarity to emphasize the suggested change. While "the interface between the spirit-world and that of men is often seen as a sort of hymenal interface, movement between the two worlds allowing a measure of control through appropriate rituals, Okri's work suggests the total

---

[15] In *Infinite Riches*, the Governor-General "rhapsodized about" the Africans' "love of music, their unscientific thinking, their explosive laughter, their preference for myth over reality, for story over fact, for mystification over clarification, for dance over stillness, for ecstasy over contemplation, for metaphysics over logic ... their deplorable habit of treating all events as signs meaning more than they do" (Okri, *Infinite Riches*, 159). This colonizer engages in "rewriting of our history", and reinventing "the geography of the nation", unwittingly effacing the natives "from creation" (*ibid.*, 110-11).

dissolution of boundaries, as if the hymen has been permanently ruptured [resulting in an] extreme esoteric fluidity".[16]

Even Azaro, who should be ontologically anchored in the eternal spirit world and immune to human weaknesses, is "filling with unease and anxiety .... nausea and bile rising in my throat" (523). He feels he is a plaything of the road (which I read as history):

> The road became what it used to be, a stream of primeval mud, a river .... There were shrines everywhere and God spoke in the bright wind and the giants spoke back in whispers .... I was both lost and blind .... I drifted in the chaos of grief and wind and rain. (330-32)

Okri here inverts the myth of origins or rather closes the cycle by returning to the image of the primordial mud.

The entire event is a dramatization of Azaro's existential confusion: "The rain made everything alien. Its persistence altered my vision" (333). In fact, his community too feels "edgy in the long spaces of an undefined expectancy" (341) and "contorted in paroxysms" (343). Azaro walks "with a terrible hunger for a destination". The road splits into a plethora of confusing roads that he cannot choose between: "I couldn't break the riddle of the market's labyrinths where one path opened into a thousand faces, all of them different, most of them hungry in different ways" (191). He meets emblematic figures such as "women of the new African churches", "prophets emerging from the forest", "sorcerers", and he hears "the passionate chants of the muezzin [which] roused the Muslim world to prayer" (133). The entire "world seemed populate with people intent on me" (133-34). Like Azaro, Dad is lost in this unfamiliar world:

---

[16] Ato Quayson, "Protocols of Representation and the Problems of Constituting an African 'Gnosis': Achebe and Okri", in *Yearbook of English Studies*, XXVII (1997), 147. While Cooper, Roy, Aizenberg, Faris, Deandrea and others, praise Okri's use of Latin American marvellous realism, Adewale Maja-Pearce deems it "a tedious exercise in the fantastic for its own sake" (Adewale Maja-Pearce, "Darkness Visible", in *A Mask Dancing: Nigerian Novelists of the Eighties*, ed. Adewale Maja-Pearce, London: Hans Zell Publishers, 1992, 103). It is important to argue that the language and imagery of the novel serve to produce the sense of confused and anguished characters. In *Songs of Enchantment*, Azaro says, "The chaos made us brain shocked .... The chaos made us hallucinate" (Ben Okri, *Songs of Enchantment*, London: Vintage, 151).

> My wife, my son, where are we going? There is no rest for the soul
> .... We must look at the world with new eyes. We must look at
> ourselves differently. (571)

The multiplicity of roads emerges from what at first sight appears to be a binary conflict between premodern and modern ideologies. At the same time, the spawning of new roads through a kind of uncontrollable hybridization and barter can, in turn, be viewed in terms of alternate modernities, foregrounded through Okri's mythical or magical realist style.

Despite his ancient age, Azaro's "feet were fresh on the paths" (134). He says:

> The worms of the road ate into the soles [souls?] of my feet .... My
> head boiled with hallucinations .... The roads seemed to me then to
> have a cruel and infinite imagination. All the roads multiplied,
> reproducing themselves, turning in on themselves, like snakes, tails in
> their mouths, twisting themselves into labyrinths. The road was the
> worst hallucination of them all, leading towards home and away from
> it, without end, with too many signs, and no directions. The road
> became my torment, my aimless pilgrimage. (134-35)

There are a number of roads to take. Azaro suffers "road-fever" (140), because he "walked on all the bad things they wash on the roads. All those witches and wizards, native doctors, sorcerers, who wash off bad things from their customers and pour them on the road, who wash diseases and bad destinies on the streets" (141). The multiple roads encapsulate all the bad intentions of the people who participated in their construction. The swaying back and forth between different roads makes Azaro lose his "sense of reality" (284), his "feet in agony" and "sense of direction askew" (285).

Okri's consistent use of material things such as disembodied body parts to describe the community increases the sense of the shocking defamiliarization with communal life in the face of "an *angst*-filled otherness machine" (465). Even the ordinary things ooze strangeness and appear threatening:

> In the darkness things merged into one another. The tables were like
> crouching animals. Benches were like human beings sleeping on air.
> (291)

One time, Azaro climbs the fetish tree to see where he is supposed to go to find his way back to his mother, but he sees "a completely different reality .... new spirit world" with a "creature ugly and magnificent like a prehistoric dragon", a "devourer of humans, of lost souls, of spirits" (286). Even the tree turns out to be a monster "awoken from a fetishistic sleep" that takes Azaro round, bursting "open a channel through centuries of bad dreams" (287).

Okri dramatizes the interplay between social and spiritual worlds implied in the Igbo proverb: the world is a marketplace and it is subject to bargain. What is at stake is not just the merchandise but political investments: "Now they want to know who you will vote for before they let you carry their load" (96). He cannot even be a slave unless he subscribes to his employers' ideology. Michael Jackson suggests that the marketplace allegorizes what Sartre understood as the mode of being of humanity, "a dynamic *relationship*" between historical circumstances beyond individual control and "our capacity to *live* those circumstances in a variety of ways".[17] It is a struggle within "unequally distributed" potentialities for being, a struggle "to strike a balance between being an actor and being acted upon" (x).

This is where authenticity comes in, as the process of creating new possibilities. Azaro and his community feel they have no agency to change their reality. They cannot envision change. The entire compound becomes "aflame with politics" brimming with "implacable enemies" (151), and "sick children, men in contorted forms of agony, women in attitudes of hungry outrage" (156).[18] More and more riots rage over his world: "the thugs and ordinary people alike poured over the road of our vulnerability, wounding the night with axes, rampaging our sleep, rousing our earth" (209). Politicians want to kill the photographer for exposing their power brokering, and because he inspires action. Yet, after the riots, Azaro feels nothing has really changed in their conditions. The conflicts remain and "the wind

---

[17] Michael Jackson, *Existential Anthropology: Events, Exigencies and Effects*, New York: Berghahn Books, 2005, xi (emphases in the original). In addition, Okri writes: "Society can be defined as the sphere in which all our hungers meet, as in a great chaotic marketplace" (Okri, *A Way of Being Free*, 7)

[18] The two parties are only called Party of the Rich, and Party for the Poor. The absence of proper names is suggestive of a number of abstractions: parents, ancestors, power, politicians, forests, spirits, ghosts, thugs, country, independence, black and white people, urbanization, etc.

of recurrence blew gently over the earth" (215). Transformative actions are still pending and more important than ever.

CHAPTER 3

HISTORY AND THE "NERVOUS CONDITION"
IN *THE ENGLISH PATIENT*

The English Patient is a drama at the margins of the largest military enterprise in the twentieth century, World War II. The characters' world is changing drastically in terms of location of power, reshaping of the geo-political structures, modes of production, economy, and ideological conflicts. Ondaatje's broken characters feel they have no say in the shaping of their identities and social conditions. The turbulent history of neo-colonialism causes their existential crises or nervous conditions.

Existential trauma and apocalyptic history
Ondaatje's focus on history has been the catalyst for the bulk of criticism on his work. While many are drawn to discuss his take on history in terms of postmodernism and the problematic of historiography, Amy Novak offers a rather Fanonian interpretation, suggesting that the novel confronts the reader with two levels of trauma: personal traumas and "the trauma of European History".[1] Marlene Goldman expands such a reading by using Walter Benjamin's understanding of history as a theoretical grid. She argues that like Benjamin's (or Klee's) "angel of history: who mournfully surveys a landscape of ruins, Ondaatje's narrative maps a wounded geography – the architectural, bodily, and psychic wreckage caused by the war .... The novel portrays apocalyptic catastrophe as irrevocable."[2]

The meaning of this apocalypse is predicated on religious paradigms. While apocalypse originally means revelation, what is

---

[1] Amy Novak, "Textual Hauntings: Narrating History, Memory, and Silence in *The English Patient*", *Studies in the Novel*, XXXVI/2 (Summer 2004), 206.

[2] Marlene Goldman, "'Powerful Joy': Michael Ondaatje's *The English Patient* and Walter Benjamin's Allegorical Way of Seeing", *University of Toronto Quarterly: A Canadian Journal of the Humanities*, LXX/4 (Fall 2001), 903.

revealed is the end of world history. Apocalypse here signifies destruction rather than a revelation of paradise. While biblical apocalypse signals divine predestination and metaphysical meaning through final ends, Ondaatje's apocalypse is, as Joseph Pesch puts it, "a secular apocalypse", which "has not revealed a new heaven or a new earth to them, but destroyed their worlds and identities".[3] Ondaatje's narrator quotes the Bible:

> *For the heavens shall vanish away like smoke and the earth shall wax old like a garment. And they that dwell therein shall die in like manner. For the moth shall eat them up like a garment, and the worms shall eat them like wool.*[4]

The biblical moth finds its counterpart in Clifton's plane, which the explorers call the "Moth" (256), whose flight over desolate lands partly prefigures the man-made nuclear holocaust in Japan. Ondaatje's language qualifies a series of modern historical events with respect to myth. His apocalypse is not just the envisioned end of history, but rather the continuous idling of history, which in my analysis contributes to the characters' nervous conditions. For Hana, "it feels like the end of the world" (292), whereas Caravaggio announces the "death of a civilisation" (286). Although the atomic attacks are on Japan, the civilization that dies appears to be the Western. What dies is the illusory supremacy of the Western Enlightenment, all "speeches of civilisation from kings and queens and presidents … such voices of abstract order" (285). The conflation of kings and presidents is a narrative gesture that permeates the entire novel, and which seems to blur the boundaries between seemingly incompatible historical phenomena. By going from kings to presidents as if there were no progress, Kip suggests that Western modernity is but a veneer to the continuous injustice: "tremor of Western wisdom" (284).

Kip experiences an existential breakdown, imagining the nuclear light as a form of modern artificial lightning, "brighter than sunlight, a flash of contained phosphorus, something machinelike" (277). This becomes a traumatic "history lesson" (285), which leads him to

---

[3] Josef Pesch, "Post-Apocalyptical War Histories: Michael Ondaatje's *The English Patient*", *ARIEL: A Review of International English Literature*, XXVIII/2 (April 1997), 122.
[4] Michael Ondaatje, *The English Patient*, London: Picador, 1993, 295 (emphases in the original. All subsequent references to *The English Patient* are given in the text).

denounce Western ideologies that have kept him in a certain socially narrow place. He enters a monastery and feels tiny and finite facing the "angel's raised arm". He "walks within the discussion of these creatures that represent some fable about mankind and heaven". They suddenly appear as "parental figures" engaged in "a debate over his fate. The raised terra-cotta arm a stay of execution, a promise of some great future for this sleeper, childlike, foreign-born" (280-81). This Christian context appears at first to be mythical, yet for Kip it has been born again through re-appropriation into new political schemes. The sacred figures participate in the modern warfare. Holding a position of the Asiatic/African Other who fights English wars, Kip suffers from *angst*, and as a gesture of some counter-modern unplugging, he plunges into "the Ofanto River" (295). Fending off his nervous condition, Kip makes an existential choice. He jumps off a bridge, which at first seems a suicide, whereas for him it is a choice of life, a hybrid form of baptism, an act as individual as resonant of other forms of ritual washing, which is also a comment on the search for the spiritual river from Rudyard Kipling's *Kim*.

The articulation of conflicts

Kip's example shows that Ondaatje's concern with World War II is not simply in terms of destruction and death, but in particular with the conflicts within Western modernity, a haunting sense that is not a true unplugging from premodernity. Although the war takes place in the twentieth century, and mainly between modern nation states, Ondaatje creates, as Susan Ellis suggests, "a rightful sense of power changing hands as a 'New Age' begins, by filling the novel with stories of the new man replacing the old, much like Rushdie: Gyges and Candaules, David and Goliath … Poliziano and Savonarola, Herodotus 'the father of history' supplemented by Almásy, Kip taking up the work of Lord Suffolk".[5] Indeed, Ondaatje posits a metaphoric polarity between Pico and Savonarola, and Poliziano and Michelangelo to qualify their own history. The patient describes them as holding "in each hand the new world and the old world" (57).

Yet, the anguished, aporetic existence is most prominent in Almásy's emphatic reference to various North African winds, most

---

[5] Susan Ellis, "Trade and Power, Money and War: Rethinking Masculinity in Michael Ondaatje's *The English Patient*", *Studies in Canadian Literature/Etudes en littérature canadienne*, XXI/2 (Fall 1996), 34.

importantly the "hot, dry *ghibli*" that causes the emblematic "nervous condition" (16). "Ghibli" is, as Peter Bekingsale explains, an Italian name for "'hot wind blowing over the Sahara desert.' The name has been frequently used since World War II for Italian combat aircraft, as well as Italian auto makers."[6] It is hardly a coincidence that the very name of the wind that causes the existential nervous condition denotes modern European battle planes employed in the imperialist war that ravishes North Africa.

The Libyan Desert changes from being a low-technological region to one being shaped by war machinery. At the same time, the desert space becomes a limbo where the explorers sink into ancient history:

> We sailed into the past. We were young. We knew power and great finance were temporary things. (142)

Furthermore, it is a place that erases history, where they lose their rationality, and deal with their nervous conditions:

> Within two weeks even the idea of a city never entered his mind. It was as if he had walked under the millimetre of haze, just above the inked fibres of a map, that pure zone between land and chart between distances and legend between nature and storyteller. Sandford called it geomorphology .... He knew during these time how the mirage worked, the fata morgana, for he was within it. (246)

The Enlightenment frameworks break down and dissolve into a kind of psychotic quagmire that pushes even a staunch atheist such as the English patient to say that there is

> God only in the desert, he wanted to acknowledge that now. Outside of this was just trade and power, money and war. Financial and military despots shaped the world. (250)

Here God is not equated with religious systems, which indeed include power relations and trade. He seems to find pleasure in "moving in ancient time" having "adapted into the breathing patterns of deep water. His only connection with the world of cities was Herodotus, his guidebook, ancient and modern, of supposed lies" (246), but "this vast

---

[6] Peter Bekingsale, "Studio Ghibli": http://mangalocity.com/studioghibliarticle.html.

and silent pocket of the earth became one of the theatres of war" (134). The explorers become true "servants and slaves" of "tides of power" (141) forming "'teams.' The Bremanns, the Bagnolds, the Slatin Pashas – who had at various times saved each other's lives – had now split into camps" (168). Almásy calls all warring sides Barbarians: "The Barbarians versus the Barbarians. Both armies would come through the desert with no sense of what it was" (257). There were

> Eight thousand men. But who was the enemy? Who were the allies of this place – the fertile lands of Cyrenaica, the salt marshes of El Agheila? All of Europe were fighting their wars in North Africa, in Sidi Rezegh, in Baguoh. (19)

The "Barbarian" qualifier draws on Herodotus, who stands for the spark of modern historiography, with his emphasis on the objective narrative that preserves deeds and suffering of men, both the Greek and the barbarians, as Arendt argues.[7] At the same time, this *pater historiae* epitomizes the historical canon that preserves the argument that splits the world into the civilized West and the barbaric East. Almásy changes, as Vernon Provencal suggests, "the imperial Herodotus" and constructs "the existential Herodotus",[8] and gives him credit for opposing "the imperial history of *progress*" and endorsing "the existential history of *process*".[9] The latter is foregrounded through the focus on propinquity of marginal personal histories; a propinquity that "appears here as an existential principle of historical patterning underlying the 'choreography of history.' Given its Herodotean context, however, the novel suggests a deeper, *fatal* connection between personal histories and the 'sweep of history.'"[10]

In fact, the characters are often swept away by the very "history they seek to escape".[11] Through a somewhat nostalgic intimacy with Herodotus, the English patient is able to show that history itself, as a concept, has changed. It is no longer, to use Arendt's words, "the story of events that affected the lives of men", but rather processes

---

[7] Arendt, *Between Past and Future*, 41.

[8] Vernon Provencal, "Sleeping with Herodotus in *The English Patient*", *Studies in Canadian Literature/Etudes en littérature canadienne*, XXVII/2 (Fall 2002), 150.

[9] *Ibid.*, 143 (emphases in the original).

[10] *Ibid.*, 152 (emphasis in the original).

[11] *Ibid.*, 153.

through which men "make history". Even further, with the uses of nuclear technology, history comes to be about changing (or splitting) reality at its subatomic level. For Arendt, this is an even bigger step from both "the pre-modern age" and the "industrial age".[12] Ondaatje's use of Herodotus is a way of expressing the immensity of historical transformations, in particular technological advancements, which in a sense leave man behind, unable to cope with the envisioned future.

Ondaatje mixes historically incongruous cultural motifs, as if to remove the history of progress and condense centuries of the West into small snippets which produce a sense of haunting. For instance, Madox's "Marston Magna in Somerset ... had turned its green fields into an aerodrome. The planes burned their exhaust over Arthurian castles." It is as if changes serve to conceal the fact that nothing has changed. Madox becomes immensely disillusioned upon meeting a priest who keeps "blessing the government and the men about to enter the war" (241). He understands that the church is not a holy, spiritual space, but a political scene in the theatres of war. Since the holy/unholy polarity has become ambiguous within the modern(ized) church, the English patient designates Madox's unholy act of suicide as holy. That is, the unholy becomes the new, supplementary holy.

Like Madox, after years of extensive solitude in the desert, the English patient is struck by the way in which his work has become instrumental for the warring sides:

> Was I a curse upon them? For her? For Madox? For the desert raped by war, shelled as if it were just sand. (257)

Ondaatje portrays the Libyan Desert against the backdrop of modern Europe. The conquering of the untillable land seems paramount for all war parties. Indeed, the English patient and his friends arrive in the desert as "the first great modern expedition" (136) signalling change. Their nationalist baggage affects their experience of the desert. They come with modern cars with "air wheels" that "ride better on sand" (139), and aircraft. More than simple material additions, Madox's and Clifton's airplanes are metaphors for entirely different understandings of existence from that of the otherwise obscure natives. In fact, Clifton was "the New Age, flying over and dropping codes" (229). His bird-eye perspective seems to yield power over the land, a scientific

---

[12] Arendt, *Between Past and Future*, 58.

objective perception, which also entails the loss of intimacy with landscape and its history that the early explorers tried to maintain. Clifton's instrumental reason mostly serves the military powers.

While the process of mapping signals objectification of natural phenomena, Almásy's trade of the maps for a plane with the Germans further stresses the surging commodification of the desert. Although Ondaatje seldom devotes attention to the natives, he presents the desert as an ancient living force that both resists, and fails to resist, modernization. In the desert, the English patient thinks he is "moving in ancient time" (246). He yearns to embrace the desert as an unspoiled, depoliticized place even though he himself has participated in its political shaping:

> *The deserts of Libya.* Remove politics, and it is the loveliest phrase I know. *Libya.* A sexual, drawn-out word, a coaxed well. (257, emphases in the original)

An old medicine man and the Bedouin tend him in ways that Hana smirks at as primitive (premodern). Despite the excruciating pain, the patient enjoys the mystical atmosphere created by the medicine man who is like a ghost using chants as much as ointments to alleviate his pains, and whose glass bottles seem to have lost their "civilisation" (10). His nostalgia for primitive, pre-political existence dissipates as yet another Romantic myth when he discovers that they have saved his life only so he could teach them about modern weaponry. They

> … knew about fire. They knew about planes that since 1939 had been falling out of the sky. Some of their tools and utensils were made from the metal of crashed planes and tanks. It was the time of war in heaven. They could recognize the drone of a wounded plane, they knew how to pick their way through such shipwrecks. A small bolt from a cockpit became jewellery. (5)

The Bedouin keep parts of plane wrecks like jewels, infusing them with mythic symbolic value besides their immediate utility, yet later on they are immensely interested in using modern weaponry. Ondaatje fuses and defuses mythological imagery with the reality of warfare. The "war in heaven" imagery is appropriately ambiguous. It disturbs the boundaries between premodern and modern frameworks. The heaven/sky is the space of a modern battle, but it also hints at the biblical angelic war from Revelations 12:7-9. The man that falls and survives is like a modern day Lucifer and yet he has hipbones of Christ. He remembers the Bedouin who anoint him (6) in terms of the Christian imagery of archangels and Baptists (9-10). Indeed, as Stephanie M. Hilger argues, he "becomes the battlefield for different historical meanings …. The characters' attempt to make the 'English' patient intelligible, to fit him into a category, is at the same time an indirect endeavor to come to terms with their own relation to a changed and changing reality."[13]

With the Bedouin he participates in ancient rituals, and they feed him like a bird would feed its chick. The way Ondaatje dramatizes the event in and outside the cave, brings forth the cave as a powerful mythical, as well as philosophical image. One cannot but be reminded of Plato's cave. Plato's cavemen, characterized by sleep of reason, are contrasted to the enlightened individuals who have walked out of the cave into the open light of ideas. It is this gesture that Žižek observes as the potential spark of modern Western thought that would come to bloom centuries later. Plato's cavemen are stymied both by chains and by their internalized myth which renders them passive *vis-à-vis* the projections before them. Even if liberated, facing the light (of reason), the cavemen are accustomed to their shackles. Ondaatje transforms Plato's cave into an ambiguous cadaverous space, a hybrid zone. When the Bedouin take Almásy out, they do it when the light is weak. This could be the sign of his inability to see the truth, but I am inclined to see the faintness of light in both places as suggestive of the dark sides of enlightenment.

Mark Cheetham and Elizabeth Harvey interpret the passages in which Almásy has a form of "necrophilic exchange" with his dead lover, as the "moment [which] evokes a tradition of the cave as passage to the underworld, the place where ghosts are encountered".[14] Indeed, for the ancient Greek and Latin poets, "caves were magical passageways between worlds, transitional meeting places of the divine

---

[13] Stephanie M. Hilger, "Ondaatje's *The English Patient* and Rewriting History", in *Comparative Cultural Studies and Michael Ondaatje's Writing*, ed. Steven Tötösy de Zepetnek, West Lafayette: Purdue University Press, 2005, 39.
[14] Mark A. Cheetham and Elizabeth D. Harvey, "Obscure Imaginings: Visual Culture and the Anatomy of Caves", *Journal of Visual Culture*, I/1 (2002), 106.

and quotidian planes of existence ... transformative microcosms of the metamorphic essence of the world order".[15]

At the same time, "the cave functions as a signifier for the artistic imperative, an endorsement of art history's place in cultural representation, and also as a mythic beginning point in the Western hegemony of the visual",[16] or the turning towards world views, what Heidegger called "world-as-picture".[17] Indeed, it is the discovery of cave drawings that signals to Almásy a civilization and history. In the novel, the cave is that ambiguous space where modernity and premodernity enter a kind of artistic theatre. This paradoxical mixing and repelling augments Almásy's *angst*.[18]

A parallel to the crucible of the desert cave is the Italian Villa San Girolamo, an oasis in the European desert created by "the last mediaeval war [which] was fought in Italy in 1943 and 1944":

> Mediaeval scholars were pulled out of Oxford colleges and flown into Umbria .... They were billeted with the troops, and in the meetings with strategic command they kept forgetting the invention of the airplane. They spoke of towns in terms of art in them. (69)

Kip "helped the mediaevalist off" (71), using "wands of gadgetry to clear mines" (73), like a magician sapper working in a world where

---

[15] *Ibid.*, 112.

[16] *Ibid.*, 106.

[17] Nancy laments "the fact that 'the world' has been secondary to the concept of a world 'view' (it was no accident that a *Weltanschauung* played by accident a major political and ideological role in Nazism). It is as if there was an intimate connection between capitalistic development and the capitalization of views or pictures of the world" (Jean-Luc Nancy, *The Creation of the World or Globalization*, tr. François Raffoul and David Pettigrew, New York: SUNY, 2007, 40).

[18] Indeed, the cave suggests a kind of "primal visuality" (Cheetham and Harvey, "Obscure Imaginings", 105), "the archetypal framework for perception and art-making in Western culture. Luce Irigaray (1985) offers a powerful critique of Western culture's visual bias, which relies ... on Plato's myth of the cave .... artists and theorists struggle with this paradoxical legacy, reproducing caves as projections of inspiration or of the mind itself and constantly interrogating the dialectic it encapsulates between interior and exterior, between materiality and transcendence, between the seen and unseen" (*ibid.*, 106). Even the Italian villa, with its connection to de Medici could be seen as a synthetic cave or grotto, a place where the dead and the living meet, a place that both evokes interiority and exteriority with its crumbled walls. The feeding scene in the cave resembles the Proustian one in which Hana peels plums with her teeth and feeds her patient.

explosives "were attached to taps, to the spines of books" and "drilled into fruit trees" (75). His awareness of the powers that keep him in place is heightened:

> [Kip] passes the Museo Archeologico Nazionale, where the remnants of Pompeii and Herculanum are housed. He has seen the ancient dog frozen in white ash …. It is the terrible silence in the empty courtyards and the dry fountains that makes him most tired. (278)

Ondaatje uses local art to draw a parallel between two types of destruction, the first being a volcano, which was in ancient times the sign of divine wrath. At the same time, the volcano image foreshadows a nuclear explosion (the rage of Man).

The crucial fact about the villa is that it is a former monastery, a place brimming with Christian meaning. Hana is a modern woman averse to premodern beliefs, which is clear both from her turning of a cross into a scarecrow and from her reaction to Kip's description of his intimacy with the Sikh tradition:

> 'Singing is at the centre of worship. You hear a song, you smell the fruit at the temple gardens – pomegranates, oranges. The temple is a haven in the flux of life, accessible to all. It is the ship that crossed the ocean of ignorance.' (271)

The temple stands for permanence of spirituality and existential meaning secured in "the Holy Book", which "lies under a canopy of brocades" (271). Hana's quietness as he tells her this reveals to him "the depth of darkness in her, her lack of a child and of faith". The loss of faith does not seem to be a mere dissemination of her Christianity, but also the faith in Modernity's man, in modern humanity which turns even an ethically idealized profession such as nursing into a care-machine. The priests Hana detests are like those that preach war in the scene when Madox kills himself. She and some other characters deal with their nervous conditions by trying to act authentically and take responsibility for their actions, as Kip does when he realizes he is implicated in the killing of people, the kind of murder for which he will not be held accountable because he is a mere cog in the machinery, and yet for which he feels he should take responsibility.

CHAPTER 4

DEATH AS A DRIVE TO MEANINGFUL EXISTENCE
IN *MIDNIGHT'S CHILDREN*

Saleem Sinai begins his life tale with his peculiar birth at the midnight inception of Indian Independence in August 1947, yet immediately the reader is made aware that the narrative is driven by his imminent death:

> … time (having no further use for me) is running out. I will soon be thirty-one years old. Perhaps. If my crumbling, over-used body permits. But I have no hope of saving my life, nor can I count on having even a thousand nights and a night. I must work fast … if I am to end up meaning – yes, meaning – something. (7)

Having faced the threat of death in war, from the Kali worshipers and language rioters, and having seen his family members killed, Saleem cannot but wonder if all this death somehow figures in a greater context in any meaningful manner? Are births and deaths planned in advance by an all-knowing divinity? Death, and by implication life, has for Saleem lost all meaning, which drives him to anguish and narrative: "What-chews-on-bones refuses to pause … it's only a matter of time. This is what keeps me going" (373). As Tim S. Gauthier argues, "narrative strains for the effect of having filled in all the gaps, of having put an image of continuity, coherency, and meaning in place of the fantasies of emptiness, need, and frustrated desire that inhabit our nightmares about the destructive power of time".[1] Rather than stultify, anguish drives him on.

Saleem's point of departure is a distrust, as well as admiration for the meaning different religions have invested in death. In order to ameliorate its impact, death is often perceived as a passage to another realm or mode of existence, or, in the case of reincarnation, a rebirth.

---

[1] Tim S. Gauthier, *Narrative Desire and Historical Reparations: A.S. Byatt, Ian McEwan, Salman Rushdie*, London: Routledge, 2006, 11.

Saleem complains that he "was not allowed to see the death of doctor Narlikar" and the doctor's corpse "lay wreathed in saffron flowers", which suggests nature, beauty and life, or a rebirth in a new form of existence. Young Saleem was told that the man's death had "taken on the qualities of water: it had become a fluid thing, and looked happy, sad, or indifferent according to how the light hit it." Another character says,

> 'It is dangerous to look too long at death; otherwise you come away with a little of it inside you .... A death makes the living see themselves too clearly; after they have been in its presence, they become exaggerated.' (226)

While this holds for all tenants of the Methwold Estate, Saleem himself becomes the greatest exaggeration.

Once the experience of mortality opens him up for radical questioning of his purpose, he embarks upon a desperate attempt to re-establish it, which leads him to exaggeration of his historical importance. In order to cope with the deaths of his family, Saleem states, "it is my firm conviction that the hidden purpose of the Indo-Pakistani war of 1965 was nothing more or less than the annihilation of my benighted family" (428). Although quite private, this placement of the family into the national history/plot/narrative ascribes their deaths a special meaning, just as some soldiers' deaths are given the meaning of martyrdom with the promise of paradise. His grief is thus emphasized but also ameliorated. The way Saleem saturates his family's deaths with meaning is a more or less orthodox, albeit vain, way of coping.

For Saleem, religious afterlife is not an option. He becomes more and more panic-stricken when he discovers he has started to crack up "like an old jug ... I shall eventually crumble into ... particles of anonymous, and necessarily oblivious, dust. This is why I have resolved to confide in paper, before I forget" (43).

Repeatedly, Saleem mentions his cracking body, which for him is also the body politic of India (311). His very death, imagined as a future event is the finalization of the cracking process, his sinking into the "vastness of the crowd ... they throng around me pushing shoving crushing, and the cracks are widening" (588). He even has a vision of the black angel of death, with the face of Indira Gandhi, which emphasizes even more intensely his disbelief in the afterlife, as well as his erasure from history (589). She was the one who ordered his and the children's sterilization and murder. A real death angel, on the other hand, would be the proof that death is the passage into the afterlife. The face of the Prime Minister suggests an affirmation of nothingness in death. That is why Saleem interprets sterilization as "Sperectomy: the draining-out of hope" (556). This is but one of the variations on the Sartrean argument that when one hears voices as Saleem does, or sees an angel, there is always an uncertainty as to the true essence of this call, and this uncertainty produces what for Sartre was the anguish in the face of freedom and an obligation to act; to choose, and to take responsibility for action.[2] I will address this in the second part of the book.

The eventual apocalypse of Saleem's world does not necessarily entail the annihilation of everything, but the rupture of his own existence. Saleem's world is, as Vijay Lakshmi puts it, one "where the boundaries of accepted morality, reality, or reason have become blurred, where the best human efforts seem but imperfect constructs, and where there is no leap of faith ... the universe of the absurd". This absurdity "exists in the banal and the mundane":

> It can strike any man in the face, as Camus says, at any street corner .... To confront our own strangeness in the mirror is to realize the denseness and strangeness of the world where our gestures become meaningless, silly pantomimes.[3]

Saleem is fascinated by historical figures such as Buddha, Moses, and Ganesh because they have all had their meaning and their personal histories preserved for centuries (207, 386-87, 445). Instead of spiritual afterlife or reincarnation, Saleem assumes the only way to transcend death is to leave a life story that encapsulates his existential meaning for future generations, in particular his son Aadam. This

---

[2] Sartre, *Existentialism Is a Humanism*, 26.

[3] Vijay Lakshmi, "Rushdie's Fiction: The World Beyond the Looking Glass", in *Reworlding: The Literature of the Indian Diaspora, Contributions to the Study of World Literature*, 42, ed. Emmanuel S. Nelson, Westport, New York: Greenwood, 1992, 149. The stronger focus on absurdity and strangeness distinguished Camus from for instance Sartre and Heidegger. In *Sein und Zeit*, Heidegger's *Eigentlichkeit* (authenticity) merges the senses of being one's own, owning one's self, and being peculiar, strange. The opposite is called *Uneigentlichkeit*. Also see Sartre's commentary on *The Outsider* (Sartre, *Existentialism Is a Humanism*, 74),

would save him from the anonymity within national life, and give him some form of immortality. He calls his desire the dream of pickling history: "Thirty jars stand upon a shelf, waiting to be unleashed upon the amnesiac nation" (586). He is trying to save his world (private and national) from crumbling to pieces by giving it "shape and form – that is to say, meaning" (587). He presents meaning as the very sustenance, pickles, to argue that it is indispensable. This gesture is no less ideological just because it is private rather than national. Saleem does not merely wish to find a meaning, but create a world in his image, or give it the meaning he wants: "I had entered into the illusion of the artist, and thought of the multitudinous realities of the land as the raw unshaped material of my gift" (222).

The end of Saleem's narrative is a summary of his life. Yet this time he narrates a future life in one last all-out attempt at imagining his end before it arrives. Since he has not managed to find or make an authentic meaning, it is a desperate, anguished effort to revert to his meaning as the allegory of India. He uses epic qualities, romanticism, and the imaginative character of Bombay-talkies. He envisions masses of population with all the familiar faces from his past, which is an imaginary gesture against dying alone. His being the one (and also no one) entails death by dissolution into that which is allegorized: the millions of the people who are, by definition, the building stones of the Indian nation. He ends up as an anonymous speck of dust in the "vastness of the crowd" (588). Saleem anticipates this outcome already when he introduces the question of "purpose, and meaning" (289) to the children. He first makes a list of possibilities: collectivism, individualism, filial duty, infant revolution, capitalism, altruism, science, religion, courage, and cowardice. Later, he concludes, "not a single one of us suggested that the purpose of Midnight's Children might be annihilation; that we would have no meaning until we were destroyed" (290). He realizes that his grand existential meaning cannot beat death, because it implies death. Death is his *raison d'etre*, his existential meaning. Again we encounter a potentially ironic construction. The question is, what happens with death or finitude under an ironic treatment?

The gravity of the issue of death is explored in an excessively ironic tone. There is hardly any issue, belief, or feeling that does not receive the equal treatment of irony. However, while the narrative is overwhelmingly ironic, death is the single issue in the novel that receives the least of Saleem's mockery, even in passages that deal with things such as the return of Mary's revolutionary lover as a ghost. Even General Dyer's darkly-comic remark after the Amritsar massacre, "Good shooting .... We have done a jolly good thing" (42), increases the horror of death. Not even the romanticized death of Aadam Aziz in Kashmir is terribly ironic. Saleem mocks his grandfather's nostalgia and the idea that it matters where one dies and is buried. Irony cancels out these elements that are supposed to tranquilize imminent death, and instead actually lift up the horror in the face of death. One claim by Kierkegaard on the characteristics of death and despair seems resonant with the novel:

> It is impossible to depict this kind of despair without a touch of satire .... It is infinitely comic that beneath all the practical wisdom that the world prizes so highly ... there is, ideally understood, total obtuseness about what the danger really is.[4]

At the same time, perhaps paradoxically, Saleem's histrionic irony has a contrary function. The overload of irony (as that which also produces laughter) is his technique of distracting the reader from his deepening anguish. Its function is to persuade his audiences that he is in control. Gauthier maintains that Saleem engages in imaginative and highly ironic "readings of the past, and hence of the present ... in order to counteract those particular feelings of existential dread" (133).[5] Rather than the erasure of anguish, his excessive irony becomes a gesture of intellectual distancing from it. Irony is typically a gesture of reason and wit, which produces the sense of the ironic narrator being in control of the existential material he deals with. In Rushdie's novel, death undermines such rational control. Read this way, each ironic gesture betrays a moment of anguished laughter, so that Saleem's life seems to progress only through a series of ironies.

Lakshmi argues that on the surface "the author seems to be satirizing the social and political systems and parodying human behavior. In doing so, he spares neither any institution nor any set of beliefs." Yet, "at a deeper fictional level" irony becomes a way of coping with "the absurdity of the human condition itself in a world where the decline of religious belief has deprived man of certainties"

---

[4] Søren Kierkegaard, *Sickness Unto Death*, London: Penguin Books, 1989, 87.
[5] Gauthier, *Narrative Desire and Historical Reparations*, 133.

invested in "closed systems of values and revelations of Divine purpose".[6] Saleem cannot be ironic both about different ideologies that appropriated death and death as a fact. If everything is ironic, nothing ultimately is. In fact, to refer back to Kierkegaard, it is the unbearable anguish in the face of finitude that produces irony, and a concern with authentic action and responsibility. In the end, finitude remains an agent of rupture, which shows the limits of ironic effects.

---

[6] Lakshmi, "Rushdie's Fiction: The World Beyond the Looking Glass", 150.

CHAPTER 5

BECOMING DEAD-TO-THE-WORLD
IN *THE ENGLISH PATIENT*

Death is like an antagonist to Ondaatje's characters. It is so present it
sometimes appears tangible, just as the deadly winds that haunt North
Africa appear both ghostly and material, such as "*aajej*, against which
the fellahin defend themselves with knives .... *khamsin* ... the ninth
plague of Egypt", and also "the secret wind whose name was erased
by a king after his son died within it" (16). The sheer hopelessness of
such actions against imminent death serves to emphasize its
insurmountable force.

The strong awareness of mortality causes or augments the
characters' existential crises. Death makes them perceive their
existence with heightened acuteness. They come to realize that the
ideologies they subscribed to are inherited, historically contingent,
and plainly false. They realize with a greater impact that meanings
traditionally employed to soothe the existential anguish in the face of
death may not have any divine origin and/or metaphysical stability.
Rather than the fear of something dangerous or life-threatening, fear
of death arises from an awareness of a more general finitude or
mortality, which is not simply one's own, as Heidegger would argue,
but rather shared, communal. Mortality, Caravaggio explains to Hana,
is discovered in the "tenderness towards every cell in a lover". In a
sense, it is experienced though acts of intimacy, community, or being-
with-others. When they develop intensive and meaningful moments of
intimacy, the central characters realize they live in a "mortal age"
(225), and that mortality is their being-in-common. The other's
mortality or death, to use Fynsk's argument, potentially calls each of
them beyond themselves and thus delivers them to their freedom. This
freedom is necessarily communal and "*shared (partagé)*, and the
experience of the other's mortality constitutes something like a

condition of this sharing. Like love (itself inseparable from an experience of mortality), it calls the subject out and beyond itself, exposing it to alterity and to its freedom".[1] Death indeed turns the characters onto themselves. Yet, mortality is often experienced when more than their own existence is at stake, as in Kip's care for Hana, and Almásy's care for Katharine.

The narrative takes place in areas that are partly isolated from the immense war machinery. Despite the illusion of peace, Villa San Girolamo is one of the

> ... last vices of war. Completely unsafe. The sappers haven't gone in there yet to clear it. The Germans retreated, burying and installing mines as they went .... The smell of the dead is the worst. (29)

There are numerous booby traps hidden everywhere: in the walls, in the book spines, the roof-damaged library, in the soil of the Italian countryside. Immense energy is spent in fighting death. In fact, as in *Midnight's Children*, death contributes to an excess of narration. Most monologues and dialogues are about dying and mortality. The awareness of mortality causes deep existential crises, which push the characters into a condition that I will call "being-dead-to-the-world". This originally religious idea indeed resembles what Bhabha calls "the colonial condition of life-in-death".[2]

All characters have a strong relationship to death. Hana, after having "removed so many pieces of shrapnel she felt she'd transported a ton of metal out of the huge body of the human that she was caring for" (50), tends a man she knows will die at any time. With the soldiers

> ... caring was brief. There was a contract only until death. Nothing in her spirit or past had taught her to be a nurse. (51)

Eventually, she "survived by keeping coldness hidden in her role as nurse", thinking, "I won't fall apart at this" (48). Once, "after three full days without rest, she finally lay down on the floor beside a mattress where someone lay dead, and slept for twelve hours, closing her eyes against the world around her". When she woke up:

---

[1] Fynsk, "Foreword", xv.
[2] Homi K. Bhabha, "Foreword", in Fanon, *The Wretched of the Earth*, xxxvi.

> [Hana] cut her hair … the irritation of its presence during the previous
> days still in her mind – when she bent forward and her hair had
> touched blood in a wound. She would have nothing to link her, to lock
> her, to death. She never looked at herself in mirrors again. As the war
> got darker she received reports about how certain people she had
> known had died. She feared the day she would remove blood from a
> patient's face and discover her father or someone who had served her
> food …. She grew harsh with herself and the patients. Reason was the
> only thing that might save them, and there was no reason. (49-50)

Hana finds no reason in the world. The library in which she finds
refuge has been characteristically blasted open "at portrait level" (11),
suggesting a void where the head (reason) and the heart (feeling/faith)
should be. Hana has witnessed dying men's agony, which she helped
relieve not with priestly rhetoric, but with soothing morphine:

> 'I know death now, David. I know all the smells, I know how to divert
> them from agony. When to give the quick jolt of morphine in a major
> vein.' (83)

This is indeed suggestive of euthanasia, but the regular morphine
injections imply erasure of consciousness of dying. Hana states her
loss of faith in religious rhetoric:

> Who the hell were we to be given this responsibility, expected to be
> wise as old priests, to know how to lead people towards something no
> one wanted and somehow make them comfortable. I could never
> believe in all those services they gave for the dead. Their vulgar
> rhetoric. How dare they! How dare they talk like that about a human
> being dying? (84)

She recognizes that religion soothes this anxiety by giving meaning
to death, for instance, a kind of afterlife communion that fulfils
infinite immanence. This immanence is not merely deferred for Hana,
but she cannot see it coming about. Often, she cannot "stop shaking",
which Caravaggio interprets as the "deepest sorrow" (44), or anguish
that turns Hana into a "twenty-year-old who throws herself out of the
world to love a ghost" (45), her "despairing saint" (3). She "disliked
his lying there with a candle in his hands, mocking a deathlike
posture. As if he was preparing himself, as if he wanted to slip into his
own death by imitating its climate and light" (62). She hates it when

he appears to be dead in this symbolic manner, lingering in some cadaverous space on the way to the afterlife: "there would be only one candle flaring into the darkness beside the English patient .... But the corridors and other bedrooms hung in darkness, as if in a buried city" (220).

As if repeating his own necrophiliac gesture towards Katharine in the Cave of the Swimmers, Hana cuddles against him and enters this ambiguous zone between existence and non-existence:

> *Felhomaly*. The dusk of graves. With the connotation of intimacy there between the dead and the living. (171, emphasis in the original)

Refusing religion, she invents private rituals:

> Each night she climbed into the khaki ghostline of hammock she had taken from a dead soldier, someone who had died in her care .... Her hammock and her shoes and her frock. She was secure in the miniature world she had built; the two other men seemed distant planets, each in his own sphere of memory and solitude. (47)

Hana deals with mortality by opening herself onto a strange kind of community in which she can at least negotiate her rituals of coping.

The English patient has miraculously survived a plane crash after having led the dangerous life of a desert explorer and mapmaker. In the present, he is slowly dying of severe burns. He has become dead to the world:

> I can talk to you, Caravaggio, because I feel we are both mortal. The girl, the boy, they are not mortal yet. In spite of what they have been through. (253)

He emphasizes his proximity to death. In Hana and Kip he still sees the possibility of embracing life/existence as something meaningful. As Bill Fledderus puts it, "finding personal meaning in structures that are shared by many is perhaps suggested by the symbolic figure of death which comes to the patient".[3] The English patient's intimations of mortality began after his arrival at the dangerous Libyan Desert. Prior to his mission, he had been a man sure of his ancestry, his nationhood, and his political allegiances. When he came to the desert, he was still thinking in terms of preconceived theories and patterns: "In the desert you have time to look everywhere, to theorize on the choreography of all things around you .... the histories in Herodotus clarified all societies" (150).

Ondaatje takes the reader between two points in his past, beginning with the arrival of the new explorers with their cultural baggage to the moment when their attitudes start dismantling. They formed a "desert society" of outsiders, increasingly isolated individuals who despised allegiance, ancestry, and nationhood, in fact all types of conformism that characterized the world around them. Their crises augmented with the "oncoming war interrupting everything" (241). He became obsessed with dying to the world. It is in the desert, that Count Almásy died before he is dead. Everything begins to look meaningless, useless, defamiliarized. Not even his lover Katharine manages to shake his attitude:

> ... he was in the zone of *limbo* between city and plateau. After six days had passed he would never think about Cairo or the music or the streets or the women; by then he was moving in ancient time, had adapted into the breathing patterns of deep water. His only connection with the world of cities was Herodotus, his guidebook, ancient and modern, of supposed lies.

After his breakdown he sinks into *angst*-ridden in-between space of *limbo*: "He knew during these times how the mirage worked, the fata morgana, for he was within it" (246). He believes he has entered the space where the world no longer matters, but where he has not entered the traditional afterlife either, sorted into either heaven or hell. This zone is neither real nor fictional, between nature and the storyteller. The world seems suspended in this ontologically instable zone. The separation makes the patient a solitary, alienated figure, similar to Okri's Azaro when he is suspended between worlds and

---

[3] Bill Fledderus, "'The English Patient Reposed in His Bed Like a [Fisher?] King': Elements of Grail Romance in Ondaatje's *The English Patient*", *Studies in Canadian Literature/Etudes en Littérature Canadienne*, XXII/1 (Spring 1997), 44.

absolutely indifferent to everything. Like Azaro, the patient must take this state as the point of departure and revert to his reality as the only space in which authentic action is possible.

This sense of limbo is further strengthened by shifts between the third and the first person narrative, often without any conventional markers as to who speaks at what point, the omniscient author, or the character. This slippage produces a form of what Novak calls "textual haunting",[4] a series of ruptures in the narrative that refracts the character's existential ruptures. One rupture arises in relation to the identity of the burned man. Although the reader might be lead into identifying him as Count Ladislaus de Almásy, in some passages he speaks about himself (or Almásy) in the third person, to which Caravaggio reacts, *"Who is he speaking as now?"* (244, emphasis in the original). The patient answers, *"'Death means you are in the third person'"* (247, emphasis in the original).

The patient soothes his anguish with fragmentary narrative, which recounts only the events in which he invested meaning. When Katharine was mortally wounded, he hid her in the cave of swimmers. As if she was incapable of the clichéd review of the past at the moment of death, he seems obliged to imagine one for her. He enacts "the spirit of the jackal, who was the 'opener of the ways,' whose name was Wepwawet or Almásy" or even "Anubis, Duamutef", the "creatures who guide you into the afterlife" (258). He perceived "a breath of death in her" and with his "tongue carried the blue pollen to her tongue" (260). He used cave colours to paint Katharine "so she would be immune to the human. There were traditions he had discovered in Herodotus in which old warriors celebrated their loved ones by locating and holding them in whatever world that made them eternal – a colourful fluid, a song, a rock drawing" (248).

While the painting-ritual would have been an ideological practice in its historical context, when the patient performed it, it lacked the elements of social domination and maintaining of power structures. He transformed the ancient ritual into something own. The old warriors wanted to appropriate the souls of their beloved ones in their social frameworks, but the patient employed art only to remove every meaning her death would have in her native England, and release her from her Christian ties. The problem was the entire cave scene was

---

[4] Novak, "Textual Hauntings", 216.

not designed around his care for Katharine's relation to death, but rather what her death did to him. Novak argues that his "effort situates both Katharine and the past as static objects, something that he might possess and that has no power to make claim upon him".[5] However, he did not do it to fix his lover as his possession. On the contrary, after having given in to the possessiveness he despised, he made one last attempt to erase every trace of his own claim upon her. Maybe he failed in his gesture. By disregarding her final wish to be named and defined through her Englishness, he did what he wished someone would do to him in the event of his death:

> We die containing a richness of lovers and tribes, tastes we swallowed, bodies we have plunged into and swam up as if rivers of wisdom, characters we have climbed into as if trees, fears we have hidden in as if caves. I wish for all this to be marked on my body when I am dead.

Indeed, anguish is too strong. The poetic language and artistry give death meanings that he believed had more authentic pathos. He did not transform her into an "anonymous, a naked map where nothing is depicted" (261), but he wrote her into their "communal book of moonlight".

The artistic gesture is repeated later in the villa. Describing Caravaggio's painting, *David with the Head of Goliath*, he says, "the true sadness in the picture" lies in the assumption that

> … the face of David is a portrait of the youthful Caravaggio and the head of the Goliath is a portrait of him as an older man …. Youth judging age at the end of the outstretched hand. The judging of one's own mortality. I think when I see him at the foot of my bed that Kip is my David. (116)

This repression of death through art is typical of this learned man from the desert. In a sense, he de-emphasizes the impact of death by ascribing it poetic/artistic meaning, which may very well be ideologically influenced.

---

[5] *Ibid.*, 217.

The Sikh sapper Kip fights death on an everyday basis, struggling to dismantle unexploded bombs found in the freed zones, and in "a time when the casualty rate in bomb disposal units was appallingly high" (183). The withdrawal of the enemy does not entail peace and safety. The remaining mines and undetonated shells present a threat to the civil population. This affects Kip to the extent that he is "unable to look at a room or field without seeing the possibilities of weapons there" (75). Later, when "the reality of the death of Lord Suffolk came to him, he concluded the work he was assigned to and reenlisted into the anonymous machine of the army". His teacher's death makes him into the one with "a map of responsibility" (195), but it also opens him up to understand that this responsibility is not authentic but an ideologically limited responsibility that does not include the Asiatic others. Eventually, death ruptures Kip's ties to the English and he experiences the meaninglessness of the world he is trying to save from destruction. After the successful dismantling of a difficult bomb, the soldiers "watched him silently, the Indian, hanging onto Hardy's shoulder, scarcely able to walk … listening to the nothingness down in the shaft" (215). His proximity to death is sometimes described in an erotic manner: "his thighs braced the metal casing, much the way he had seen soldiers holding women in the corner of NAAFI dance floors" (210), but a single "spark and Kip would be in a shaft of flames" (213).

Often, the entire world seems to him to be on the verge of extinction: "as he lay there the mined bridge exploded and he was flung upwards and then down as part of the end of the world" (60). Kip uses European cultural nodes such as paintings and statues as fixed points that keep him from immense anxiety as in the scene where he enters into intimacy with Hana: "he felt he was now within something, perhaps a painting he had seen somewhere in the last year. Some secure couple in a field" (104).

However, with the nuclear attacks on Japan, and the "death of a civilisation" (286), Kip "feels all the winds of the world have been sucked into Asia", where "the living witness the death of the population around them" (287). The atomic bombs are to him more than just material destruction and annihilation. In fact, Kip stresses the viciousness of that which brought about the events. He blames it on the English racial superiority and global influence:

American, French, I don't care. When you start bombing the brown races of the world, you're an Englishman …. You all learned it from the English. (286)

Kip is at first pushed outside the world. Like Hana and the patient, he finds everything unfamiliar and meaningless. Then he assumes the position of his brother, the critic of Western Enlightenment. He mounts a motorbike and leaves the villa "like somebody unable to enter the intimacy of a home" (291). The nuclear annihilation contributes to Kip's final existential rupture, and his immense awareness of the shared human mortality or finitude. He faces a choice between continuing his life as it is, or reverting to his Sikh culture: "he had brought out a photograph of his family and gazed at it. His name is Kirpal Singh and he does not know what he is doing here" (287). After years of disagreement with his brother, Kip is shaken out of his English element. If death turns him onto himself, it makes him revaluate his situation. At surface his choice is to re-subscribe to his Sikh traditions. I will later address the ambiguities in his choices.

CHAPTER 6

IDEOLOGICAL RE-APPROPRIATION THROUGH DEATH
IN *THE FAMISHED ROAD*

> Much as death-confrontation / Paralyses
> some with despair / Makes others poison
> / Themselves with emptiness / But
> releases in the fortunate few / A quality
> of enlightenment / A sense of the limited
> time we have / ... / To explore our
> potential to the fullest / And to lose our
> fear of death.[1]

In *The Famished Road*, as well as in its two sequels (*Songs of Enchantment* and *Infinite Riches*), Okri's protagonist Azaro constantly dwells in close proximity to death, which hurls him into a questioning of the meaning of his very being-abiku. Abiku is a spirit that incarnates in a human body, only to will its own death because of the hardships of human existence. Human death should be a moment of rejoicing in the prospect of re-inscription into the happy spirit existence. Therefore, different from Rushdie and Ondaatje's treatment of death against the religious idea of the Hereafter, Okri introduces an additional twist to the existential issue of death or finitude. He weaves this existential concern into the texture of the happy abiku spirit world. At first sight, it appears absurd that an eternal sprit like Azaro should dread death. Yet, death is closely tied to his very being and causes immense traumas. It makes Azaro realize that the meaning of his being, which is characterized by perpetuating a cycle of incarnations into the human existence, is not a matter of his nature or essence, but rather something resembling a spirit culture, a form of burdensome spirit tradition introduced by the king and "the serene presences of [their] ancestors" (4). By dramatizing animism as a fact

---

[1] Okri, *Mental Fight*, 4.

of reality Okri dramatizes *angst* even in a character who should not be able to experience it in principle, and in this manner highlights the question of authentic choice, action and responsibility. In an interview with Deandrea, Okri maintains that Azaro has "doors of death perpetually open inside him" which affects his perception of everything.[2] Azaro knows that what is waiting for him on the other side is not the kind of freedom and joy he values the most. He refutes the premises of his type of animism.

As an abiku, he is perceived as nothing but the bringer of death. Able to "will [their] deaths" (4), the abiku cause "much pain to mothers". The mothers' "anguish" in turn becomes for them "an added spiritual weight which quickens the cycle of rebirth. Each new birth was an agony for us too, each shock of the raw world." Their birth is in fact their death-to-the-spirit-world, and their death in existence is their re-birth to the spirit world. The abiku are born and die at the same time. Their human birth is "agony" (5), because it is their (spirit) death as well.

What happens next is that Azaro starts feeling *angst* in the face of his human death, rather than joy. This anguish tips the scales for Azaro and makes him want to stay in the human world: "I wanted to make happy the bruised face of the woman who would become my mother" (6). Azaro's love of his human mother, and in fact his desire to understand humanity opens him up for the possibility of human death-anguish. He can no longer stay "indifferent to the long joyless parturition of mothers" (5). He knows, unlike the humans who can only believe, that there is an afterlife in the spirit world, even though there is also an implied uncertainty as to the performability of the transition. Enflamed by the king's speeches, the spirits prepare to make "the passage alone. Alone [they] hade to survive the crossing – survive the flames and the sea, the emergence into illusions". Azaro's transition is different from the Judeo-Christian-Islamic transition into afterlife. In fact, he might die for good in this birth/death transition, which is not a mere crossing of thresholds between worlds. Although birth and death are here both the same, there is a possibility of another death of being altogether, and the end of interworldly travels. There is no explanation as to what this other death entails in the spirits' "myths of beginnings" (6).

---

[2] Deandrea, "An Interview with Ben Okri", 80.

Azaro questions the principle of transformation. His rebellion might be a battle lost before it even began, but Azaro finds it necessary to mark his contempt of the principle:

> How many times had I come and gone through the dreaded gateway? How many times had I been born and died young? And how often to the same parents? I had no idea. (5)

After he has explained how he and his spirits dislike existence because of "the fact of dying" (3), he realizes his kind have caused this fact since the beginning of human history. The abiku cycles of rebirth (or rather re-death) appear as "paradoxes" (7). He decides to explore possible meanings of human existence through love, care, and even suffering. To speak of cycles of birth and death can give us the illusion that everything moves smoothly, as if there is no risk, and no responsibility in the flow of events. Azaro's latest cycle, however, shows all the hard edges, cuts and gaps. Humanity does not become just another phase. Rather through his love for his parents Azaro decides to take a leap into mortal life, to experience the full brunt of being-human. Questioning his abiku essence, Azaro endorses existence as a way of becoming free. Another abiku asks him, "'What are you doing here?'" He replies, "'Living,'" but he does not know for what. The abiku insists, "'Why don't you know? Haven't you seen what lies ahead of you?'" Then, the abiku "showed me images which I couldn't understand. They showed me a prison, a woman covered with golden boils, a long road, pitiless sunlight, a flood, an earthquake, death" (8-9).

His kin want him to believe that human existence amounts to anguish about being-mortal, which is the opposite of the eternal spirit joy. Azaro's human death would entail a re-appropriation into his spirit world. The spirits ensure him he retains his essence and spirit meaning only as long as he returns and maintains the abiku orthodoxy. Due to his refusal to capitalize on abiku spirituality, his companions consider him a traitor. They apply different strategies to cause his death: "they called me from across the road with the voice of my mother. As I went towards the voice a car almost ran me over". After Azaro falls ill, the spirits try to trick him, "the longer they kept me there, the more certain they were making my death". They "managed to shut me out of my life. I cried for a long time into the silver void till our great king interceded for me and reopened the gates of my body"

(9). After two full weeks of lingering "between not dying and not living" he wakes up brimming with anguish. As a token of their gratefulness to God, his parents give him the most emblematic name that will forever remind him of his proximity to death: Lazaro. The Herbalist summoned to bring him from the other side says, "This is a child who didn't want to be born, but who will fight with death" (10).

Azaro does not want his parents to perform a costly ceremony and find his charmed objects to sever him from the spirit world. He wants to be able to re-enter eternity once again in case he does not like the human world. Severed from his spirit world, he would become human and therefore also finite. He would become like anyone else, dreading mortality and not knowing what awaits him beyond. Azaro constantly fears two deaths, one that is a painful transformation from existence to spirit life (and back), and the second that could be the final nothingness of being. His spirit companions tell him existence is meaningless and call on him to return: "Deep in me old songs began to stir. Old voices from the world of spirits" (266). Only the spirit king, who has undergone the most and the longest transformations in existence, gives Azaro leeway in order to let him rediscover the value in being-abiku. Only through an act of genuine willing-his-death will Azaro be fully re-assimilated. Although the King too will try to force Azaro's return, he is aware of the kind of imbalances (doubts) this will bring into their world. This is why he called Azaro the mischievous one even before the incarnation. He knows Azaro must submit unquestionably. Yet, the more the spirits emphasize mortality, the more Azaro feels alienated from the spirit world. He feels more "joys of homecoming" (34) when he returns to his human mother than facing the prospect of returning to the spirit world. The prospect of death makes the entire non-human world terrifying and unhomely.

After he was kidnapped, Azaro says, "I couldn't move. I felt transfixed, as if I were suffering a living rigor mortis" (127). Then:

> The blankness of death came upon me. I shut my eyes. It was no different when I opened them. At one point I fell into a strange sleep in which the figure of a king resplendent in gold appeared to me and vanished. My spirit companions began singing in my ears, rejoicing in my captivity and in the fact that I would soon be joining them. I could not shut out their singing and I'm not sure which was worse: being bundled away by unknown people to an unknown destination or hearing my spirit companions orchestrate my passage through torment

> with their sweet and excruciating voices .... I called to our great king, and I said: 'I do not want to die.' (131)

The passage of re-appropriation is anything but free and sweet, as the spirit songs promise. The length and torture of the passage only increases with years, which is depicted through ghosts that come to fetch him. Azaro is "contorted in paroxysms" (343). He immediately becomes feverish and cannot move. Still, he says, "I won't come". The mother warns him "If a spirit calls you ... don't go, you hear? Think of us" (352). Azaro's resistance to the spirits weakens when the mother hits him (365), and the father flogs him "mercilessly", saying, "If you want to return to the world of spirits, return! But if you want to stay, then be a good son!" Pinned between different demands for his submission, Azaro says:

> I went into a curious state of being. I began to feed on my hunger .... I dipped myself and found other worlds waiting. I chose a world and lingered. There were no spirits there. It was a world of wraiths. (373)

He enters a limbo without "feelings, sentiments, sympathies", where neither the human nor the spirit world can claim him:

> I smelt the world of holidays, the world of spirits .... I willed myself away, wanting to leave, singing the song of departures that only my spirit companions can render .... Mum's face was far away. The distance between us grew. Dad's face, large and severe, no longer frightened me. His assumption that the severity of his features gave him power over anything made him look a little comical.

Dad's power diminishes as Azaro sinks "into the essential indifferent serenity of the spirit-child's soul". The three-headed spirit forces him to become "at home with death", with respect to "the unintended callousness of human beings, their lovelessness, their forgetfulness of the basic things of existence" (374). Yet, the spirit does not offer love and freedom, care and happiness.

During this death journey of re-appropriation, two worlds are connected through the channel of his body/soul. His father's breath is felt as the strong wing that makes him hover above and swerve from the road to the spirit world (376). Once the mother shows affection and openness, Azaro reconnects with the human world:

> Mum pressed her warm face to mine and lifted me up. The spirit leapt into the chasm .... The spirit said: 'Don't be afraid.' I wasn't any more. Mum's voice was in my soul. (383)

The road to the other world becomes more and more a torture, which serves to kill Azaro's body and release his spirit from human bonds. The great river they must cross is an enormous mirror that seems "like nothing, emptiness, air" where "the ferryman of the dead" waits beside a canoe (385). The death-driver turns out to be an old woman with strange animalistic features. Her blows to the spirit are synchronized with the ritual sacrifice enacted to draw Azaro back (390).

Yet, it is not the ritual that empowers Azaro, but Dad's new way of being. Dad's "words offered me water and food and new breathing". More importantly, "to my utter astonishment, Dad knelt by the bed" (386). Azaro has not seen such behaviour before. Although his companions advocate love, they prove merciless. They deprive Azaro of agency. The father, in his vulnerability, opens up to the possibility of love:

> Love is crying in my flesh, singing strange songs .... I see great happiness in our future. I see joy. I see you walking out of the sun. I see gold in your eyes. (386)

The father is ready to accept Azaro's choice:

> They say you are an abiku child, that you care nothing for your parents, that you are cold, and that you have eyes only for that special spirit who is a beautiful young girl .... But I do not believe them. You have wept for us and watered the tree of love. (387)

In his last speech, Dad says:

> 'All roads lead to death, but some roads lead to things which can never be finished .... Death has taught me the religion of living.' (572).

By the same token, this is what Azaro does as well. Tracing a possibility of action, and a way of being free, Azaro returns to the human world, rambling about, "the mystery of being, of births within births, death within births, births within dying, the challenge of giving birth to one's true self, to one's new spirit" (559). As Okri suggests in the epigraph to this section, death can paralyse, expose a self to a kind of nothingness, but for some like Azaro and Dad it comes to be a release and enlightenment, that which opens them up for their freedom and spur to action, and in fact, "the possibilities of a new pact with [his] spirit". He begins to believe that "no true road is ever complete, that no way is ever definitive, no truth ever final". Despite innumerable conflicts in the human world, Azaro finds it a place of unexpected possibilities for freedom. Among humans, he is an exile who needs to negotiate his way of being free.

Azaro's case brings up the question of self-willed death, which Nietzsche for instance developed in *Thus Spake Zarathustra* and other writings – "freiwilliger Tod".[3] As Sean Ireton puts it, Nietzsche "calls for the individual to *will* his death as the ultimate yea-saying to life".[4] To will the death of one's self is, for Nietzsche, not to commit suicide, but rather to overcome one's ties to the world. In the novel, the ideal spirit world seems to offer Azaro something that appears very much like Nietzschean ultimate relish in the freedom. Yet, for Azaro, the supposedly ideal spirit world betrays freedom by turning these ideals into enforceable orthodoxy. Once he refuses to will-his-physical-death, he denies the supremacy of the abiku, and in a sense wills-his-death-as-abiku. Even though Azaro will die one day and perhaps return to the spirit world, he seems to suggest he will not continue the cycle of reincarnations, thus breaking with the pacts of the spirits. In a sense, if the Nietzschean point is the overcoming of one's inherited being, Azaro seems to perform a true self-overcoming by refusing to die at the wrong time set by his spirit companions. He cultivates an entirely new relation to death, in a desperate attempt to find ways of being free.

---

[3] Friedrich Nietzsche, *Thus Spake Zarathustra*, tr. Thomas Common, Ware: Wordsworth Classics, 1997.

[4] Sean Ireton, *An Ontological Study of Death: From Hegel to Heidegger*, Pittsburgh: Duquesne University Press, 2007, 23 (emphasis in the original).

PART II

AUTHENTICITY

AUTHENTICITY: INTRODUCTION

> In the name of certainties, nations and individuals had come to regard themselves as gods. This certainty, whether its name be religion, imperialism, ideology, class, caste, race, or sex, has been the great undoing of our measureless heritage.[1]

> ... it's a dangerous business to try and impose one's view of things on others .... a little uncertainty is no bad thing. Cocksure men do terrible things.[2]

The nervous conditions and identity crises caused by death and violent conflicts (ethnic, national, racial etc.) make the characters in Ondaatje's, Rushdie's and Okri's novels deeply concerned with their personal selfhood as well as their place in the world. What they often perceive as the conflict between premodern and modern ways of being turns out to be a form of alternate or counter modernity, which brims with historical meaning and yet also produces a sense of absurdity, or what Bhabha calls "postcolonial non-sense". In the face of the world they cannot fully grasp, let alone control, they feel what Jackson calls "existential imperative"[3] to engage creatively with their particular historical moments, with their pasts and the envisioned (national) futures. As a way of coping with their *angst*, they desire to convert the given situations into new possibilities of personal development, often *vis-à-vis* different forms of social bonding. This desire, together with the actions they take, constitutes their particular ways of being free

---

[1] Okri, *A Way of Being Free*, 30.
[2] Rushdie, *Midnight's Children*, 212.
[3] Jackson, *Existential Anthropology*, xxii.

and authentic. To argue that this is something entirely new would be to reinvent the wheel.[4]

In the main introduction, I discussed the idea of authenticity as a prominently European critical and historical concept, which has mainly come to be understood in terms of two strong desires: communalism and individualism. Although these are opposed to each other, both arise in relation to certain historical conditions (social oppression, and a form of disorientation and estrangement).

Individualism has developed in part from Romantic personalism, which is the search for essential personal selfhood. We can see this in the character of the English patient who seeks refuge in the solitary desert life from all the habits he has grown up with, from the world defined along racial and national lines, the world that seems to offer only the possibility of role playing, that is, an acting based on dogmas, orthodoxies, authoritative and diffuse forms of power. In some postcolonial contexts in the novels, this attitude is considered Western heritage. Thinkers as varied as Fanon, Taylor, Bhabha, Heidegger and Appiah have labelled this stance "individualism". As its name indicates, the individual is deemed the indivisible/atomic residue of a decomposition of community.[5]

In contrast, postcolonial history, under the sway of authoritative and diffuse powers, has produced a need that has been called "nativism", "communalism", or even "indigenism", which has figured strongly in the articulation of various nationalisms. As in Romantic

---

[4] Sartre claimed, "reality exists only in action" (Sartre, *Existentialism Is a Humanism*, 37), and that the individuality of (Cartesian) cogito is not isolated in the mind but is constituted by being in the world.

[5] For Heidegger, "Only where man is essentially already subject does there exist the possibility of his slipping into the aberration of subjectivism in the sense of individualism" (Martin Heidegger, *The Question Concerning Technology*, tr. William Lovitt, New York Harper and Row, 1993, 133). According to Benjamin D. Crowe, Heidegger "attacked the totalizing, homogenizing effects of metaphysics and ideology" with a view of "a free community of individuals, each of whom realizes his or her own personal vocation" (Benjamin D. Crowe, *Heidegger's Religious Origins: Destruction and Authenticity*, Bloomington: Indiana University Press, 2006, 92, 168). Still, as Fynsk argues, Heidegger remained under "the pressure of a long tradition that thinks the 'Authentic' individual as isolated", and to think that death was what ultimately severed one from every relation. Even though "*Mitsein* [being-with] and *Dasein* [being-there] are co-originary" (Fynsk, "Foreword", xvi) these ontological markers remain quite abstract. Also see Marjorie Grene, *Dreadful Freedom: A Critique of Existentialism*, Chicago: University of Chicago Press, 1948, 68.

personalism, there is a desire for the original identity, communal rather than individual, which is clean from colonial influences. Communalism too evinces a strong desire for freedom in relation to something that is articulated as a menace. It uses the Romantic rhetoric of essence for communitarian politics of belonging. Just as for an individualist, freedom is primarily "freedom from". The difference is that individualism defines itself in opposition to social commitment *per se*, while communalism is a need to preserve essential relations, meanings and habits. To a certain extent the basic assumption is that authenticity is something that was lost or stolen or hidden and that needs to be to be won back.

In the novels, we find both these tendencies and also something more. We can trace a strong focus on the singular in opposition to social forces, and yet we also find that the Romantic understanding of selfhood does not hold. There is a movement towards a more existential idea of the creation of selfhood through various forms of social action. This view too places a great deal of emphasis on the individual asserting his freedom from bad faith. As Sartre argued, "'why shouldn't he choose bad faith?' My answer is that I do not pass moral judgment against him, but I call his bad faith an error."[6]

Given the emphasis on personal development, community is initially treated negatively. The novels stress that certain choices are already made for the characters, and that if there are choices then characters must opt for one of the already articulated alternatives. As Saleem puts it: "Even a baby is faced with the problem of defining itself" and it can be "bombarded with a confusing multiplicity of views on the subject" (165). To begin with choice seems to be defined in terms of two categories, conformity and non-conformity. As Crowe suggests, "two possibilities are open to each and every individual: 1) acceptance of the 'danger' or 'threat' of living one's own life, or 2) abdication of self-responsibility through identification with 'worldly' concerns and occupations".[7] The distinction between the two "is not one of 'what,' but one of 'how'".[8] Bad faith is tempting because it

---

[6] Sartre, *Existentialism Is a Humanism*, 47. In Rushdie's *The Ground Beneath Her Feet*, the narrator says, "Freedom to reject is the only freedom. Freedom to uphold is dangerous" (Salman Rushdie, *The Ground Beneath Her Feet*, London: Vintage, 2000, 146).

[7] Crowe, *Heidegger's Religious Origins*, 92.

[8] *Ibid.*, 96.

offers the path of least resistance in coping with reality.[9] It is symptomatic of ideologically coloured "common sense", which exercises "a hidden tyranny over the ways individuals in a particular community think and act".[10] Indeed, "human beings grow up into inherited contexts of meaning".[11] Everyday existence "gravitates towards tranquil convenience"[12] because "our heritage or tradition is the repository of all the possibilities that are available to us at a particular time".[13] In a sense, at best, one chooses between the options already there. In the end, one does what everyone does. In this way the responsibility for singular actions is diluted. Everyone is to blame, and no one in particular.

This way of acting is not due only to the idea that identities are scripted roles, as Appiah has argued. Rather, as Chakrabarty has suggested, identities come to individuals as

> ... taste, as embodied memories, as cultural training of the senses, as reflexes, often as things that I do not even know that I carry .... I am to some extent a tool in the hands of pasts and traditions; they speak through me even before I have chosen them critically or approached them with respect.[14]

While for Chakrabarty, this social training is not entirely negative, in the novels, this embodiment is extensively connected to what Sartre called bad faith. Identity helps one to discriminate and show preference. It helps one identify certain values. Ondaatje dramatizes this quite effectively through the figure of the English patient, who resists identity, identification and recognition. Identity as such seems to be communal or in any case social. It means, as Ferrara has argued, to participate in the same division of labour, to be located in the same socio-political stratification, to share certain codes of status and interests, to recognize that everyone is subjected to the same systems of obligations and authorities.[15] Identity revivifies itself through

---

[9] *Ibid.*, 79.

[10] *Ibid.*, 101.

[11] *Ibid.*, 104.

[12] *Ibid.*, 85.

[13] *Ibid.*, 115.

[14] Dipesh Chakrabarty, *Habitations of Modernity*, Chicago: The University of Chicago Press, 2002, 46.

[15] Ferrara, *Reflective Authenticity*, 109.

certain rites and continuity of shared myths.[16] Collective identities, which can be viewed from cultural, sociological, political and psychological perspectives, do not "collapse or give way to new ones any time a conflict of interest arises among the participants. On the contrary, they do possess mechanisms for integrating diverging interests and preventing them from degenerating into conflict."[17] As I have shown in the first chapter, communal identities are both shattered and yet they remain a burden because there is a desire for their revivification. In the novels, communal and individual identity loses its primary place and turns out to be a problematic and not entirely desirable level of selfhood. The characters' identity crises are not only due to the fact that their communities stymie their freedom, but also to the sense that social ties and communitarian belonging stop making full sense, or even stop working. This disruption confuses them, but it also opens them up for potential reworking of their selfhood, as we can see in the most telling scene in which Rushdie's Aadam Aziz is unable to reconnect with his Islamic religion. This leads the characters to what I have described as individualist resistance to community.

Reworking (and un-working) community
Despite the main focus on individuality in the novels, there is certain resistance to the idea of individuals as (in-divisible) social atoms. Arguing against the notion of "individual", Nancy proposes:

> Neither 'Personalism' nor Sartre ever managed to do anything more than coat the most classical individual-subject with a moral or sociological paste: they never *inclined* it, outside itself, over that edge that opens up its being-in-common. An inconsequential atomism, individualism tends to forget that the atom is a world. This is why the question of community is so markedly absent from the metaphysics of the subject.[18]

In the novels we find as much contention to such personalism or atomism as to social orthodoxies. The characters can be said to be singular in Nancy's sense of the term, that is, their subjectivity is singular only insofar as it is always open to the other. This openness,

---

[16] *Ibid.*, 119.
[17] *Ibid.*, 111.
[18] Jean-Luc Nancy, *The Inoperative Community*, tr. Peter Connor, Minneapolis: University of Minnesota Press, 1991, 4 (emphasis in the original).

which also evinces the alterity of their selves, seems also to be the space of their enunciation. The characters also seem to rework the sense of communal bonding, and reclaim community as the space for personal development. They present a desire for authenticity that partly stands out as the third thing, distinct from both individualist and communalist needs and responses. They experiment with different ways of being free, being themselves, and bonding with others. They posit no essential kernel or substance, but argue for an existential process of creation through action. There is a movement away from the sovereignty of selfhood (be it individual or communal), and an opening onto its alterity. Authentic selfhood comes to be articulated in terms of becoming within communal space. This is, for instance, clear in the way Azaro moves from the space of the limbo – which is in fact his total detachment from the worlds of humans and spirits and an escape into some inner space – and his return, his entering into a relation with Dad and Mum, with the ghosts and politicians. The self is here not the subject that positions itself always in relation to an object, but rather it becomes, as the narrator of *The English Patient* puts it, like echoing sound: *"exciting itself in hollow places"* (21, emphasis in the original). Ondaatje's image is reminiscent of Nancy's example of the kind of sharing and exposure that constitutes singular selves (rather than in-dividuals) among the Inuit Eskimos who "sing by making their own cries resonate in the open mouth of a partner".[19]

The novels seem to bring to crisis both the ideas of individuality and community. There is an exploration of the possibility of communal bonding that is not binding, a form of sharing and struggle that sustains personal growth and responsibility. Ondaatje manages more than the other two authors to dramatize a number of different ways of bonding between the four characters in the villa. The question is how to form a community that articulates difference (rather than essentialist diversity), a community that can live with such difference without either turning into a common work (an idea, an essence, a myth), or losing all sense of affiliation, caring and sharing. Once identity's essential status is undermined, the question arises, can there be a community without shared identity, and what happens with singular ways of being free? The basic contradiction that unsettles as well as gives openness to these novelistic explorations is the one

---

[19] *Ibid.*, 31.

between the characters' sense of the value of sharing, of the facticity of singular freedom as something that needs to be asserted in community, and the tendency in their social spheres to convert, as Berman put it (in relation to Rousseau), "all human relations into mutual exploitation".[20]

In *Midnight's Children*, Saleem's authenticity is dramatized as a struggle against a plethora of conflicting forms of power in the postcolonial subcontinent. It is mainly negotiated in terms of meaning or purpose of existence, and action in politically charged times. The political aspects of existence dominate the modern history of India. Saleem himself is initially defined politically (in relation to the Partition). He comes to be suspicious of partitions of different kinds, not because he supports unity, but because the kind of diversity instigated by partition creates purportedly homogenous unities. Already in the beginning he comes to understand the importance of community based on difference, or even a form of freakishness or deviation. Saleem grows suspicious of the Nehruvian vision of national community as a form that contains diversity, and entertains the thought of shared difference that forces each and every singular member to open to the alterity of the other (which is why all the forms that try to hold unities eventually crack).

The Famished Road, which begins with Azaro's rebellion against the pacts among his kind, foregrounds a sharing of a fundamental freedom in community. There is an emphasis on imagination and creativity (but not *ex nihilo*), and dreaming as a form of action. Okri articulates authenticity as a way of practising freedom. Freedom is taken to be factual, and not only a shared goal (national liberation), even though freedom is a political and revolutionary issue. Authenticity is negotiated through a revolution that takes place on several different planes. This revolution is supposed to break the idling of history, the cyclical returns of the same suffering and oppression. It pertains to singular responses to history, as well as to the communal sharing of both mortality and freedom. Dad's experience of freedom feeds his political passion. It is his historical situation that helps him articulate his stance. The particulars of Dad's struggle are not irrelevant, but what is important to capture is both the relational value of his actions and the very dynamics in them. While

---

[20] Berman, *The Politics of Authenticity*, 188.

Azaro does not articulate his freedom as much in political terms as his father, the moment his abiku-being is interpreted metaphorically by Dad, his way of being free becomes politically significant. Azaro's primary struggle is indeed related to the abiku ontology, but this very conflict has political overtones because he discovers that the abiku are not defined simply by nature. Rather, the cycles turn out to be tied to a form of abiku ideology and politics. This struggle has resonances in the world of the humans because their historical situation demands that they rework that which Dad calls their spirit, their essences, their traditions and habits.[21]

In *The English Patient*, authenticity is first constricted to strong escapist drives. Different characters want to shed the skins of their societies, their national history, and often choose seclusion over sociality. This changes when they begin to have a strong sense of their shared mortality or finitude. Death indeed forces them to introversion, but eventually they come to experience mortality as something shared, something that makes them commune, and enter intimacies of love and friendship. Their personalities come to be articulated through their opening unto the strangeness and the mortality of others. I will call this community "inoperative", using Nancy's phrase, because it arises from the dissolution of myths, dogmas, and ideologies of immanence, and yet there is a strong focus on sharing, caring, and bonding. Mortality in particular comes to constitute the condition of this very sharing. Mortality calls them out and beyond themselves, exposing them to their alterity, freedom, and leads them to some form of inoperative community.

---

[21] In *Mental Fight*, Okri reacts against "the self-mythology / Of a people, a race" (Okri, *Mental Fight*, 32), against living "As if in Plato's cave, / Watching the shadows". Furthermore, "The most authentic thing about us / Is our capacity to create, to overcome, / To endure, to transform, to love" (*ibid.*, 61). In the end: "after the gospels, / After the human and divine comedies, / After the one thousand and one nights, / After crime and punishment, / War and peace, pride and prejudice, / The sound and the fury, Between good and evil, / Being and nothingness, / After the tempest, the trial, / And the waste land, / After things have fallen apart, / After the hundred years of solitude, / And the remembrance of things past, / In the kingdom of this world, / We can still astonish the gods in humanity / And be the stuff of future legends, / If we dare to be real, / And have the courage to see / That this is the time to dream / The best dream of them all" (*ibid.*, 68).

CHAPTER 7

FROM SELF-SUFFICIENCY TO INOPERATIVE COMMUNITY
IN *THE ENGLISH PATIENT*

The English Patient stages an existential experiment which mainly involves three characters from different cultural backgrounds, classes, races and gender: Hana, the English patient, and Kirpal Singh. All three are partly escapists who mull over death and their untoward historical predicaments. They often dwell in the state of existential anguish, which pushes them to revaluate their existences, and articulate their ways of being free through action in a world that is reshaped by war. Yet, despite certain individualistic aspects, they enter a form of "inoperative community", which denotes a kind of community that refrains from grounding itself in common being, essence or substance.[1] I will structure my analysis around the three main characters separately while examining the ways in which they form a community.

Before I proceed with the analyses, I want to contextualize my reading in contrast to some critical work. Aitor Ibarrola-Armendariz argues that Ondaatje "fails to unshackle his characters from their ethnic origins and traumatic pasts".[2] Rufus Cook understands the novel in terms of Hillis Miller's idea of evolving backwards, perpetual back and forth reverberations, the repetitions of images and scenes, which "give unity to the novel's 'scrambled narrative fragments,'" but

---

[1] "Inoperative community", as Nancy has argued, is defined insofar as it resists the fascist desires for immanence of the members of a community, immanence that is the sacrifice of singularities for the sake of unity. Nancy also finds problematic the communist ideal when it defines human beings as "the producers of their own essence in the form of their labour or their work" (Nancy, *The Inoperative Community*, 2). It is for this reason he highlights a certain un-working or inoperativeness of community, which does not operate with a view of a particular common project, as we will see in the allegory of the heavenly builders in *The Famished Road*.

[2] Aitor Ibarrola-Armendariz, "Boundary Erasing: Postnational Characterization in Michael Ondaatje's *The English Patient*", in *Tricks with a Glass: Writing Ethnicity in Canada*, eds Rocío G. Davis and Rosalía Baena, Amsterdam: Rodopi, 2000, 42.

"also contribute to the feeling that the present is actually only a replica or reenactment, and that genuine identity or meaning is always to be found elsewhere, in some experience remembered from the past, some sort of 'original pattern' prototype".[3]

Cook locates the topos of desired meaning in the "original" prototypes, suggesting that the characters always move using their old footsteps, trails, roads, and most importantly, memories, and that "their own meanings depend on mimetic or referential associations".[4] However, this reverberative backtracking is a way of moving forward. That is, the doubling of events and images does not evoke, as it does for Cook, Baudrillard's simulacrum and perpetual wallowing in self-reference. The backtracking reminds one rather of Heidegger's idea of *Holzwege*, walking the same paths, but walking them differently, and thus transforming them. This image suggests a destructive/creative process in relation to the past that is not behind but rather meets the characters from the future. By retracing their steps, characters seek to transform the meaning of their actions. The backtracking, which for Cook is evolving backwards "to some 'original identity,' some timeless and essential secret'",[5] is in fact a process of translation and a transformation. In a search for authenticity, such repetition is a way out of endless repetition. As Crowe explains it, repetition can be understood as "an activity that 'responds [*erwidert*]' to the past as a possibility, i.e., an activity that takes the past as a challenge for the future rather than something intrinsically valuable as such. It is thus simultaneously a 'disavowal [*Widerruf*]' of 'that which is effective in the today as the past'."[6]

Ibarrola-Armendariz suggests that the characters' main advantage "in this challenging task of re-reading their existence is that they can rely on their own interpretative potential and use their skills in whatever way they please. In this microcosm, they are responsible only to themselves for their acts of revision .... Predictably, the reader is frequently bewildered by the form that those regenerating 'rituals' take."[7]

---

[3] Rufus Cook, "Being and Representation in Michael Ondaatje's *The English Patient*", *ARIEL: A Review of International English Literature*, XXX/4 (October 1999), 38.

[4] *Ibid.*, 40.

[5] *Ibid.*, 43.

[6] Crowe, *Heidegger's Religious Origins*, 193.

[7] Ibarrola-Armendariz, "Boundary Erasing", 47.

He further suggests that the characters' freedom evinces a "monologic merging of their four voices [which then] radically reduces the potential constellation of Ondaatje's discourses and themes".[8] The characters' rituals do not isolate the demand on responsibility for their actions, but emphasize the responsibility for singular choices. They are stripped naked. They cannot blame anyone for their actions. While Cook judges Ondaatje's betrayal of "one of the main goals of the narrative, which is to let each of the characters give shape to his or her story",[9] Ondaatje shows that giving shape to one's own story in such an individualist fashion is a modern myth. Hana, for instance, participates in the forming of a new, motley community, which indeed turns out short-lived, but it undeniably provides space for the different characters' singularity as well as new ways of bonding, possibilities of new social alignments that rearticulate alignment along national, racial, religious, tribal, class or profession lines.

Hana: nursing authenticity

For Hana, being a nurse implies conforming to a social, ideologically limited role, or what Appiah calls a life script.[10] She decides to pull out of the war machinery and nursing as her national duty in order to reshape "this universe of hers" with a "burned man to care for, some sheets to wash in a fountain, a room painted like a garden" (33). To nurse authenticity might then sound like an oxymoron, a paradox. However, in her pertinent choice to alter the life script of a nurse, her awareness of her own responsibility is heightened. Nursing this one man becomes in a sense a nursing of her freedom and responsibility that is not reduced to duty.

While most critics, reviewers, as well as the film's director Anthony Minghella, foreground the English patient, Hana comes across as perhaps the most authentic. It is her actions that serve as the catalyst for the formation of the villa-community. It is into her story that the other three characters enter. Hana's authenticity is worked out not only through dramatized encounters and conflicts with the other characters, but also in a prominently intimate and tense relationship

---

[8] *Ibid.*, 54.
[9] Cook, "Being and Representation", 42.
[10] Kwame Anthony Appiah, *The Ethics of Identity*, Princeton, NJ: Princeton University Press, 2005, 22.

with the narrative voice. Even though the narrator leaves the English patient a mystery, in the final passages Hana is the one whom the narrator is unable/unwilling to fix in any traditional way, as if she had agency to resist this third person narrator.

Hana carried out "her duties while she secretly pulled her personal self back. So many nurses had turned emotionally disturbed handmaidens of the war, in their yellow-and crimson uniforms with bone buttons" (178). Devastation has contributed to Hana's existential crisis:

> Throughout the war, with all of her worst patients, she survived by keeping a coldness hidden in her role as nurse. I will survive this. I won't fall apart. (48)

She had used the role as nurse as an established and meaningful beacon of identity, to slow down her falling apart. Still, "her body had been in a war and, as in love, it had used every part of itself" (81). She decides to draw "her own few rules" and skip being "ordered again or carry out duties for the greater good" (14). The "greater good" has lost its meaning and turned into mechanical following of directives. While the "greater good" should be the end of the mayhem, the nurses' work does not merely alleviate pain and mend wounds. It sustains the progress of war. Hana decides to leave the moving armies and the nursing establishment, and take on a burned man, tending him in a ruined Italian villa. Having been "trained at Women's College" (49), she wants to break with her traditional female role:

> I was considered a snob. I worked harder than others …. I wanted to go home and there was no one at home. And I was sick of Europe. Sick of being treated like gold because I was female. (85)

This decision makes her feel "safe here, half adult and half child" (14). She tends the burned man because with him "she could turn away from being an adult" (52), and have womb-like feeling under heavy blankets (49). Childhood suggests a Romantic return to innocence, when she was still not entirely spoiled by adult schemes. Yet, when she was young,

> … there was her mother Alice her father Patrick her stepmother Clara and Caravaggio …. She used them like authorities in a book she could

refer to on the right way to boil an egg, or the correct way to slip garlic into a lamb. They were not to be questioned.

Now, in the Italian villa, Hana

> ... was evasive, veering Caravaggio away from stories that involved some moment of life. She wanted Kip to know her only in the present, a person perhaps more flawed or more compassionate or harder or more obsessed than the girl or the young woman she had been then. (268)

Eleanor Ty suggests that freedom for Hana "means days without routine, without rules, without limits".[11] When she withdraws into the villa and rests, Hana wants

> ... to receive all aspects of the world without judgment. A bath in the sea, a fuck with a soldier who never knew your name. Tenderness towards the unknown and anonymous, which was a tenderness to the self. (49)

At the same time, it is not simply the question of judgment or the lack of it, but rather an ecstasy of the self, in the sense of standing out of oneself, reaching out and beyond the limits of a self (*ec-stasis*).

Caravaggio was positively surprised by the fact that "he loved her more now than he loved her when ... she was the product of her parents" (222). Now she was

> ... what she herself has decided to become. He knew that if he had passed Hana on a street in Europe she would have had a familiar air but he wouldn't have recognized her. The night he had first come to the villa he had disguised his shock. Her ascetic face, which at first seemed cold, had a sharpness .... He could hardly believe his pleasure at her translation. Years before, he had tried to imagine her as an adult but he had invented someone with qualities moulded out of her community. Not this wonderful stranger he could love more deeply because she was made up of nothing he had provided. (222-23)

---

[11] Eleanor Ty, "The Other Questioned: Exoticism and Displacement in Michael Ondaatje's *The English Patient*", *International Fiction Review*, XXVII/1-2 (2000), 12.

Hana is a translated woman, liberated from her communal identity. In this passage, Hana's looks and her selfhood seem to reflect each other; both are transformed and are still transforming.

Only as an afterthought does Hana realize that even her stepfather was something of a non-conformist, who tried to (re)imagine the world at a slight angle:

> ... her father was never fully comfortable in the world. His conversations lost some of their syllables out of shyness. In any of Patrick's sentences ... you lost two or three crucial words. But Hana liked that about him, there seemed to be no feudal spirit around him. He had a vagueness, an uncertainty that allowed him tentative charm. He was unlike most men. Even the wounded English patient had the familiar purpose of the feudal. But her father was a hungry ghost .... He was the least furious man she knew, hating argument .... He had never attempted to convert anyone in his life, just bandaging and celebrating events that occurred near him .... Her father loved a city of his own invention .... He never truly stepped out of that world. She realizes everything she knew about the real world she learned on her own or from Caravaggio or ... Clara. (90-91)

With time, Hana has come to despise the reality and rhetoric that purported to give sense to it:

> Who the hell were we to be given this responsibility, expected to be wise as old priests, to know how to lead people towards something no one wanted and somehow make them comfortable. I could never believe in all those services they gave for the dead. Their vulgar rhetoric. (83-84)

Hana opposes the rhetoric of Christianity, and the rites that give special meaning to death and thus bring comfort and alleviate the agony of dying, both for those on their deathbed and those around them. She detects a certain falsity in such gestures. Indeed, as David Roxborough argues, Hana's transformation of a crucifix into a scarecrow is a "poignant, perhaps even sacrilegious relegation of the cross to the position of repellent or frightening totem [which] violates the sanctity of the image and suggests a similar resistance in Hana's mind". This act is parallel to the narrator's technique of immersing the narrative in Judeo-Christian (and even Islamic and Sikh) symbolism. Roxborough traces a plethora of religious motifs, which are not simple meaning oases in which existentially broken characters find ground for their identity. On the contrary, when one and the same person "may become both saint and Satan in the space of a few pages [this] presents uncertainty that is symptomatic of internal struggle".[12] The Saint/Satan characteristic does not sustain the idea that individuals have both good and evil sides. Rather, it is "a provocative statement concerning the loss of sacred origins and the diminishing potential of humanity to create or recover a dynamic, meaningful myth".[13] Ondaatje creates characters who are not "passive recipients of religious dogma". Instead they "question the myth's ideological basis".[14] They question the ways the myth produces and maintains a world. The loss of the sacred origin constitutes the interruption of myth, where myth is severed from its meaning and therefore loses its power to convert its own fiction into foundation. It has lost its flow, its ability to transcend time/generations. The myths in question are not simply premodern. While old myths already imply their fictionality and metaphoricity, the new mythologies seem to tend even more towards transparency and naturalization, increasingly ignoring this implied irony of premodern myths.

Now that Hana has begun distrusting myths and ideologies, she also transforms the role of the female nurse who altruistically and heroically takes care of someone she does not even know. Hana abandons this role as a general duty.[15] To use West's words, "organizations appealing only to a sense of duty presumably depend on less obvious sources of satisfaction. Where satisfactions are not apparent, we begin to suspect the existence of other motives: lust for power or revenge, or the longing for the security of a dogma or a

---

[12] David Roxborough, "The Gospel of Almásy: Christian Mythology in Michael Ondaatje's *The English Patient*", *Essays on Canadian Writing*, LXVII (Spring 1999), 244.

[13] *Ibid.*, 239.

[14] *Ibid.*, 243.

[15] This gesture is reminiscent of Rousseau for whom the politics of authenticity, as Berman sums it up, "demanded radically liberal social reforms designed to make men free and equal, happy and beneficent". However, to institute care, to form institutions that are supposed to release human potentials runs a greater risk of repressing these very human energies. The idea of a free institution is a contradiction in terms: "To take away the sweetness of a good deed, all you need to do is make it a duty" (Berman, *The Politics of Authenticity*, 221). If duty made Rousseau want to do the opposite, someone like Hana can do the dutiful deed only after she has renounced the demand of duty.

faith."[16] It is "an impoverished conception of politics which can only appeal to duty".[17] Hana wishes she had nursed her stepfather Patrick, but not out of duty, or for a higher cause. She wonders if he was "nursed by a stranger?" (90), the way she is a stranger to the English patient. Here there is a trace of Christian duty to show kindness to strangers, as well as the projection of her burnt stepfather onto Almásy. However, instead of settling on either of these most typical explanations, Hana evinces some transformative action in her decision to keep nursing him:

> A man not of your own blood can break upon your emotions more than someone of your own blood. As if falling into the arms of a stranger you discover the mirror of *your own choice*. (90, emphasis in the original).

Here, Hana is not moving in the direction of individualism for which hell is generally other people. Her patient's otherness, his disturbing strangeness and alterity opens Hana up to her own alterity and becomes a ground of communication and a relation. Her singularity, her choices, her freedom, her self are articulated not so much in those moments of isolation, but through her surprising connection with and openness to her patient. There is a sharing between them, a bond that does not tie them to each other, as Caravaggio seems to believe.

The experience of freedom is also the experience of a community. Her acts of freedom cannot be possessed but only dispossessed of insofar as Hana is dispossessed of herself. By keeping with her patient Hana does not sink into individualist egoism, nor does she remain the dutiful nurse acting on orders.

Seeing how Hana has grown attached to the patient, Caravaggio believes she conforms to the role of a female nurse, eternally caring for an eternally dying patient, as if stuck in a time loop. He says, "I want to kill the Englishman, because that is the only thing that will save you, get you out of here" (122). He talks about the patient as an old guru whose intellect seduced her into this strange disciple position. Indeed, she identifies with "the young boy in the story [*Kim*]" who follows a guru, but the reverse is true as well, "it was

---

[16] West, *Authenticity and Empowerment*, 108.
[17] *Ibid.*, 174.

Hana in the night who stayed with the old man, who guided him over the mountains to the sacred river" (111). Contrary to Caravaggio's view, the patient understands he cannot preach freedom, because such a gesture would defeat its purpose. That is why she is annoyed with both Caravaggio and Kip when they try to protect her from her self, as if they had the right way, while the patient shows no such intentions. The patient says to Hana, "You're surrounded by madmen", upon which she answers, "Yes, I think we are all mad" (266). Madness is positive here because it signals non-conformity, and a certain instability and divisibility of the self.

Yet, she also sometimes plays a saviour. She wants to save the patient from his lost-ness. At the same time she indeed understands that his chaotic rambling is his way of negotiating his own selfhood *vis-à-vis* the attacks like those of Caravaggio. The patient does not offer Hana meaning, but a certain blank/black mirror in which her own existential experiment is reflected and refracted: "There was no defense but to look for truth in others" (117). The truth in others is, to use Nancy's words, the truth of their finitude/mortality as well as the necessity of a communal bonding for freedom:

> Freedom cannot be presented as the autonomy of a subjectivity in charge of itself and of its decisions, evolving freely and in perfect independence from every obstacle. What would such an independence mean, if not the impossibility in principle of entering into the slightest relation – and therefore of exercising of the slightest freedom.[18]

This is why authenticity is only ever realized through action and singularity through relation. Hana's freedom is not at bottom "a struggle for recognition and self-mastery of a subjectivity" but rather "what throws the subject into the space of the sharing of being".[19]

Hana bonds with, but is not tied to the patient even though she "sleeps beside him virtuous as a sister" (126). Here we find what Nancy calls "a bond that forms ties without attachments, or even less fusion, a bond that unbinds by binding, that reunites through the infinitive exposition of an irreducible finitude".[20]

---

[18] Nancy, *The Experience of Freedom*, 66.
[19] *Ibid.*, 70.
[20] Nancy, *The Inoperative Community*, xl.

Given that Ondaatje's characters all love jazz, it might be valuable to evoke Eagleton's use of a jazz band as a metaphor of their community. In a jazz band, unlike in a philharmonic orchestra, there is singularity and freedom, and yet a communal (dis)harmony:

> There is no conflict here between freedom and the 'good of the whole', yet the image is the reverse of totalitarian. Though each performer contributes to 'the greater good of the whole', she does so not by some grim-lipped self-sacrifice but simply by expressing herself. There is self-realization, but only through a loss of self in the music as a whole. There is achievement, but it is not a question of self-aggrandizing success.[21]

In such a community members care for themselves, but their care is communicated through others. Just as in jazz music, there is a sense of history, of the past, of heritage that ties and burdens them, but this relation is most importantly transformative and translational.[22]

The communal jazz-banding can be contrasted to Hana's solo singing of a national anthem:

> She was singing it as if it was something scarred, as if one couldn't ever again bring all the hope of the song together. It had been altered by the five years leading to this night of her twenty-first birthday in the forty-fifth year of the twentieth century. Singing in the voice of a tired traveller, alone against everything. A new testament. There was no certainty to the song anymore, the singer could only be one voice against all the mountains of power. That was the only sureness. The one voice was the single unspoiled thing. (269)

Hana sings the anthem with certain tiredness, marring the nationalist zeal, the power of its rhetoric, practically mocking the way the anthem is supposed to make her a part of a larger entity, instead feeding her sense of isolation. The relation to the nation is captured in the image of the individual that stands alone against the world, always already lost and defined through this binary opposition.

---

[21] Terry Eagleton, *The Meaning of Life*, Oxford: Oxford University Press, 2007, 173.

[22] Since authenticity entails, as Crowe suggests, "sensitivity to the demands of the present situation, authentic individuals participate in one way or another in the resolution of common problems or in the realization of common goals" (Crowe, *Heidegger's Religious Origins*, 203).

The English patient: shedding skins

The most striking aspect of the English patient arises from his belief that "the world burns around them with only a few crucial rules" (125). He totally refuses identity with respect to nationality, class, race and culture:

> We were German, English, Hungarian, African – all of us insignificant to them. Gradually we became nationless. I came to hate nations. We are deformed by nation-states. Madox died because of nations. (138)

Like his crew, he "seemed to be interested only in things that could not be bought or sold, of no interest to the outside world" (143), and "the river that is trade" (145). He sees the world as governed by capitalist, nationalist and racist ideologies. His rejection of the national ties, and a resistance to identity as such, has been the nexus of critical attention to the novel.

The patient's severe burn scars aid his struggle against different forms of social affiliation and identity formation. He is a man with no name, no past, no ancestry and no nationhood:

> A man with no face. An ebony pool. All identification consumed in fire …. There was nothing to recognize in him. (48)

Ondaatje's description reminds one of a deterritorialized body without organization, "a body that breaks free from its socially articulated, disciplined, semioticized, and subjectified state (as an organism), to become disarticulated, dismantled, and deterritorialized, and hence able to be reconstituted in new ways", as Stephen Best and Douglas Kellner put it following Deleuze and Guattari.[23] According to Elizabeth Kella, "Almásy is saved from being reduced to a corporeal object by his ability to create meaning", and "the extremity of his physicality serves to bring out his essential subjectivity".[24]

The question is, what is this essential subjectivity? The narrative identifies him both as Almásy and suggests, "everything about him

---

[23] Stephen Best and Douglas Kellner, *Postmodern Theory: Critical Interrogations*, London: Macmillan, 1991, 90-91.

[24] Elizabeth Kella, *Beloved Communities: Solidarity and Difference in Fiction by Michael Ondaatje, Toni Morrison, and Joy Kogawa*, Acta Universitatis Upsaliensis, Studia Anglistica Upsaliensia, CX, Uppsala: Uppsala University, 2000, 87.

was English except that his skin was tarred black, a bogman from history among the interrogating officers" (96). Is his true subjectivity something hidden under the masks he uses to provoke those who try to identify him: "You should be trying to trick me … make me speak German, which I can" (95)? He appears blank, but he is no *tabula rasa*. There is enough vague information to lure people around him into conducting their own small investigations into his secret past. Not who he is, or wishes to be, but who he was with respect to his past: "He had rambled on, driving them mad, traitor or ally, leaving them never quite sure who he was …. All that is missing is his own name" (96). The interrogators' demand that he identifies himself emphasizes the burden of heritage. The war circumstances augment their urge to conformity. More than ever, they are forced to choose their affiliations at every level of their existence. Wrong connections can lead to death, as when the Allies refuse to help him save his lover Katharine because he gives them the wrong name:

> I was yelling Katharine's name. Yelling the Gilf Kebir. Whereas the only name I should have yelled, dropped like a calling card into their hands, was Clifton's …. I was just another possible second-rate spy. Just another international bastard. (251)

In his evasive answers to the interrogators, be they friends or foes, the English patient fends off every attempt to classify him. The third person narrator shifts between the telling of Almásy's past and letting him narrate for his company. It is never clear who knows what, how much, and speaks with what authority. In several places, the narrative slides from the third to the first person, without conventional markers, without hints as to who speaks at what point, the implied author or the characters. Although the novel offers several clues that identify the burned man as Count Ladislaus de Almásy, in certain passages he speaks about Almásy in the third person, upon which Caravaggio reacts, "*Who is he speaking as now?*" (244, emphasis in the original).

Later, Caravaggio watches him, thinking, there is

> … more to discover, to divine out of this body on the bed, nonexistent except for a mouth, a vein in the arm, wolf-grey eyes. He is still amazed at the clarity of discipline in the man, who speaks sometimes in the third person, who still does not admit that he is Almásy. (247)

Since the patient's narratives move back and forth in time, often lingering on feelings rather than following a plot, Caravaggio

> … stays alongside him reordering the events. Only desire makes the story errant, flickering like a compass needle. And this is the world of nomads in any case, an apocryphal story. A mind travelling east and west in the disguise of sandstorms. (248)

In the end, Caravaggio "wants to rise and walk away from this villa, the country, the detritus of a war." He is merely a thief who feels he

> … must get out of this desert, its architecture of morphine. He needs to pull away from the invisible road to El Taj. This man he believes to be Almásy has used him and the morphine to return to his own world, for his own sadness. (251)

The more Caravaggio insists, the more the English patient withdraws into his interiority (he is infinitely more open with Kip). He resists being claimed or owned, like the desert, which

> was a piece of cloth carried by winds, never held down by stones, and given a hundred shifting names long before Canterbury existed …. All of us, even those with European homes and children in the distance, wished to remove the clothing of our countries. It was a place of faith. We disappeared into landscape …. Erase the family name! Erase nations! I was taught such things by the desert. (138-39)

Posed like a human black hole, he devours any meaning given to him. By doing so he in fact mocks the ideologues who cannot keep the desert/cloth their object. He says:

> When we are young we do not look into mirrors.[25] It is when we are old, concerned with our name, our legend, what our lives will mean to the future. We become vain with the names we own, our claims to have been the first eyes, the strongest army, the cleverest merchant …. But we were interested in how our lives could mean something to the

---

[25] Annick Hillger aptly argues that Hana's own resentment of mirrors is her way of "refusing an identification of the self in the very traditional manner of self-reflection" (Annick Hillger, "'And this is the World of Nomads in any Case': The Odyssey as Intertext in Michael Ondaatje's *The English Patient*", *Journal of Commonwealth Literature*, XXXIII/1 [January 1998], 31).

past. We sailed into the past. We were young. We knew power and great finance were temporary things. (141-42)

For him, youth is synonymous with exploration. Later, the explorers start thinking what legacies they will leave for posterity. They become vain and possessive; they want to shape the world and hand it down to future generations, thus in a sense denying the new generations their own freedom. The patient's friends start naming things after themselves, a fossil tree, a dune type, and even a tribe. By entering the desert to erase history, he also brings history to the desert. This is why the novel situates itself in ambiguous topoi such as caves, shifting landscape of the desert, the shattered/open monastery/villa, and muddy holes. It is as if one needs to cross a plane of nothingness to face all that selfhood means in spaces between worlds, none of which is real or imaginary in the simple sense of this dichotomy, "that pure zone between land and chart between distances and legend between nature and storyteller" (246).

Marilyn Adler Papayanis analyses the trope "desert" as typical for Western seekers of authenticity: "intimidating desert frontiers produce dread and the ideal conditions for radical existentialist experimentation".[26] Indeed, the patient says, by "the time war arrived, after ten years in the desert, it was easy for me to slip across borders, not to belong to anyone" (139). He always strives to find alternate names, because to name is also to label. He wants to erase his family name because it has become a suffocating confinement. Conversations with him begin as if in the middle, rather than formally by calling of a name. When he says, "There was a time when mapmakers named the places they travelled through with the names of lovers rather than their own" (140), he seems to argue that there are unselfish ways of naming, naming that is not claiming the object but opening oneself in relation to it. To name something after a lover is a sign of a self that defines itself by means of a detour, and an exposure to otherness.[27]

---

[26] Marilyn Adler Papayanis, *Writing in the Margins: The Ethics of Expatriation from Lawrence to Ondaatje*, Nashville, TN: Vanderbilt University Press, 2005, 207.

[27] Nicola Renger argues that "the problem of identity 'is not so much that of knowing one's identity as it is that of how to relate that newly evolving identity to its inherited or given names'" (Nicola Renger, "Cartography, Historiography, and Identity in Michael Ondaatje's *The English Patient*", in *Being/s in Transit: Travelling, Migration, Dislocation*, ed. Liselotte Glage, Amsterdam and New York: Rodopi, 2000, 116).

The trial of the patient, by now often fixed as the Hungarian Count who aided the Germans in their North-African enterprise, blossoms outside the frameworks of the novel in various reviews of the book and the film, as well as scholarly articles. Troy Jollimore and Sharon Barrio offer a practical-philosophical analysis in which his connections to Nazi Germany are interpreted as treason. What is more, "the fact that Almásy fails to think beyond a very limited horizon, and is completely indifferent to the effects of his actions on those who live beyond this horizon – that is in fact the most powerful consideration in favour of the claim that he is an evil person", because "we should accept that evil can proceed from indifference as well as malevolence".[28] This argument strongly resembles the judgment of the interrogators in Camus' *The Outsider*[29] and Coetzee's *Disgrace*[30] in which indifference borders on evil. While Camus' Meursault meets his persecutors with silence, the patient "talks all the time" (28) about anything but what the interrogators want. It is as if he enacts the saying that the "surest way of being mute is not to hold your tongue but to talk".[31] Unlike Meursault, he encounters characters that admire his single-mindedness, and unconventionality. Even Hana disregards his past sins:

> I think we should leave him be. It doesn't matter what side he was on, does it? .... No, David. You're too obsessed. It doesn't matter who he is. The war is over .... Leave him alone. He's my patient. (165-66)

The patient acts on the basis of other values than those that shape the world he wants to abandon. His ambivalent existence prevents him from thinking tactically *vis-à-vis* the politics of the war. As Alice Brittan points out, he helps the Nazis not because of political preference, but because the English prevented him from saving Katharine.[32]

The patient was not like any other explorer. Despite his strong connections to the British imperial machinery, he was more of a

---

[28] Troy Jollimore and Sharon Barrios, "Beauty, Evil, and *The English Patient*", *Philosophy and Literature*, XXVIII/1 (April 2004), 27.

[29] Albert Camus, *The Outsider*, London: Penguin, 2000.

[30] J.M. Coetzee, *Disgrace*, London: Penguin Book, 1999.

[31] Sartre, *Existentialism Is a Humanism*, 87.

[32] Alice Brittan, "War and the Book: The Diarist, the Cryptographer, and *The English Patient*", *PMLA*, CXXI/1 (January 2006), 206.

nomad that struggled within different systems of power. Hillger suggests

> [his] nomadism is his strategy of escaping his heritage. He identifies with the nomads from Herodotus and then with the nameless nomadic tribe that saved him in the desert. The '— tribe' parallels the '— wind' .... [The] removal of this sign opens up a blank in his identity, which could also have made him into the '—' patient. By deciding to bring 'their' patient to the British base, the — tribe establishes his identity as British.[33]

Best and Kellner explain how Deleuze and Guattari advocated nomadism because a "nomad-self breaks from all molar segments and cautiously disorganizes itself. Nomad life is an experiment in creativity and becoming, and is anti-traditional and anti-conformist in character".[34] Nomadism does not absolute arbitrariness of direction that the self takes. Rather it evokes openness to change.[35]

In the novel, the idea of non-conformity is articulated with respect to the historical figures of Herodotus and Poliziano. For the patient, Herodotus is the historical example of a nomad, a desert man who can

> ... travel from oasis to oasis, trading legends as if it is the exchange of seeds, consuming everything without suspicion, piecing together a mirage. 'This history of mine,' Herodotus says, 'has from the beginning sought out the supplementary to the main argument.' What you find in him are cul-de-sacs within the sweep of history – how people betray each other for the sake of nations, how people fall in love. (118-19)

The patient's Herodotus, if not the historical one, is a rebel against the powers of his time. He seeks alternative histories rather than fixity of the mainstream narrative. The other figure is "Poliziano ... Brilliant, awful man. A genius who worked his way up into society" (57).

---

[33] Hillger, "'And this is the World of Nomads in any Case'", 40.

[34] Best and Kellner, *Postmodern Theory*, 103.

[35] Hillger suggests that by "freeing itself from the 'category of the root, the origin, [which] is a category of dominion', nomad thought tries to let itself not be blind to its immediate surroundings because some faraway place must be reached. In contrast to sedentary thought, it is prepared to acknowledge whatever may be found on the way during the process of thinking" (Hillger, "'And this is the World of Nomads in any Case'", 24).

Poliziano was a self-made man who paved his own path in history as the opponent of the religious zealot Savonarola who cried out

> *'Repentance! The deluge is coming!'* And everything was swept away – free will, the desire to be elegant, fame, the right to worship Plato as well as Christ. (57, emphasis in the original)

The tension between conformity and freedom is further dramatized through the patient's relationship with Katharine Clifton. Like Rushdie's Aadam Aziz, the English patient falls for a woman who loves her own legacies, which she locates in England:

> ... she was a woman who ... loved family traditions and courteous ceremony and old memorized poems. She would have hated to die without a name. For her there was a line back to her ancestors that was tactile, whereas he had erased the path he had emerged from. He was amazed she had loved him in spite of such qualities of anonymity in himself. (170)

Except that she breaks the law against adultery, Katharine desires a conventional relationship.[36] The patient's strangeness attracts her, but she wants to nurse him back into the real world, despite his "wishes to burn down all social rules, all courtesy" (155). His non-conformity is even more foregrounded when he pretends to play by the rules:

> At the hotel he was excessively polite. When he behaved this way she liked him even less; they all had to pretend this pose was courtesy, graciousness. It reminded her of a dog in clothes. (151)

---

[36] Hsuan L. Hsu suggests, "Almásy, Katharine, Hana, and Kip embody and enact desires that transgress both national and familial boundaries .... Whereas marriage is public and official, adultery is by definition private and illicit, a violation not just of societal laws, but of vows voluntarily undertaken" (Hsuan L. Hsu, "Post-Nationalism and the Cinematic Apparatus in Minghella's Adaptation of Ondaatje's *The English Patient*", in *Comparative Cultural Studies and Michael Ondaatje's Writing*, ed. Steven Tötösy de Zepetnek, West Lafayette, IN: Purdue University Press, 2005, 50). However, as Vladimir Nabokov has said in his lecture on *Madame Bovary*, adultery is a most conventional way to rise above the conventional (Vladimir Nabokov, *Lectures on Literature*, Harcourt, CA: Brace Jovanovich, 1980, 133). Ondaatje seems to have integrated Julian Barnes' suggestion that any "history of adultery would doubtless quote Emma's seduction" (Julian Barnes, *Flaubert's Parrot*, London: Pan Books, 1985, 102).

Even though she wants him to be more conventional, she knows his mimicry is merely a mockery:

> I began to be doubly formal in her company. A characteristic of my nature. As if awkward about a previously revealed nakedness. It is a European habit. It was natural for me – having translated her strangely into my text of the desert – now to step into the metal clothing in her presence. (235-36)

There is a dose of irony in his emphasis on "nature" and "habit", which is why Katharine "looked down on [him] quizzical as if [he] were a planetary stranger" (236). She hates his posing as a bitter and self-sufficient outsider (172), but when he behaves regularly, she is even angrier because he is playing the game, mocking her:

> You think you are an iconoclast, but you're not. You just move, or replace what you cannot have. If you fail something you retreat into something else. Nothing changes you .... I left you because I could never change you. You would stand in the room so still sometimes, so wordless sometimes, as if the greatest betrayal of yourself would be to reveal one more inch of yourself. (173-74)

What Katharine argues against is his way of maintaining the image of a self-sufficient individual who cannot imagine overstepping "the norms of his own anomaly", to use Maurice Blanchot's phrase.[37] She tells the patient that he is not really a self-sufficient iconoclast and that the world is not simply some raw material he can use for his personality. He cannot see this because he is so positioned in terms of the individual/society binary: "'Ownership,' he says. 'When you leave me, forget me.'" (152). For her, it is something quite different. "'You slide past everything,'" she says, "'with your fear and hate of ownership, of owning, of being owned, of being named. You think this is a virtue. I think you are inhuman'" (238). Katharine's statement is similar to Appiah's theoretical claim that complete independence of mind "would mean ... to have no fixtures, no horizons of decision making, no pregiven ends or values or interests or goals. Such a creature starts to look distinctively inhuman."[38]

---

[37] Maurice Blanchot, *The Unavowable Community*, Barrytown, NY: Station Hill Press, 1988, 39.
[38] Appiah, *The Ethics of Identity*, 53.

Almásy's detachment and estrangement make him more desert-like, more inhuman. To truly become a self-sufficient individual he would have to abandon every relation, every communication, and assume a total independence. This would be to stop being human. However, this individualism is dismantled through a community with Katharine, the smallest community of two lovers. The community of lovers immediately comes in conflict with society. It pushes them outside the norms and duties. Through this community "she realized suddenly that wondrous thing about the human being, it can change. She did not have to remain a socialite who had married an adventurer." He says, "She was hungrier to change than I expected" (230), while her husband:

> ... was a man embedded in the English machine. He had a family genealogy going back to Canute. The machine would not necessarily have revealed to Clifton ... his wife's infidelity, but it began to encircle the fault, the disease in the system. It knew every move she and I made from the first day .... Clifton was as innocent as we were about the great English web that was above us. But the club of bodyguards watched over her husband and kept him protected. Only Madox, who was an aristocrat with a past of regimental associations ... warned me about such a world.

It is at this moment, "far too late to avoid the machinery we had set in motion", that Madox gives his friend a hint by trying to "explain Clifton's world in terms of Anna Karenina's brother" (237).

The world against which the patient defines himself is described in terms of machines, diseased systems, and great conspiratorial webs, that is, the stereotypes of control and systematic oppression. It is from such a world he endeavours to escape into "the zone of *limbo* between city and plateau ... that pure zone between land and chart between distances and legend between nature and storyteller". He starts appreciating "the place they had chosen to come to, to be their best selves, to be unconscious of ancestry. Here, apart from the sun compass and the odometer mileage and the book, he was alone, his own invention" (246).

The patient's desire for self-sufficiency enters another phase in the cave of the swimmers, where he and Katharine "had come together and spoken once more as lovers, rolling away the boulder they had placed between themselves for some social law neither had believed in" (171). After the crash, he "pulled her body free, carrying it out of the plane's crumpled grip, this grip of her husband" (173). He makes his dead lover "anonymous, a naked map where nothing is depicted" and he disregards her wish to be named and known. He makes her into what he wants to be, what he wishes someone would do with him:

> And all the names of the tribes, the nomads of faith who walked in the monotone of the desert and saw brightness and faith and colour. The way a stone or found metal box or bone can become loved and turn eternal in a prayer. Such glory of this country she enters now and becomes part of. We die containing a richness of lovers and tribes, tastes we swallowed, bodies we have plunged into and swam up as if rivers of wisdom, characters we have climbed into as if trees, fears we have hidden in as if caves. I wish for all this to be marked on my body when I am dead. I believe in such cartography – to be marked by nature, not just to label ourselves on a map like the names of rich men and women on buildings. (261)

The desert cave is holy to the patient because it allows him to perform the communal rite of painting and eternalizing his lover in the manner he finds suitable to their relationship, rather than the manner which his family or community would have recommended. He is anguished because he suspects that his desire for absolute autonomy has brought back the "world" into their lives with a vengeance:

> Had I been her demon lover? Had I been Madox's demon friend? This country – had I charted it and turned it into a place of war? (260)

This is where he realizes that his voluntary exile does not cancel out the world he wishes to escape. His escapism turns out to be a form of bad faith, a lack of awareness of his actions and a failure to take responsibility for the complicity in making the desert into a place of war. What Novak describes as the trauma of the lost and unattainable past is here not so much the loss of the desired object (a woman), but a trauma following the realization of his failure to take responsibility for his actions.[39] His understanding of authenticity as self-sufficiency

---

[39] Novak is wrong in claiming the novel "stages the struggle to bring forth and give meaning to that which escapes our ability to know and comprehend" (Novak, "Textual Hauntings", 213). Memory is the memory of that which is always carries a

folds back upon himself, and, as Papayanis has argued, he seems to arrive at a "universalist ethic", [40] which consists in "radical identification with the cosmos and humankind, and, indeed, a sense of Bataillian rupture and communication". [41] This ethic is "a reformulation of the modernist project of self-dismantling along postmodern lines". It is "an expatriate ethos" "that aspires almost to global subjectivity, although in an entirely decentered way". This "global ethic", however, does not seem quite universal or global. There is not much in the narrative that suggests a certain universality of the patient's stance, which in any case is not stable. There is indeed an existential process. There are new forms of bonding closer to what I referred to as inoperative community. The patient says, "we were the thin edge of a cult she had stumbled onto" (230-31). The intonation on the "we" is crucial. Although he is a loner, he still participates in a peculiar community he denotes "thin edge of a cult" to stress the strangeness, outsider-ness, difference, as well as fanaticism in their praxis. Finally, he says:

> We are communal histories, communal books. We are not owned or monogamous in our taste or experience .... I carried Katharine Clifton into the desert, where there is the communal book of moonlight. We were among the rumour of wells. In the palace of winds. (261)

Yet, this community is not society. His insistence on the cult quality of such communities or communal books shows that existential freedom is not founded in some sort of extreme isolation. Having begun his life as a man of labels and the world, the man who belongs to the Geographical Society (230), he enters an "oasis society", in which they know "each other's intimacies" (136). While this oasis society is still close to the world he wants to abandon, it is later in the company of the villa that he finds a community that is even more removed from the notion of society. The point is that they do not commune on the basis of common being or essence. Just as we saw in Hana, he was pulled out of the illusion of self-sufficiency and began opening himself unto the otherness of his lover: "their foreignness

---

meaning. The past has meaning only when it is appropriated for fulfilment of existence.

[40] Papayanis, *Writing in the Margins*, 236.

[41] *Ibid.*, 237.

intimate like two pages of a closed book. He has been disassembled by her" (155). The two pages (of their communal book) are singular, but not self-sufficient unto themselves. They are separate and yet there is a touch, a communication, a relation that constitutes their singularities.

Kip and the ambiguities

The Sikh sapper Kip presents a challenge when it comes to the question of authenticity. As a colonial subject, Kip engages with the discourse of Western imperialism, South Asian communalism, and, through his relationships with the villa crew, with individualism. His presence potentially relegates their desire for individual self-sufficiency to being a modern Western whim, and yet not. His sheer presence and actions reveal the devastating ideological and economic workings of the world, and the shortcomings of authenticity when it is understood as the private chiselling of the self.

As Ibarrola-Armendariz argues, Kip "begins to feel the first symptoms of existential alienation when he joins the British Army".[42] Indeed, his profession ties him to the war and the world he struggles to protect, but at the same time, he finds a haven in the villa community. He oscillates between it and his duties to the Allies, and the memory of his past life. Kip remains an ambivalent figure. He does not reveal much of "his past or qualities" as if it "would have been too loud a gesture. Just as he could never turn and inquire of her [Hana] what deepest motive caused their relationship" (197). Indeed, "there isn't a key to him" (270).

This half-in-half-out movement is strengthened by the use of specific imagery. Kip does not sleep in the house but in the gardens, which are "like further rooms" (43). He sleeps with half his body inside and half outside his tent. He "seems casually content with this small group in the villa, some kind of loose star on the edge of their system" (75). Furthermore, he often walks around with "just one earphone attached to his head, so he can hear sounds from the rest of the world that might be important to him" (76). It is as if he wants to remain in contact with both his immediate reality and that larger history of which he is a part but with which he has no true intimacy as he would perhaps have in a smaller community in his birthplace. His

---

[42] Ibarrola-Armendariz, "Boundary Erasing", 45.

listening to the radio also has certain doubleness. News broadcasts are indeed a way of keeping himself informed of the global perspective. At the same time, he listens to radio music as a way is of shutting out the world. It is also an escapist channel, which helps him "towards clear thought" (98-99).

In the beginning, Kip is a foreigner serving the English. While Europeans conceive of his identity mainly in terms of his race and culture, his nativist brother – who searches for Sikh roots and is an insurgent against English colonizers – perceives him as a traitor. Kip is claimed by and yet also estranged by different, conflicting discourses. He often comes across as a mere tool or a commodity for the English. At most, he is a semi-heir, despised for not following certain English traditions. Yet, when he does remain loyal he is not granted safety and intimacy. Upon his arrival in his unit, he

> ... had no idea what a kipper was, but the young Sikh had been thereby translated into a salty English fish. Within a week his real name, Kirpal Singh, had been forgotten. He hadn't minded this.

He prefers the demeaning nickname to being subject "to the English habit of calling people by their surname" (87-88). He might be ashamed to express his background in a racist context, or he may be like the patient who wants to erase his family name, which is the sign of both filial and ethnic bonds within and over generations.

To his company, Kip gives an air of self-sufficiency, which both amazes and irritates Hana, just as the patient affected Katharine: "She lies there irritated at his self-sufficiency, his ability to turn so easily away from the world" (128). He seems more independent from her than the other soldiers. He "will not eat the food she gathers", and "does not need or want the drug in the needle she could slide into his arm" (126). He disturbs her image as a nurse and thus in fact aids her in her attempt to shed this particular skin. Kip is suspicious of all gestures from the characters tied to the English. Hana's loving approach could in his eyes be politically and culturally charged, indeed a part of an ethos that has made him an outsider and not a part of any community. Indeed, he was "the foreigner, the Sikh. His only human and personal contact was the enemy who had made the bomb and departed brushing his tracks with a branch behind him" (105). Even with the people at the villa he starts off as a foreigner, an outsider among outsiders. Hana

> ... will realize he never allowed himself to be beholden to her, or her
> to him .... *Beholden. To be under obligation.* And he, she knows,
> never allowed that. If she crosses two hundred yards to him is her
> choice. (128, emphases in the original)

At times, Kip's "self-sufficiency seems rude to them, though no
doubt he feels it is excessive politeness" (127). Kip's self-sufficiency
is far more complex than they suspect. We have seen how the English
patient came across as rude and inhuman when he boasted his
independence from the social sphere of the Europeans in Africa. But
Kip is not simply trying to advocate his individualism, a conscious
attempt at shedding his inherited skins. Nor is his self-sufficiency a
simple matter of learnt politeness. Rather, the

> ... self-sufficiency and privacy Hana saw in him later were caused not
> just by his being a sapper in the Italian campaign. It was as much a
> result of being the anonymous member of another race, a part of the
> invisible world. (197)

Indeed, even though Kip is indispensable in his group of sappers,
he is anonymous and invisible. His presence is mostly known in the
moments when his difference shines up against the norms he is
expected to meet: "I knew if I lifted a teacup with the wrong finger I'd
be banished. If I tied the wrong kind of knot in a tie I was out" (283).
In a sense, Hana and the patient misinterpret Kip's social
estrangement as self-sufficiency.

However, his seclusion is not merely a matter of social ostracism.
It is also a matter of choice. He broke with the "old tradition in his
family", which prescribed that he as the second son "be a doctor", and
"volunteered himself into a unit of engineers" (182), becoming
something of a "*fato profugus* – fate's fugitive" (273). Within the unit
he indeed experiences racial profiling and is measured and marked,
which he knows would make his brother furious, but he "did not feel
insulted" because he had this side to his "nature which saw reason in
all things" (200). Having chosen and mastered "the strangest
profession his century had invented, a sapper" (182), his very skills
make him crucial to his fellow sappers as well as to soldiers, the
medical staff, patients and civilians. Whether or not they want it, the
other soldiers must see him, his work and even his heroism. Devon
Campbell-Hall interprets Kip's self-sufficiency with respect to the

idea of a "dangerous artisan [who] is able to move independently, free from many of the collective responsibilities of established societies, including those of his traditional community".[43] Indeed, Kip appears an essentialist when he ascribes his unique skills to his Sikh being – "He had come from a country where mathematics and mechanics were natural traits" and where people recycled everything, like the Bedouin that the patient meets:

> Most people in his village were more likely to carry a spanner or screwdriver than a pencil …. Antidotes to mechanized disasters were easily found …. What he saw in England was a surfeit of parts that would keep the continent of India going for two hundred years. (188)

Such a relation to technology is, as Campbell-Hall puts it, "spiritualised". It provides him "modest protection against the vacuum of the dehumanising war machine".[44]

However, until he meets Hana, Kip does work rather mechanically, proficiently, almost like a machine. Then he starts changing, re-examining his choices, and what they have turned him into. For instance, he becomes annoyed that

> … the girl had stayed with him when he defused the bomb, as if by that she made him owe her something. Making him feel in retrospect responsible for her, though there was no thought of that at the time. As if *that* could usefully influence what he chose to do with a mine. But he felt he was now within something, perhaps a painting he had seen somewhere in the last year. Some secure couple in a field … with no thought of work or the danger of the world …. If he were a hero in a painting, he could claim a just sleep. (104, emphasis in the original)

Indeed, a dismantling of a bomb is not aided by a sudden surge of care for one particular woman. Yet, her presence gives him a greater sense of the implications of his work and responsibility. The possibility of her death frightens him more than his own. Her possible death calls him beyond himself and thus delivers him to his freedom, as Nancy would claim. This freedom, like death, is necessarily "shared

---

[43] Devon Campbell-Hall, "Dangerous Artisans: Anarchic Labour in Michael Ondaatje's *The English Patient* and *Anil's Ghost* and Arundhati Roy's *The God of Small Things*", *World Literature Written in English*, XL/1 (2002-2003), 45.
[44] *Ibid.*, 50.

(*partage*), and the experience of the other's mortality constitutes something like a condition of this sharing. Like love (itself inseparable from an experience of mortality), it calls the subject out and beyond itself, exposing it to alterity and its freedom."[45]

In such deadly "communication are singular beings given – without a bond and without communion, equally distant from any notion of connection or joining from the outside and from any notion of a common and fusional interiority".[46] Kip and Hana then become a community (of lovers) whose freedom and authenticity is articulated through their sharing of finitude.

The patient suggests:

> Kip and I are both international bastards – born in one place and choosing to live elsewhere. Fighting to get back to or get away from our homelands all our lives. Though Kip doesn't recognize that yet. That's why we get on so well. (176-77)

He interprets Kip as a likeminded non-conformist, only not aware of it. For Novak, such identification oversimplifies their differences: "A well-educated European who consciously erases past and nation has very little in common with a colonial subject fighting the war of his colonizers."[47] Shannon Smyrl has argued that the patient glosses over the difference between his and Kip's approaches to selfhood and identity, and that he limits the horizon of possibilities and denies him "the complexity of self-determination".[48] For Smyrl, the patient

> ... erases their particular relationships to the process of cultural decentralization – Kip's emerging opportunity for self-invention is a crisis of legitimacy for the English patient – and thus neutralizes the nascent opportunity, represented in Kip, for a new understanding of identity organized around difference and disunity .... The English patient's self-construction as "international bastard" is produced in terms of the indeterminacy of language, and thus suggests an unlimited possibility of identification. Kip, in contrast, signifies as

---

[45] Nancy, *The Inoperative Community*, xv.

[46] *Ibid.*, 29.

[47] Novak, "Textual Hauntings", 221.

[48] Shannon Smyrl, "The Nation as 'International Bastard': Ethnicity and Language in Michael Ondaatje's *The English Patient*", *Studies in Canadian Literature/Etudes en littérature canadienne*, XXVIII/2 (Fall 2003), 34.

"international bastard" through the naturalization of his experiences of exclusion within Western culture.[49]

By merely expanding the meaning of the word "bastard", Smyrl ends up basically repeating the patient's gesture. If the patient is merely engaged in linguistic play, made possible by the indeterminacy of language, then her continuous use of the same name albeit expanded only aids the same play. Indeed, the patient's denomination is hardly unambiguous. He is not an "international bastard" just because he has chosen it but because his actions have placed him both inside and outside power struggles. He can see that Kip too is struggling to move away from his origins while he is also pulled back. Also, like Kip, he himself is a dark man not quite English and not entirely something else. What makes them "international bastards" is their struggle between different social and political frameworks, and also the fact that they arrived in this position from quite different points of departure, which both Novak and Smyrl seem to ignore. Secondly, like many other critics, they do not grant Kip any agency. It is in fact the patient who refrains from seeing Kip as nothing but a colonial subject, a perpetual victim. Indeed, Kip's family was not really the wretched of the earth. Also, Kip could be a marginal figure in his South Asian context because he is a Sikh, and not just due to his relation with the colonizer.

Kip is aware of the question of his agency:

> I believed I could fill myself with what older people taught me. I believed I could carry that knowledge, slowly altering it. (283)

Since he "hated confrontation", he

> … had discovered the overlooked space open to those of us with a silent life. I didn't argue with the policeman who said I couldn't cycle over a certain bridge or through a specific gate in the fort – I just stood there, still, until I was invisible, and then I went through. Like a cricket. Like a hidden cup of water. You understand? That is what my brother's public battles taught me. (200)

---

[49] *Ibid.*, 10-11.

His revolutionary brother "refused to agree to any situation where the English had power. So they dragged him into their jails" (200). Kip believes he has discovered a form of non-violent protest, which is "the trick of survival, of being able to hide in silent places" (201), which "didn't stop [him] doing whatever [he] wished or doing things the way [he] wanted".

Kip's strategy of silence and invisibility at first resembles the desert tactics of the ostrich catchers, which we find in a scene omitted from the final version of the film. An old desert Arab explains to the English patient this trick of appearing one with the landscape, so the bird cannot distinguish one from a rock. According to the Arab, one should "Beware of the one who doesn't move". In this story the invisibility is not a mere ignoring of the problem, but a form of ambush. The catcher turns invisible in order to attack and not to remain invisible. If Kip turns invisible it is not simply because he refuses to engage with the power, but also because the power ignores him. He poses no threat whatsoever. For Ellis, his "individualistic silence can no longer be seen as an act of sociopolitical rebellion, but an act of sociopolitical surrender".[50] As an invisible man he cannot be loved or hated, or even recognized.

Although he seems to enjoy his invisibility and his self-sufficiency, he does not remain invisible. When he becomes the only man who can dismantle the bomb that killed his teacher, he is infused with the immense "map of responsibility" and yet he remains uninterested "in the choreography of power" (195). He "was expected to be the replacing vision" and temporarily he was "a king, a puppet master", but it was

> … strange to him. As if he had been handed a large suit of clothes that he could roll around in and whose sleeves would drag behind him. But he did not like it. He was accustomed to his invisibility. (197)

When he arrives at the villa he cannot be ignored. His otherness pulls the other characters out of themselves. They have to relate to him, and even feel their own alterity. Hana, for instance, "crawls in against his body like a saint …. It is his world. She feels displaced from Canada during these nights" (127). Their love relationship

---

[50] Ellis, "Trade and Power", 25.

becomes the small community within which he articulates his authenticity.

In the end, Kip comes to the point when two nuclear attacks bring him closer to his brother's nationalist attitude. At first he "looks condemned. Separate from the world, his brown face weeping" (283). It is as if he is observing the world from a detached place, analysing it in terms of the powers that give it its character:

> I grew up with traditions from my country, but later, more often, from *your* country. Your fragile little island that with customs and manners and books and prefects and reason somehow converted the rest of the world. You stood for precise behaviour .... Was it just ships that gave you such power? Was it, as my brother said, because you had histories and printing presses. (283, emphasis in the original)

Kip funnels all his anger at the patient as the allegory of the entire British nation:

> If he closes his eyes he sees the streets of Asia full of fire. It rolls across cities like a burst map, the hurricane of heat withering bodies as it meets them, the shadow of humans suddenly in the air. This tremor of Western wisdom. (284)

He remembers his brother who told him:

> Never turn your back on Europe. The deal makers. The contract makers. The map drawers. (284-85)

Kip grieves for the "Indian soldiers [who] wasted their lives as heroes so they could be *pukkah*" (283), that is "authentic", "genuine", "superior". If this refers to being genuinely English it is nothing but their conformity. Also, Kip's identification with the Japanese seems strange given that the Japanese slaughtered the Sikhs. Still, Kip

> ... does not feel he can draw a match out of his bag and fire the lamp, for he believes the lamp will ignite everything. In the tent, before the light evaporated, he had brought out a photograph of his family and gazed at it. His name is Kirpal Singh and he does not know what he is doing here. (287)

There is a sense of immense closeness and sharing of death with those who are so removed from him that he will never know their faces, their voices and stories. His fear of using a harmless match in contrast to the atomic fire produces this sense of sharing of death that opens him up unto his own otherness.

The nuclear attack is an extremely melodramatic way of destroying the villa community, and, as Hilger puts it, "forcefully reconstructs the binary which the characters have gradually and painfully deconstructed in an attempt to emerge from their solipsism. The world of the Villa San Girolamo is destroyed as the outside world breaks in".[51] Indeed, their "half-dark room crowded now with the world". The world invades "their world" (285-86). This world-intrusion seems to entail that this community has been an existential bubble, isolated from the world (or within it), just as the English patient was isolated in the desert, extremely private and individualistic: "Perhaps this villa is a similar tableau, the four of them in private movement, momentarily lit up, flung ironically against this war" (278). Hana even exclaims,

> ... it feels like the end of the world. From now on I believe the personal will forever be at war with the public. If we can rationalize this we can rationalize anything. (292)

However, it was above all Kip whose oscillation between the villa and the world outside thwarted the other characters' desire for detachment and self-sufficiency. After he leaves the villa, Kip travels "against the direction of the invasion, as if rewinding the spool of war, the route no longer tense with the military" (290). On the way, two things are with him, the patient's spirit and the Bible:

> ... he carries the body of the Englishman with him in this flight. It sits on the petrol tank facing him, the black body in an embrace with his, facing the past over his shoulder, facing the countryside they are flying from .... Isaiah and Jeremiah and Solomon were in the burned man's book, his holy book, whatever he had loved glued into his own. He had passed this book to the sapper, and the sapper had said, we have a Holy Book too. (294)

---

[51] Hilger, "Ondaatje's *The English Patient* and Rewriting History", 46-47.

There is a contrast between two books, a holy one and a Holy one. The patient's holy book is the record of his existential struggle. The biblical passages are, to the patient, a way of working his path through his heritage, whereas to Kip this signals a bondage to Christian ideologies. Therefore, Kip refuses this gesture of the dying man by pointing out that the Sikhs have a Holy Book. Although Kip positions himself *vis-à-vis* their cultures, the patient does not leave him. His presence during the ride shows their bond.

Kip's ride ends with a plunge into "the Ofanto River" (295), which is a repetition of the search for the spiritual river from *Kim*. For Mark D. Simpson, "Kip's unforeseen plunge serves as a reminder of what Suleri terms 'colonial dischronology' – of moments at which performative slips expose vulnerable catches in an empire's machine".[52] The question is whether or not he has found his river through a return to his native country and his heritage? Indeed, as Fledderus argues, "Kip's rejection, while the most dramatic, is not unqualified, for his motorcycle accident occurs on a bridge while he is trying to remove his goggles, a possible sign of enlightenment as to his inability to escape complicity, first in his birth culture and second with the empire".[53] The narrative throws the reader decades into the future, like a "stone of history skipping over the water" (299), and juxtaposes Kip and Hana's separate lives. Kip is a doctor, all according to his family tradition: at his

> ... table all of their hands are brown. They move with ease in their customs and habits. And his wife has taught them all wild humour, which has been inherited by his son.

Yet, at the same time, he remembers his life in the villa and envisions Hana as someone who

> ... has moved from being a young woman into having the angular look of a queen, someone who has made her face with her desire to be a certain kind of person. He still likes that about her. Her smartness, the fact that she did not inherit that look or that beauty, but that it was

---

[52] Mark D. Simpson, "Minefield Readings: The Postcolonial English Patient", *Essays on Canadian Writing*, LIII (Summer 1994), 232.
[53] Fledderus, "'The English Patient Reposed in His Bed Like a [Fisher?] King'", 40-41.

> something searched for and that it will always reflect a present stage
> of her character.

Kip imagines Hana as a risk-taker, struggling against her baggage, asserting herself through her actions:

> … a woman of honour and smartness whose wild love leaves out luck, always taking risks, and there is something in her brow now that only she can recognize in a mirror. Ideal and idealistic in that shiny hair. (300-301)

As Cook argues, although Kip "is apparently firmly ensconced again in his traditional cultural roles", he has not "achieved the state of complete self-containment that he seeks: people and events around him still function, in considerable part, as signs and substitutes for some absent reality, for some portion of himself that has been lost in time".[54] It is through his admiration of Hana that Kip keeps a window open, aware of the implications of his choices: "Singh. And the ambiguities" (188).

Fledderus argues that the villa community "functions as a way of experiencing transcendence from the here and now, though the transcendence, like the community, is temporary".[55] The long or short life of a community does not mean much for its character. For Kella, this community is based primarily on "Western humanism" and "reinforces a romantic view of pure love relationships, of the authenticity of desire as at war with the corruptive forces of societies and nations".[56] She also argues that this "affective community" is characterized by a "copresence of subjects" who accept each other unconditionally and are transparent to one another.[57] There is indeed an attempt to refrain from prejudices, but there is never any transparency and unconditional acceptance of subjects. There are no fully-fledged subjects to begin with. A transparency or even communion between characters is the total opposite of what happens. It cannot be argued that the novel itself endorses the "pathos of her [Hana's] solitude" and "affirms an existentialist individualism".[58] The

---

[54] Cook, "Being and Representation", 41.

[55] Fledderus, "'The English Patient Reposed in His Bed Like a [Fisher?] King'", 47.

[56] Kella, *Beloved Communities*, 90.

[57] *Ibid.*, 96.

[58] *Ibid.*, 110.

problem is not only that Kella equates individualism and existentialism. She interprets the end of the story as if it were a logical conclusion of a philosophical argument. Even if we understand the novel as an argument, the end cannot be anything but just another premise. To argue that the villa community is formed in relation to nothing but a Western ideology of love is not only to assume a simplistic understanding of love, but also to deny Kip any sense of agency. It is to cocoon him in the position of a suffering underdog. It is to overlook the fact that most people in his vicinity depend on him for life, that even his smallest actions demand that they position themselves *vis-à-vis* him, that they stand in some relation to him (even if it be in racist terms). It is not only Kip that changes under the influence of his English teachers and European environment. His love for the patient and Hana alters the ways of love and romance as they might see them, as in the scene when he cuts the wire of the patient's hearing aid as if it was a ticking bomb that would bother him when he makes love to Hana. It is as if he cuts off the love conceptions that the patient has been feeding to them by telling them love stories. What is more, to assume that community is only based on love is to forget that they enter a relation because of their sharing of death, or rather their finitude.

Community and death

The inoperative community that I have argued for in this section is closely connected to what I analysed in the first chapter, death. I have argued that death causes the characters' existential anguish, which in turn opens up characters to the exploration of freedom and authenticity. Death turns each singular character unto him- or herself. Even though it is an individual's "ownmost" possibility, as Heidegger expressed it, in Ondaatje's novel death is also shared. While this is partly explored in Rushdie's novel, where Saleem proposes that the meaning of the M.C.C. is death, it is particularly Ondaatje's novel that draws certain force from the sharing of mortality.

Each character in the villa, for instance, is singular and can work on his or her selfhood because they all share what Blanchot described as the unshareable solitude of being-towards-death. They share that which appears impossible to possess and share. Indeed, as Blanchot puts it, to "remain present in the proximity of another who by dying removes himself definitively, to take upon myself another's death as the only death that concerns me, this is what puts me beside myself, this is the only separation that can open me, in its very impossibility, to the Openness of a community".[59] Finitude provokes a kind of ecstasy of the self and thus delivers it onto its freedom. At the same time, "holding the hand of 'another who dies,' 'I' keep up with him, I don't keep up simply to help him die, but to share the solitude of the event which seems to be the possibility that is most his own and his unsharable possession in that it dispossesses him absolutely". For Blanchot, only finitude constitutes community of mortal beings because it precludes communal immanence, and any common being or essence. It has no production value as aim and serves no particular purpose.

Blanchot's general statements resonate with the kind of opening unto self-and-community that Hana, for instance, presents through her decision to nurse the dying English patient, or when she aids Kip in the dismantling of a difficult bomb. Mortality, Caravaggio explains to Hana, is discovered in the "tenderness towards every cell in a lover" (225). The patient at first only sees Caravaggio in this way, saying:

> I can talk to you, Caravaggio, because I feel we are both mortal. The girl, the boy, they are not mortal yet. In spite of what they have been through. (253)

On a more general level of the narrative, all four characters share mortality, or the awareness of it, and in the end, they are all forced into a kind of global sharing of mortality, when the nuclear attacks on Japan make all the disparate local worlds into something of "the world". The possibility of a community in relation to finitude works paradoxically with its impossibility in the proximity of death. If the sharing of death constitutes the villa community, it is also what destroys it. The villa company is shattered after a nuclear holocaust that seems impossible to share at the same time as it is shared. The deaths of the anonymous others pull the singular characters out of themselves. The sharing is evident in their concern with the deaths of others whom they know only as (inter)national enemies (the hell that is other people). This sharing also reveals the impossibility of sharing (and shouldering the sense of immense responsibility).

---

[59] Blanchot, *The Unavowable Community*, 9.

Community, as Nancy has argued, is "revealed in the death of others; hence it is always revealed to others". Furthermore,

> ... death itself is the true community of *I*'s that are not *egos*. It is not a communion that fuses the *egos* into an *Ego* or a higher *We*. It is the community of *others*.[60]

There is a difference between this argument and the claim that the death in the name of community or nation is supposed to bring about the immanent life. What Nancy calls for is the idea that the death of another shatters the individualist atomism of the ego or "I" (*ergo sum*), and makes possible the ecstasy of singular beings. Indeed,

> ... finitude itself *is* nothing; it is neither a ground, nor an essence, nor a substance. But it appears, it presents itself, it exposes itself, and thus it exists as communication .... finitude *co-appears* or *compears* (*comparaît*) ... finite being always presents itself 'together,' hence severally.[61]

The sharing "comes down to this: what community reveals to me, in presenting me to my birth and death, is my existence outside myself .... It is the community of finite beings, and as such it is itself a *finite* community." Community is not limited as opposed to infinite, but "a community *of* finitude, because finitude 'is' communitarian".[62] If we assume that single beings are constituted through such sharing, then we skip the hierarchy between singulars and their communal life. In communitarian models, community is the ruling project and operation. In various individualist models, the opposite is held true.

Although Ondaatje's novel dramatizes the operative-ness of states as grand communities (which demand sacrifice and death as a way of maintaining their mythologies), it also introduces a certain inoperative or unworking company based in the sharing of mortality. Community, as is obvious from the ending of the novel, is finite itself. It is not a failure because it does not meet the ideal demands that some critics envision. I have sought to see what and how this constellation is dramatized, rather than postulating what it must be, and then judging

---

[60] Nancy, *The Inoperative Community*, 15 (emphases in the original).
[61] *Ibid.*, 28 (emphases in the original).
[62] *Ibid.*, 26 (emphases in the original).

its success or failure according to such parameters. Once the narrative induces us to no longer think about individuals as social atoms and unwork the operational models, we lose certain hierarchies. We can begin to think singularity and community beyond the oppositional models. We come to think a finite community instead of the community of death.

CHAPTER 8

REVOLUTION REVISITED IN *THE FAMISHED ROAD*

> … there are corpses in the consciousness of all peoples, all histories and all individuals, dead things that need to be acknowledged and buried, dead habits, dead ways of seeing, dead ways of living, things that weigh us down and draw us towards death and prevent us from growing.[1]

The protagonist of *The Famished Road*, Azaro, is an addled abiku spirit who is "an unwilling adventurer into chaos and sunlight, into the dreams of the living and the dead" (558). Through Azaro, Okri dramatizes the implications of choices and actions within oppressive historical circumstances. Azaro is a revolutionary spirit in several senses of the word. His coming among the humans is like a materialization of inspiration that Dad desires for his community. However, he is also the abiku, traditionally seen as an evil spirit that revolves through history, moving back and forth between two worlds. As an abiku, he symbolizes recurrence of the suffering and injustices. In the course of this narrative (and the two sequels), Azaro re-examines and reworks the idea of revolution and his cyclical character through a struggle with the living and the dead. He and even his father try to make real progress possible and preclude further fascist domination as well as inspire the reformation of their social sphere. Their singular revolutions always also implicate the communal space. This is how they articulate their ways of being free.

In this section, I will first lay out and elaborate on Azaro's existential problematic, and use "road" as an overarching metaphor

---

[1] Okri, *Songs of Enchantment*, 289.

for both freedom and authoritative power. Then I will analyse the emphasis on social action, which even includes dreaming. Dreams are not dramatized as purely individual, but also social phenomena.

Azaro is, as Cooper puts it, "buffeted between existential issues: Life and Death, Good and Evil, personal uniqueness and the predictability of the human condition, the unjustness of the division between rich and the poor, and the creation of the new social divisions in independent Nigeria".[2] Given that Azaro is a spirit, it is as if once he becomes human he cannot escape grappling with existential issues. Azaro's problematic relationship to the ideal spirit world can be taken as a way of undermining the primacy of the spirit over existence, of essence over existence, or at least it may be a way of surpassing this dichotomy and rooting spirit in mundane human existence, its materiality. Azaro's decision to remain in the human world is an act that escapes instituted orders of meaning. His action creates a site where the questions of meaning, existence, community and even politics are opened for revision. He lives in a world that Wole Soyinka describes in terms of the animist integrated essentiality of all things. Traditionally, the abiku are the scourge of human beings. They enter the human world only to steal whatever they deem valuable and have no qualms about killing children whose bodies they possess. Many noted Nigerian writers have dealt with the abiku in poetry, prose and plays, typically describing inherited and visceral fear. By dramatizing an unorthodox vision of the abiku realm, Okri maintains a critical distance to the Nigerian mythopoesis. Following Soyinka's emphasis on non-conformity in self-determination, Okri uses the abiku as an inlet into the exploration of freedom and the possibility "to alter the way in which we perceive what is valid and what is valuable", as he expresses to Wilkinson.[3]

By referencing Azaro's impulses to authenticity, I seek to expand and even subvert the implications of what Cooper calls Azaro's search for the "understanding of the spiritual meaning of life".[4] While "spiritual" here seems to suggest a storage of essential meaning, Azaro faces "the challenge of giving birth to one's true self, to one's new spirit, till the contradictions are right for the new immutable star within one's universe to come into existence, the challenge to grow

---

[2] Cooper, "Out of the Centre of My Forehead, an Eye Opened", 99.
[3] Wilkinson, *Talking with African Writers*, 87.
[4] Cooper, "Out of the Centre of My Forehead, an Eye Opened", 67.

and learn and love, to master one's self; the possibilities of a new pact with one's spirit" (559).

Azaro's primordial covenant forces him to follow the abiku orthodoxy of cyclical incarnations into the human world, with the purpose of tasting hardships of existence and eventually returning to the spirit "land of beginnings" and "origins". Initially he qualifies human existence as a limited and un-free sphere constricted by material and ideological factors. He desists "the rigours of existence, the unfulfilled longings, the enshrined injustices of the world, the labyrinths of love, the ignorance of parents, the fact of dying, and the amazing indifference of the Living in the midst of the simple beauties of the universe". In the spirit world, under the aegis of a sapphire-adorned king, there is

> … feasting, playing, and sorrowing. We feasted much because of the beautiful terrors of eternity. We played much because we were free. And we sorrowed much because there were always those who had just returned inconsolable for all the love they had left behind, all the suffering they hadn't redeemed, all that they hadn't understood. (3)

The spirit world is posited as an ideal realm. Yet, it seems as if Azaro is merely rambling through some spirit world manual that explains why he should dislike human existence. Although being-human entails an exposure to "agony", the abiku must incarnate as soon as they become too happy in the spirit world. They need to taste the bitterness of human life to better appreciate their origins. For this, they are "disliked in the spirit world and branded amongst the Living". Azaro grows tired of this wavering between "exile" (5) and home because it is "terrible to forever remain in-between". The constant "coming and going" (6) is a primordial covenant turned into a dogma, which he refutes. In the realm of freedom, he realizes, there are strict rules of conformity:

> I was a spirit child rebelling against the spirits, wanting to live the earth's life and contradictions. Ade wanted to leave, to become spirit again, free in the captivity of freedom. I wanted the liberty of limitations, to have to find or create new roads from this one which is so hungry, this road of our refusal to be. I was not necessarily the stronger one; it may be easier to live with the earth's boundaries than to be free in infinity. (558)

At first sight, by choosing humanity, Azaro seems to tie himself to the world characterized by un-freedom. Yet, he claims he endorses freedom. Azaro's perplexing decision to break with "the captivity of freedom" (559) shows that the unlimited freedom of the spirits conceals fundamental un-freedom. This freedom is not a mere factuality of the spirit realm but also a part of an ideology that is supposed to obscure some forms of oppression. In contrast, for Azaro, if in the spirit world there truly are no limitations against which choices are defined as choices, there is nothing to prove the purportedly absolute freedom. Azaro's embracing of life contradictions evokes Nietzsche's idea that "the ability to contradict … is still more excellent and constitutes what is really great", which is "the step of steps of the liberated spirit".[5]

Furthermore, Azaro makes it clear that the land of origins does not provide definitive answers to the mystery of being. In the human world, where social contracts cause immense suffering, Azaro comes to understand that similar forces regulate the spirit world as well. This becomes obvious once his spirit companions launch frequent attacks on him, contradicting their supposed penchant for freedom, love, and compassion. The abiku "who broke their pacts were assailed by hallucinations and haunted by their companions. They would only find consolation when they returned". If he is absolutely free, then he should be free to choose human existence. It is as if the spirits too have ideologies to remind them of their place in the world. If the "cycle of rebirth" (5) constitutes their being, they surely need no "pacts" to "return to the spirit world at the first opportunity" (4). Their king is the one whose "love of transformation" sets the precedent, or an ideal principle the other abiku must live up to.

These cyclical transformations are indeed the "doom of repetitions", as Wright points out, "a reversion to something that existed before, a change that makes things the same again", which is "not a transformation at all".[6] The change is not progress by default. Okri demonstrates this aesthetically as well, structuring his novel as a concatenation of short chapters each repeating the same old violence, struggle, and failures. It is as if no new chapter relies on the fact that

---

[5] Friedrich Nietzsche, *The Gay Science*, tr. Josefine Nauckhoff and Adrian Del Caro, Cambridge: Cambridge University Press, 2001, sec. 297.
[6] Derek Wright, "Pre- and Post-Modernity in Recent West African Fiction", *Commonwealth* XXI/2 (Spring 1999), 13.

something has happened and belongs to the past, that something has already been said and done, but rather as if there is one choppy and prolonged present of suffering, the present still-born. Temporality is not exclusively causal-linear. Rather everything simply is, and the only things that give the sense of duration are the fluxes of anguish that extend into the past and the future.

Azaro becomes sensitive to orthodoxies, which keep the world idling. It is much easier for him to see through human ideologies and refute them as in the scenes where he mocks various chieftains and politicians (279), than it is for the humans who have grown up immersed in their social situation. As an equivalent, his greatest fear is from his spirit world:

> I listened to the many voices in me .... I shut my eyes and, within, everything was black. A deeper shade of black unfurled within the blackness. I was drawn into a vortex. (255)

If Romantic personalism advocated the attention to the inner voice of one's spirit, Azaro's introspection reveals a plurality of voices that tear him apart. Just as Dad feels incumbent upon him the heritage of his own father, the priest of the road, so Azaro must keep extraordinary focus to refrain from the calls of the spirits. All "contorted in paroxysms" (343), Azaro meets the three-headed spirit with an unorthodox response: "I won't come". The "mischievous one" chooses to break the pact: "I wanted to taste this world, to feel it, suffer it, to make a valuable contribution to it, and to have that sublime mood of eternity in me as I live the life to come" (6). Azaro seems to see the human world as the stage for his becoming. For this reason, he can feel "joys of homecoming" (34) among humans, while the spirit world becomes alien and horrific:

> I was home .... No spirits plagued me. There were no ghosts in the dark spaces. (40)

Azaro's world consists of two worlds, which mix and repel. As Robert Fraser suggests, Okri's "almost mystical philosophy of signification means that we must treat with some caution the view of Okri's writing as divided into 'realistic' and 'esoteric' episodes, with phases of transition joining them. Such an approach, tempting at first reading, ultimately fails because it sets up the reader as the standard of authenticity."[7] Given Okri's pronounced aversion to metaphysics entailed in incarnation (Wilkinson), I find the blurring and occasional merging of the two worlds a striking resemblance to Heidegger's argument that existence entails "no decision about whether the human being in a theologico-metaphysical sense is merely a this-worldly or another-worldly creature".[8] Okri seems to renounce the certainty of affiliation grounded in ontology, metaphysics or theology. He can dramatize Azaro as all too human, a new human, or perhaps even a radically new humanist who articulates his freedom in relation to the famished road.[9]

The road

Okri explores the metaphoric potential of the trope "road" along the notions of freedom and authenticity. In her comparison of Rushdie and Okri, Jacqueline Bardolph suggests that for Okri the road is "an allegorical *topos* inherited from Soyinka", which stands "for the uncertain path to independence, the moment when new political forces emerge at the same time as the symbolic forest world is encroached upon".[10] I suggest a complementary intertextuality. Okri's dramatization of roads in opposition to trees draws on Rousseau's idea that individuals are like trees standing in the heavy traffic of enormous highways.[11]

---

[7] Robert Fraser, *Ben Okri: Towards an Invisible City*, Tavistock: Northcote House, 2002, 81.

[8] Martin Heidegger, *Pathmarks*, ed. William McNeill, Cambridge: Cambridge University Press, 1998, 266.

[9] In Cooper's reading, Okri "liberates his fictional sites from the organicist traditions by rendering them wholly kinetic – they literally shift position as political developments on the cusp of independence dictate their interaction and transform their differing levels of meaning" (Cooper, "Out of the Centre of My Forehead, an Eye Opened", 284).

[10] Jacqueline Bardolph, "Azaro, Saleem and Askar: Brothers in Allegory", *Commonwealth Essays and Studies*, XV/1 (Winter 1992), 45. Indeed, Soyinka's poem "Death in the Dawn": "the mother prayed. Child / May you never walk / When the road waits, famished" (Wole Soyinka, *Idandre and Other Poems*, London: Methuen, 1967, 10).

[11] Jean-Jacques Rousseau, *Emile*, tr. Barbara Foxley, London: Everyman, 1955, 11. Indeed, as Berman puts it, for Rousseau and the Romantics that came after him, "the Tree represents all man's capacity for life, freedom, spontaneity, expressiveness, growth, self development – in our terms, authenticity" (Berman, *The Politics of Authenticity*, 164).

Okri shows that in the course of history roads and cities have been built where trees and forests used to be. While Azaro seems to yearn for the natural state of being akin the Romantic vision, to use Berman's words, he learns to nourish his self on the world as it is, because his roots are in "the middle of the highway, the road which history has laid out".[12] At the same time, he discovers that the trees are outgrowths of the road or roads. The modern roads are different but in the novel they seem to carry same implications as the mythical hungry road.

At the same time as the road is symbolic of social oppression and inauthenticity, it also signifies freedom. Azaro opens his story with: "In the beginning there was a river. The river became a road" (3). The master myth of the road suggests that the conditions of the world have already been set for those born into it. The road is always threatening. Indeed, if the mythical road swallowed travellers, the modern roads are suggestive of colonialism. As Cezair-Thompson shows, fifty years before Okri, Joyce Cary's *Mister Johnson* describes the building of a road that "signifies the colonizer's appropriation, not only of Africa, but, more importantly, of the faculty for 'imagining' Africa".[13] Okri's novel expands this signification to include "the probability that ... no true road is ever complete, that no way is ever definitive, no truth ever final" (559). For Cezair-Thompson, such an authentic road, given its openness, "symbolically appropriates the natives' rights to 'imagine' their own destiny".[14] As Okri argues with Jean Ross:

> Our worldview is not just aesthetic; it's functional. You have a song in which somebody says, "Don't walk on the hungry road," and it's saying very simple things, but at the same time, because hungry has got very many meanings, and road has got very many meanings – and it can be the road that human beings travel and the road that spirits travel or the road that destinies travel or the road that thoughts and feelings travel – all of these are resonant in one's being at the same time one is using a simple word like that.[15]

---

[12] Berman, *The Politics of Authenticity*, 166.

[13] Cezair-Thompson, "Beyond the Postcolonial Novel", 33.

[14] *Ibid.*, 35.

[15] Jean Ross, *Contemporary Authors Interview*, Vol 138, Detroit: Gale Research, 1993, 338-39.

The connection between authoritative and diffuse powers and roads is most clear when Azaro is lost in a marketplace:

> I couldn't break the riddle of the market's labyrinths where one path opened into a thousand faces, all of them different, most of them hungry in different ways .... I walked round and round the market spaces, unable to go any deeper, unable to find my way out ... and unable to stop because of the perpetually moving crowds who pushed me on or shoved me aside or trampled me or shouted at me and I was confused by everything. (191)

Azaro faces all kinds of people who try to peddle their ideologies as much as their merchandise:

> 'If you don't belong to our party you don't belong to this space in the market .... Leave. Go. We don't want people like you.'

Paying the dues does not help, because this market is not ruled by economy only. In it, "no single voice, unless it were louder than all the voices put together, could make the market listen" (198). In the market, the faces fade into disembodied voices that speak to Azaro:

> 'Maybe he is mad.'
> ... 'They say he is looking for the spirit of Independence.'
> 'They say he is looking for himself.'
> 'For his own spirit.'
> 'Which he lost when the white man came.'
> ... 'Maybe what is to come is already driving him mad.'

One voice makes him the spirit of Independence, which has lost its true sense. Yet, Azaro is not primarily there to give metaphorical sustenance to nationalism. Instead, Azaro is intent on articulating new roads that lead him out of "the riddle of the market" (196-97). Proper to the suggestion that existence is a set of paradoxes that neither the living nor the dead can solve, his hungry road metaphorizes both ideologies that burden the traveller, and what Quayson calls "existential hunger".[16]

Having refuted Romantic essentialism, Azaro uses the image of an unfinished road to Heaven with a population of road builders

---

[16] Quayson, *Strategic Transformations in Nigerian Writing*, 122.

(working for two thousand years, as instructed by their great prophet) to refute the idea that authenticity is about the creation of a work, or the prize that awaits at the end of the road. To reach Heaven is to

> ... have nothing to do, nothing to dream for, and no need for a future. They will perish of completeness, of boredom. The road is their soul, the soul of their history. (397)

This is why each time the road is nearly finished cataclysmic series of events demolish it. Every new generation

> ... begins again from the wreckage ... with nothing and everything. They know all the earlier mistakes. They may not know that they know, but they do. They know the early plans, the original intentions, the earliest dreams. Each generation has to reconnect the origins to themselves. (379)

New generations are conditioned by earlier plans, but they must recreate their road to Heaven. The allegorical story does not reveal the source of the frequent demolitions, but Azaro comes to understand that creative destruction is a task on his own hands and his community. Talking with Wilkinson, Okri elaborates: "for anything new, for something good to come about, for it to reach the level of art, you have to liberate it from old kinds of perception, which is a kind of destruction. An old way of seeing things has to be destroyed for the new one to be born."[17] The emphasis here is on conscious creative destruction rather than forgetting, or psychological suppression. Total forgetfulness deprives characters of the social frameworks within which their choices can be asserted as choices, and changes as changes.

The road of creative destruction is a step away from Romantic ideals and the idea of authenticity as the work, the perfect society that one must eventually reach. Bill Hemminger uses Heidegger's discourse on the road or path to argue that the authentic life recovers "the 'openness of the possible and of our own responsibility as individuals in articulating and bringing to realization the worldly

---

[17] Wilkinson, *Talking with African Writers*, 81.

contexts in which we find ourselves'".[18] Indeed, "authenticity involves a full and rich 'form of participation in the public context .... Living authentically implies living with understanding .... like Kierkegaard, Heidegger argues that our primary access to reality is through our involved action."[19] Since Azaro is very much an observer, the question is what constitutes his involved actions?

Authenticity and action

Although Azaro's spirit world is supposed to allow for unlimited freedom, it is in the human world of countless limitations that Azaro finds the space in which to articulate his freedom and "create new roads" (558).

Azaro walks the unfamiliar roads that proliferate in the country, and are trafficked by any kind of horrible creatures and things. Although there are moments of pure solitude in limbo-like realms, these are short and transitional phases that help Azaro figure out his relation to the world. Azaro shuns neither the world, nor solitude. Both isolation and action have place in his process of becoming. Although the estrangement and anxiety seem important elements and phases in this process, action in the social sphere carries more value.

At first, Azaro comes across as a wandering observer of the human world. He seldom engages with humans. He does not use spirit powers to change history. He does not start a revolutionary movement like his father. However, his destructive creation of his self, implicates spirits and his human family, and eventually also the history of the ghetto through his engagement with Madame Koto. The whole of Book Five is devoted to Azaro's actions against the parents and the three-headed spirit, actions which involve all aspects of existence, as Cooper puts it, "at the level of perception and language, persuasion and vision", and not only "as in the epics of old, at the level of great physical battles and feats of strength".[20] After Dad flogs him, saying:

> 'You are a stubborn child, I am a stubborn father. If you want to return to the world of spirits, return! But if you want to stay, then be a good son!' (373)

---

[18] Bill Hemminger, "The Way of the Spirit", *Research in African Literatures*, XXXII/1 (Spring 2001), 69.
[19] *Ibid.*, 77-78.
[20] Cooper, "Out of the Centre of My Forehead, an Eye Opened", 102.

Azaro begins to "feed on [his] hunger". He enters a kind of limbo, a "world of famine, famishment, and drought" (373), where neither the human nor the spirit world can claim him. Later, tempted by spirit songs, and "feeding on the diet of the other world", Azaro ignores his mother's anguish, and reverts to the "indifferent serenity of the spirit-child's soul". On the journey back, the two worlds struggle through the channel of his body/soul so that Dad's breath is felt as the strong wind that makes him hover above and swerve from the road-to-spirit-world (376). Mum and Dad's increasing crying and begging for forgiveness disturb the spirit's force:

> Mum pressed her warm face to mine and lifted me up. The spirit leapt into the chasm .... The spirit said: 'Don't be afraid.' I wasn't any more. Mum's voice was in my soul. (383)

As opposed to the spirit who demands absolute obedience, the parents suddenly allow for Azaro's choice, and so allow for his authenticity.

The songs of enchantment, like those of mermaids, produce in Azaro "a terrible ecstasy" (374), which is supposed to dull his sense of agency and allure him back to his origins. This ecstasy transforms into an ecstasy of his self in a communication with his parents. This being exposed undermines their egos, their subject positions and yet it constitutes both their singularities and their small community. They remain singular, acknowledged as such, and yet they are singular only insofar as they are open to each other in this relationship. The spirit, on the other hand, wants to maintain the strict power structure between them: "Be grateful. When we cross the river there is no turning back" (385). While both sides begin with the use of force to win him over – Dad even employs a herbalist – Azaro returns to existence only when Dad refrains from his egoism. To Azaro's "utter astonishment, Dad knelt by the bed" (386). Dad's pages-long speech serves to show Azaro that whatever he decides it is by his choice. In the end, Azaro does not merely choose between two alternatives, but opts for something else. He chooses a family that has changed through a relation to him. The family as he knew it was recreated. This example is how Azaro presents the first step in the reworking of authenticity, community, singularity and his revolutionary spirit.

Back in existence, Azaro experiences everything with fresh eyes, as if he has been born again:

> It seemed that our lives would know a new dawn, take on new colours of sweetness, and that in the warm spirit our miseries would be transformed into something miraculous and tangible like the birds in heaven. The world was new too, everything was fresh. (393)

Everything appears miraculous: the "fact that human beings talked, laughed, wept, sweated, sang, without some visible thing which made all the animation possible, the fact that they were alive in their bodies, contained this thing called life in their flesh, seemed incredible to me". Standing in "an absolute awe of the world", and "lightning-struck by life" (396), he says, "it dawned on me that I had been granted a greater freedom, so long as I stayed alive" (399). This freshness arises from Azaro's re-immersion into the world from another angle. The world is not solely the place of un-freedom and suffering, but also a space of freedom, of possibilities, of wonder. It is important that Azaro does not find his essence or his self through pure introspection, but develops into something new through a relation with his parents. His authentic singularity is not about total independence and autonomy of himself as a subject, as an indivisible individual. It arises in and through this relation with his parents.

Reworking revolution

In the human world, Azaro's engagement is most visible in contrast to Dad's own revolutionary spirit and Madame Koto's political conversion. Like Azaro, Dad goes through severe trials before he proclaims his plan to improve the living conditions in the ghetto. Dad's existential transformation is acted out as political engagement.[21] When "party supporters" like his landlord start "terrorising everyone" who is "on the wrong side of politics" (238), Dad responds, "Even God can't tell us who to vote for. Don't be afraid. We may be poor, but are not slaves" (237). Dad's interest in politics has the ring of Rousseau's politics of authenticity. Dad seems to show that, to use Berman's summary, "the personal needs and aspirations of the individual man could not be fulfilled except through political activity and involvement".[22]

---

[21] Golomb has used Camus' inversion of Cartesian cogito: "I rebel – therefore we exist" (Golomb, *In Search of Authenticity*, 192), to propose that in general "authenticity is rooted in revolution" (12), and that rebellion "makes authenticity socially viable and awakens the individual's self-respect" (191).
[22] Berman, *The Politics of Authenticity*, 216.

Although Azaro does not articulate his authenticity as much in political terms as his father, the moment his abiku being is interpreted metaphorically by Dad, his ways of being free become politically significant: "Dad found that all nations are children; it shocked him that ours was an abiku nation ... the child of our will refuses to stay till we have made propitious sacrifice and displayed our serious intent to bear the weight of a unique destiny" (567). Azaro's primary struggle is in relation to the abiku, but this very conflict has political overtones because he discovers that the abiku are not defined simply by nature, but rather by abiku ideology. This struggle has political resonances in the world of the humans because their historical situation demands that they rethink that which Dad calls their spirit, their essences, their traditions and habits. Azaro's abiku-ness serves to highlight these needs and desires. Although he seldom acts physically, Azaro still participates in communal struggles against bad-milk politicians. His very presence as the ambiguous figure, both real and metaphorical, is the nexus in which struggle is articulated:

> In the diabolical heat of that afternoon six illegitimate sons of minor warlords ... enacted a battle of ascendancy .... They all looked alike. They were the interchangeable faces of violence and politics. (225)

The clone-like thugs conform to the "codes they were fighting for .... They are the madmen of our history" (226). They wave their shirts "like monstrous flags ... chanting the songs of their ascendancy, the songs of the Party of the Poor, or was it of the Rich. No one could be certain" (227). Azaro recognizes "the new incarnation of their recurrent clashes, the recurrence of ancient antagonisms, secret histories, festering dreams". He fears "that all over the world thugs with fire in their brains were pounding one another in a weird delirium of history" (228). Here Okri uses broad, un-nuanced social categories such as poor, rich, crowd, masses and party. The rich are both Koto and the landlord who are closest to what could be called middle class, and filthy rich entrepreneurs and imperialists who quarry Nigerian natural wealth. Okri seems to suggest that the homogenization of social categories works to the point of rich/poor appearing imaginary, almost mythical. He shows how authoritative and diffuse powers divide a suffering population, and how hard it is to shake them off in order for particular cases such as Azaro's family to shine. By employing such wide social categories, Okri shows they are politically usable even though utterly unsound.

Crooked politicians, whether they belong to the Party of the Rich or Party of the Poor, target the population and politicize their hunger in order to harvest the countless votes they need to assume power. The Party of the Rich strategically distributes powdered milk to temporarily appease their constituents and gain political upper hand. Only after the people suffer massive poisoning from the rotten milk do they come together in their escalating rage and attack the politicians. In the next instance, Okri expands this by turning to existential hunger. After the riots, the crowd

> … were angry but they were also helpless and they couldn't decide on the best course of action. They talked, could find no solutions, and as night fell they dispersed to their rooms, hobbling, wracked by spasms. (156)

However, the local photographer's hunger "couldn't extinguish his spirit and in the afternoons he still went up and down the place, taking pictures with demented eyes" (168). On the verge of dying, he keeps trying to draw national attention to the ghettos, reverberating with sounds "like the celebration of an old pain, an ancient suffering that has refused to leave". The ghetto population, which is described as "the worshipers at the shrine of suffering", are struggling to transform "anguish into power", so they

> … invoked names of destiny-altering deities, gods of vengeance, gods of wealth, womb-opening gods. They too made me afraid of life. They too had come from hunger, the wretchedness of our condition. (324)

The new historical situation has weakened their old ideologies, so they cannot quite articulate and cope with the new circumstances. The population employs their beliefs as forms of empowerment. Dad evokes the god of authentic revolution (53), which evinces a peculiar barter between the idea of a revolution and divinity. It is not a way of re-mystifying or mythologizing the idea of a revolution, but rather a way of demystifying the belief that revolution is secular as such. Olatubosun Ogunsanwo argues, "Okri's neo-traditional art is not merely making a nostalgic return to the African folktale. It is actually a re-writing of the socio-cultural past in the present in a way that demands critical re-interpretation in anticipation of the future."[23] The novel describes that which Ogunsanwo calls the non-assimilationist stance, which is implied in the African Way. In *Songs of Enchantment*, Okri evokes

> The African Way – The Way of compassion and fire and serenity: The Way of freedom and power and imaginative life; The Way that keeps the mind open to the existences beyond our earthly sphere, that keeps the spirit pure and primed to all the rich possibilities of living .... the valuable truths in our stolen heritage, our dispersed legacy.[24]

This view, as Quayson maintains, reminds strongly of animism as the spiritual belief in the possibility of openness. At the same time, I lean more towards Lim's reading of Okri's evocation of Senghorian African Way as non-essentialist. This anti-essentialism does not merely arise from Okri's sensitivity to historical contingency. Indeed, as Quayson suggests, Okri dramatizes "defamiliarization of indigenous beliefs rather than a true replica of such belief in reality".[25]

As the first revolutionary move, Dad resumes boxing, which once caused him to disobey his father's wish that he become the priest of the road. Here, Okri transforms the traditional tale that Achebe discusses in *Morning yet on Creation Day*. Achebe's tale is about a wrestler who beats everyone in his way only to end up beating his own *chi*. While Achebe makes up a "cautionary tale" designed to

---

[23] Olatubosun Ogunsanwo, "Intertextuality and Post-Colonial Literature in Ben Okri's *The Famished Road*", *Research in African Literatures*, XXVI/1 (Spring, 1995), 45.

[24] Okri, *Songs of Enchantment*, 160.

[25] Quayson, *Strategic Transformations in Nigerian Writing*, 148. Quayson highlights Karin Barber's study of Yorúbá's "high level of 'porosity and incorporativeness ... the proliferation of alternative perspectives, the holding open of possibilities, the deferral of final ideological resolutions" (Ato Quayson, "Orality – (Theory) – Textuality: Tutuola, Okri and the Relationship of Literary Practice to Oral Traditions", in *The Pressures of the Text: Orality, Texts and Telling of Tales*, ed. Stuart Brown, Birmingham: University of Birmingham, 101). In a sense, the Yorúbá culture pre-empts essentialist nativism. Unlike Tutuola, Okri maintains, "a rich ambivalence towards the traditional resource base" (*ibid.*, 114), using the repository of myth to "heighten the ambiguities inherent in the dispossession of real world existence" (*ibid.*, 115). According to Cooper, Okri rewrites the ancestral limits found in Achebe's work, and breaks with "the Tutuolan universe" and its heroes whose "mythopoeic character derives strength from being a representative of a communal ethos" (Cooper, "Out of the Centre of My Forehead, an Eye Opened", 77).

show "a limit to man's aspirations",[26] Azaro and Dad assume that no limits should be left unchallenged. Dad argues, "you have to overcome things first in the spirit world, before you can do it in this world" (416). Back from "the Land of the Fighting Ghosts", Dad has the eyes of "a man who has stared into the deepest pits of existence" (464). His contenders, Yellow Jaguar and Green Leopard are both human and ghostly. Green Leopard, in particular, fights for the Party of the Rich. After the defeat, the Leopard's followers "left with their philosophy in disgrace. The pamphlets they had distributed, which were scattered about the street, flew all about as the van sped off over them" (459).

Dad then begins talking "of becoming a politician and bringing freedom and prosperity to the world and free education to the poor" (467). Despite his meagre accomplishments, he shows some breakthrough within a short period of a year. As if his entire life has been one long prelude to activism, this illiterate man is driven by a strong will to break loose:

> A new idealism had eaten into his brain with the freshness of his recuperation …. He conjured an image of a country in which he was invisible ruler … and in which every citizen must be completely aware of what is going on in the world, be versed in tribal, national, continental, and international events, history poetry and science; in which wizards, witches, herbalists and priests of secret religions would be professors at universities. (468)

Although he is running out of money, Dad throws a party for the poor, promising "political miracles" (478), similar to religious miracles. He thinks he can feed starving beggars with one, un-multiplied chicken (479), an ironic simulacrum of Jesus' fishes and loaves. He "thought of getting a delegation of Madame Koto's prostitutes to go and protest to the Colonial Administration" (469). The invisibility of Dad as the ruler is not suggestive of a secret, conspiratorial tyrant, but a ruler who wants to refute the master-slave dialectic. Dad's rule is more about lifting "up the spirit of the people" to fulfil their "need for world inspiration" (510), which they lacked on the nights of the riots: "With the abundant energy of a man entering a

---

[26] Chinua Achebe, *Morning yet on Creation Day: Essays*, London: Heinemann, 1975, 95.

new destiny". Dad "went up and down the road shouting about the poverty of our will" (514). "'This is why our road is hungry,' Dad hollered. 'We have no desire to change things!'" (517). Dad keeps shifting between fistfights and brainstorming-aloud. This is the way authenticity is chiselled out for him. He grapples with the paradox of benevolent rulers, free institutions, the turning of good deeds into a matter of duty, the transparency of a political representative or proxy (or the futility of it). He encourages his neighbours to

> ... think differently ... and you will change the world .... remember how free you are ... and you will transform your hunger into power. (479)

He hopes to help his community, locate their potentialities, and prevent them from burning out in rage. Given the use of the phrase "wretched of the earth" in later abiku narratives, the critique of blind rage seems to be a reference to Fanon's endorsement of the rage of the colonized. Or more precisely, the reference might be to Sartre's glorification of the colonial whirlwind, which may not have been Fanon's agenda. Once the accumulated energies are exhausted, the wretched of the earth fall back into even greater misery. They even forget what has happened. Their fire does not enter history, not until the Photographer shows it to the rest of the country.

Dad demands new forms of thinking and action. He challenges limits, breaks with orthodoxies of the past and the present. He seems to both endorse and transform his heritage, which consists of gods and ancestors' demands on the people. Only by breaking with them can he respect them and build up his new life:

> It is the spirit which invites things in, good things, or bad. Invite only good things, my son. Listen to the spirit of things. To your own spirit. Follow it. Master it. (572)

On this point, his nascent idealism differs from Azaro's insight. We have seen how Azaro refused the call of his spirit once he found it full of voices that called him back to the land of origins. Unless the mastering of the spirit means transforming its voice, Dad is very much an essentialist at this point. Still, it is significant that Dad's high-spirited idealism, which rages from the local context to imply global significance, begins with small everyday actions such as cleaning the streets. While it seems to be a form of thinking globally and acting locally, Dad's commitment is to the everydayness of life. He does not become the idealist leader who can potentially turn into a fascist. The ambitions and grand-scale political agendas must not blind him to the possibilities of more modest actions and accomplishments. This is one implication in the shift from elevated rhetoric to picking up of garbage.

Azaro fears that all roads (to political freedom or not) are hungry, and that all paths demand sacrifice and blood:

> ... most of our real troubles started that night .... With the blood mingling with rain and flowing right into the mouth of the road. I heard the slaking of the road's unquenchable thirst. And blood was a new kind of libation. The road was young but its hunger was old. And its hunger had been reopened. (484)

Okri seems to evoke Fanon's description of "retarded, rebellious, and recalcitrant" rural masses who are continuously exploited by both imperialists and native, urban nationalists, but who are not properly politicized in their struggle.[27] In *The Famished Road*, Okri seems to refute the idea that there should be a unified political front, but rather that the ghettos must develop according to their own drives as well. The question is, if any political programme, for instance of the Party of the Poor, can change the social conditions in the ghetto, why put such stress on existential freedom? Okri's often-contradictory narrative is about the opening of new possibilities. It is a movement from sedimentation of meaning, orthodoxy and certainties that ground tyrannical actions. Even the very idea of freedom, as Azaro shows when he leaves the free realm of the spirits, can come to mean un-freedom. As Esther de Bruijn suggests, "when Dad defeats his *chi*, he displays the cosmopolitan imperative to tackle one's own self-imposed and culturally-imposed limitations in order to open up new avenues of understanding".[28] Indeed, most of "Okri's characters are very much works-in-progress, none of whom arrive at complete 'self-actualization,' all of whom struggle in the process of trans-

---

[27] Fanon, *The Wretched of the Earth*, 71.
[28] Esther de Bruijn, "Coming to Terms with New Ageist Contamination: Cosmopolitanism in Ben Okri's *The Famished Road*", *Research in African Literatures*, XXVIII/4 (Winter 2007), 180.

formation".[29] Dad's as well as Azaro's "spirit was restless for justice and more life and genuine revolution" (566), which was a sign that "new forces were being born to match the demands of the age" (569-70). Dad's engagement seems to show that his political movement must not only satisfy the principles of empowerment but also those of singularity and authenticity. As West has argued, "liberation, unlike the socialization of the economy, cannot be carried out on behalf of the oppressed by a knowledgeable elite or a powerful vanguard. Liberation involves a transformation of each individual. But it is nevertheless not an individualistic process".[30] Indeed, an "individual's increased self-confidence and freedom is discovered in an act which is irreducibly both political and celebratory, empowering but also pleasurable".[31]

We could argue that Dad undergoes a form of education. Like a child, he feels powerless and his initial reaction is to box. At the same time, when he starts defining his revolutionary project, it becomes clear that he wants to articulate his freedom but not by assuming authoritative power. In this way, he and the other poor can do more for themselves without necessarily demanding too much from each other. It is not the question of the balance of power, the choice between ruling or obeying, but rather the undermining of power as such through different articulations of freedom. Once Dad refuses to obey the authorities (unlike for instance Madame Koto), his initial self-interest and practical selfishness (which is obvious from his treatment of Mum and Azaro) leads him towards community. His fights are not individual events, and his wins are not means of amassing money (by participation in the politics of the game, and game of politics).

When Dad wakes up from his final dream, he says,

> 'My heart must be open. My life must be open. Our road must be open. A road that is open is never hungry .... Our lives are changing. Our gods are silent. Our ancestors are silent .... My wife, my son, where are we going? There is no rest for the soul. God is hungry for us to grow .... We must look at the world with new eyes. We must

---

[29] *Ibid.*, 181.

[30] David West, *Authenticity and Empowerment: A Theory of Liberation*, London: Harvester Wheatsheaf, 1989, 100.

[31] *Ibid.*, 77.

look at ourselves differently. We are freer than we think .... Wars are not fought on battlegrounds but in a space smaller than the head of a needle. We need a new language to talk to one another.' (571-72)

Arguing that they are freer than they think, and that they need a new language to articulate their current conditions, desires and ways of being free, Dad seems to stress that freedom is not a goal. Rather, it is a fact of life. For Dad there is no gap between free will and action, a gap that only paralyses acting and thus the capacity to be free. His principle of openness and incompleteness is not about arbitrariness of choice. On the contrary, it is about trying to preclude a dead end in the development of singulars and communities. Following Nancy, I understand "the term 'incompletion' in an active sense ... as designating not insufficiency or lack".[32] In *Retreating the Political*, Nancy includes the idea of openness of the world, "it is necessary at one and the same time to affirm and denounce the world as it is – not to weigh out as best one can equal amounts of submission and revolt, and always end up halfway between reform and accommodation, but to *make* the world into the place, never still, always perpetually reopened, of its own contradiction, which is what prevents us from ever knowing in advance *what* is to be done, but imposes upon us the task of never making anything that is not a world."[33]

The principle of incompletion and openness is anti-teleological, yet there is still the sense of direction that is not absolutely arbitrary. In fact, Okri's use of "road", which means the world of the characters, is more evocative than Nancy's "world" because "road" implies a sense of direction and movement, which Nancy indeed wants to foreground. Azaro partly learns the lesson about incompletion and openness when he meets with the heavenly road-builders whose road to heaven is never completed despite their meticulous plans. If such goal-defined movement is fundamental for the unnamed people, then the continuous destruction of their goal marks a different kind of communal path, a path that is progressive but not in the technological sense (as in building/making/producing).

---

[32] Nancy, *The Inoperative Community*, 35.
[33] Jean-Luc Nancy, *Retreating the Political*, Florence: Routledge, 1997, 158 (emphases in the original).

In "Esoteric Webworks", Quayson proposes that Azaro is too passive in comparison to Dad.[34] Indeed, Azaro shows meagre action in the human world, and displays no spirit powers that he could use to alter human reality. However, the passivity claim demeans his choice to abandon the abiku. The lack of spirit powers is indeed the biggest sign of his decision to cut himself off from his kind. As Maggie Phillips suggests, he does not, like other mythical heroes reworked by modern authors such as Tutuola, "derive strength from being a representative of a communal ethos", human or spirit.[35] One cannot accuse Okri's Azaro of passivity because he does not lead a revolution. To read Azaro as too passive is to read him too symbolically, as the allegory of that which Wright describes as "the infinite deferral of the postcolonial nation's political maturity and true independence".[36] Rather, "Okri has not in fact simplified and flattened his paradoxical motif into allegory or archetype but has retained all of its complex contradictions".[37]

For Azaro, although "the spirits and our ancestors will hold a great meeting to discuss the future of the world" (547), what counts in the first place is "the challenge of giving birth to one's true self" (559). At the same time, as we have seen, this self is not entirely cantered on subjectivity or individuality. The singular way of being free is always articulated through an opening onto community. It is a freedom for, and not merely freedom from. Authenticity as a way (or ways) of being free is in Okri's work a recognition of the fundamental freedom that is shared (even if the sharing might always be incomplete in the sense of there never being a full communion in communities). Furthermore, it is immediately political and revolutionary. Dad's experience of freedom is practically indistinguishable from his political passion. It is his historical situation that partly articulates his struggle in this manner. The particulars of Dad's struggle are not irrelevant, but what is important to capture is not only the relational value of his actions, but also the very dynamics in them. That is, all

---

[34] Ato Quayson, "Esoteric Webworks as Nervous System: Reading the Fantastic in Ben Okri's Writing", in *Essays on African Writing 2: Contemporary Literature*, ed. Abdulrazak Gurnah, London: Heinemann, 1995, 144-58.

[35] Maggie Phillips, "Ben Okri's River Narratives: *The Famished Road* and *Songs of Enchantment*", *Contemporary African Fiction, Bayreuth African Studies*, XLII, ed. Derek Wright, Bayreuth: Breitinger, 1997, 173.

[36] Wright, "Pre- and Post-Modernity in Recent West African Fiction", 14.

[37] *Ibid.*, 15.

action is an expression of freedom as something factual, but no action becomes by implication a fixed model or a paradigm of freedom, not even for the particular characters. While action can take many forms, in this novel it is politically charged, or rather political passion arises from physical and existential hunger. I would even go as far as to say that it is not easy to pry apart these types of hunger, but rather claim that they co-originate authenticity as political passion and action.

Through Dad and partly also Azaro, Okri seems to argue for a revolutionary kind of community that does not revolve around a leader, a myth, or a common being, but remains open to that which Blanchot called the "unknown spaces of freedom", which make "us responsible for new relationships, always threatened, always hoped for, between what we call work, *oeuvre*, and what we call unworking [inoperative-ness], *désoeuvrément*".[38] What is clear from the allegory of the heavenly road-builders is that they conceive of Heaven as their goal that gives meaning and justifies the means. But as soon as they approach it cataclysms destroy it and they have to start anew. In a sense, Heaven is always postponed. We could argue that big plans whose realization always lies in the future indeed spur the builders to action and gives them meaning. Their community is then based in "the work" (*oeuvre*).

The implied critique of the road builders opens up the possibility of un-working (*désoeuvrée*). After each catastrophe (a recurring apocalypse), the builders lose the sense of their original plans, which they must recreate before they can set on the task of building again. They keep forgetting that the original plans have been changed many times, and yet they still try to accomplish the work their predecessors began. Their history repeats itself albeit with some changes. They are stuck in the metaphysics of goals and means, where the goal justifies and gives meaning to the means. The means and the production in turn do the same to the goals through actualization of abstract ideas. Their goal gives meaning and justification to their actions. Like Penelope's tapestry, the road is done and undone. It basically self-destructs once it approaches fulfilment. If this allegorical story is supposed to serve as a lesson to Azaro then what it teaches him is that the revolution must not revolve back to old injustices and suffering, that liberation

---

[38] Blanchot, *The Unavowable Community*, 56.

must not turn into tyranny. As Ade says to Azaro: "I have seen the future. The Koran says nothing is ever finished" (547).

In contrast to the road builders, Dad does not deliver political predictions, only vague musings on the possible futures. True predictability eliminates freedom, choice, and responsibility, and thus eliminates that which is political in the discourse on existence. The political presupposes freedom. There seems to be a kind of quantum thinking in this novelistic discourse. The novel does not simply imply that an individual can make a difference but actually that the individuals and their communities do not stand in opposition. Instead, both are variables of existence that can affect each other in discontinuous ways. Such an understanding of community has a different temporality, which moves away from the linear models of social causality, but does not fall into the Orientalist understanding of cyclical time. Instead, we find a kind of ecstatic model of time in which the present, the past, and even the future stretch into each other. Azaro exclaims:

> I realised that an invisible space entered my mind and dissolved part of the interior structure of my being. The wind of several lives blew into my eyes. The lives stretched far back and when I saw the great king of the spirit-world staring at me through the open doors of my eyes I knew that many things were calling me. It is probably because we have so many things in us that community is so important. (511)

After having resisted his abiku kind, Azaro endorses the importance of community. We can at different points notice that Azaro and Dad grapple with the question how to remain an authentic individual and yet at the same time be a building block of a viable social unity. However, they move away from the binary of individual/communal. They seem to suggest that singularity can only ever be actualized in a community. There is a tension but not an opposition. By juxtaposing the images of his open eyes and the gaze of the king who would perhaps want to re-appropriate him for the abiku society, Azaro shows that there is a certain tension between resistance to orthodoxy and an ecstatic openness to the other, whether this other is equally open or malevolent. Azaro's open-eyes, which entail his open being, become a part of a communal sharing of alterity, the past, and the inkling of a future. Azaro works, in Fraser's explanation, as both a soloist and a choir.[39] He also refuses to be, as Wright puts it, "at the mercy of supernatural powers" which try to "hold supreme command over his loyalty and attention".[40]

Given that Okri's emphasis lies on action and that it calls for a reworking of both community and individuality, both the politics of freedom and the spirit of revolution, the question is, what are we to think about the complementary insistence on dreaming and the claim that "a dream can be the highest point of a life" (774)? Does the novel, in the final analysis, merely call for imaginary escapades and escapism as critics such as Andrew Smith maintain?

Communal spaces of dreaming and imagination
In *The Famished Road*, the resistance to orthodoxy and ideological muddling of consciousness is also characterized by dreaming and "experiments in imagination".[41] The peculiar aspect of dreaming is that it often takes place in the communal space.

Dreaming and imagination are strongly connected to the opening onto what Azaro calls "our immense possibilities".[42] In *The Famished Road*, the notions of dream and imagination overlap. Dad says:

> I travelled on a road till I got to a place where the road vanished into thin air. So I had to dream a road into existence. (501)

Later, he proclaims they "can redream this world and make the dream real" (572). At this point, Dad suggests that dreaming does not signify an activity in a sleeper's mind, something which the sleeper merely experiences or even suffers (in case of nightmares). Nor is it a dream waiting to be realized. Rather, dreaming entails imaginative and creative action. The characters use creative imagination to change nightmares that haunt them. As Corey has argued, dreams and imagination also contribute to the constitution of "an indigenous connective tissue through which the world [and] self are concernfully manifest and taken under care".[43] Indeed, "imaginative activities and

---

[39] Fraser, *Ben Okri*, 68.
[40] Wright, "Pre- and Post-Modernity in Recent West African Fiction", 11.
[41] Okri, *Infinite Riches*, 75.
[42] *Ibid.*, 162.
[43] Anton Corey, *Selfhood and Authenticity*, Albany, NY: SUNY, 2001, 45.

their correlates are natural to the world; they are part of the way objects, events, and persons show themselves".[44]

In the novel, the fact that dreams are taken seriously seems to be a response to the colonial understanding of Africa that we for instance see in Joseph Conrad's Marlow, for whom Africa is a dream from which he wants to wake up in the modern, secular, dreamless, cynical Europe: "It seems to me I am trying to tell you a dream – making a vain attempt, because no relation of a dream can convey the dream-like sensation."[45] For Okri, Africa is the place where social power of dreaming is crucial, where dreams are anything but immaterial. Okri suggests to Wilkinson:

> Dreams are a part of reality. The best fiction has the effect on you that dreams do. The best fiction can become dreams that can influence reality. Dreams and fiction blur the boundaries. They become part of your experience, your life.[46]

Renato Oliva aptly claims that for Okri dreaming "is itself action. Dreams can activate hidden energies",[47] and "in dreams begins responsibility".[48] In the novel, dreams are social and not merely individual phenomena of the suppressed unconscious. This is why Madame Koto's dreams swamp the ghetto and become yet another sphere for ideological struggles. Politicians "waged their battles in the spirit spaces, beyond the realm of our earthly worries. They fought and hurled counter-mythologies at one another" (568). The two political parties distribute pamphlets in the day, but at night, people's dreams are haunted by their incendiary messages. The monstrous figure of Madame Koto "was initiated into another secret society that was famous for its manufacturing of reality" (567). Having "incarnated all her legends into her new spirit, joined with her myths" Koto flies around at night "drawing power from our sleeping bodies .... sapping our will" (568). As a result, "our dreams became locked

---

[44] *Ibid.*, 48.

[45] Joseph Conrad, *Heart of Darkness*, Boston: Bedford/St Martin's, 1996, 42.

[46] Wilkinson, *Talking with African Writers*, 82.

[47] Renato Oliva, "Re-Dreaming the World: Ben Okri's Shamanic Realism", in *Coterminous Worlds: Magical Realism and Contemporary Post-Colonial Literature in English*, eds Elsa Linguanti, Francesco Casotti and Carmen Concilio, Amsterdam: Rodopi, 1999, 189.

[48] *Ibid.*, 194.

out of the freedom of the air. Our yearnings became blocked out of the realms of manifestation" (569). In this respect, as Anna Smith argues, Okri departs from a Western secular belief in dreams as intra-personal and presents dreaming as "cultural disturbance".[49] Smith also broadens the general implications of dreaming by referring to Charlotte Beradt's case study of totalitarianism in the Third Reich. The study indicates substantial "changes in the social environment brought about changes in the nature of dreams". Indeed, "totalitarianism penetrates so deep that its ultimate effect is to remove the desire to protest even at an unconscious level".[50] Since "dreaming is indispensable for a society's health", to liberate dreams is to open up for social change, and "start a revolt in a place where power is still dispersed in pockets, rather than unitary, or homogenized". Smith also quotes a social study, *Dreaming, Religion and Society in Africa*, to argue for "the connection between dreams and social action",[51] and that "the productions of dreaming do actually become absorbed and transformed into culture".[52]

Okri does more. He treats dreams as the field for authentic possibility due to their fluency. Indeed, dreams can be under the influence of strong ideological forces that integrate themselves into individual/communal identities at the instinctive, unconscious levels, but also a field of greater singular contribution to invention of new roads.[53] John C. Hawley calls this "the politics of the interior".[54] We could call it the politics of dreaming. In the novel, "rebellion" often starts in the dream space. When the spirits make Azaro's "wretchedness more sublime", he enters a state that cannot easily be called a dream or reality, if we maintain this binary opposition. What is important is that a certain transformation takes place, "a rebellion of joy" (266).

---

[49] Anna Smith, "Dreams of Cultural Violence: Ben Okri and the Politics of the Imagination", *World Literature Written in English*, XXXVIII/2 (Winter 2000), 46.

[50] *Ibid.*, 51.

[51] *Ibid.*, 50.

[52] *Ibid.*, 51.

[53] See Iain R. Edgar, *Dreamwork, Anthropology and the Caring Professions*, Aldershot: Avebury, 1995.

[54] John C. Hawley, "Ben Okri's Spirit Child: *Abiku* Migration and Post-modernity", *Research in African Literatures*, XXVI/1 (Spring 1995), 34.

Okri does not keep Azaro or Dad in the esoteric dream realms only to lapse "into visionary vagueness", as Wright suggests.[55] On the contrary, at one point the entire community "had awoken into an unholy rage and had crossed over the barrier of ordinary awakening. We had entered the fullness of power and spirit ... we became chaotic gods ourselves" (250-51).

Bardolph has argued that Okri's existentialism implies an unarticulated desire for "a common structural cause to these aborted allegorical journeys".[56] Andrew Smith proposes that Okri's is a merely "culturalist" emphasis on dreaming and imagination and therefore "a 'disinvestment', an oblique celebration of freedom from the more urgent imperatives of material survival".[57] For him, Okri is overwhelmingly concerned with "the imaginative and symbolic parameters", and refuses "to recognize these as having a determinate relationship to a specific historical and social context", and summons "back into existence that very fetish of culture whose exorcism was the first necessary step for James and Fanon". I explained earlier how Okri stresses the imperatives of material survival, the struggle against the famished road, which he expands to include a stress on dreaming. Smith attacks this gesture calling it Okri's critical orthodoxy, "the romantic privileging of a great act of imagination" which "holds power and conviction only where the dominant metaphor for the social world is a textual one or where social change is understood to be a cultural matter rather than a question of systems of material production".[58] Smith claims the overarching demand of the novel is some form of idealist realm of infinite freedom and possibilities. However, if this were true then Azaro would be flying around in the spirit world, feasting and playing imaginative games. Instead he chooses the struggle and pain in the human world. I would agree if he were referring to *Starbook*, where this emphasis on imagination goes over into vague musings. Smith misses therefore to historicize Okri with respect to his disillusionment with African peoples' unwillingness to self-transformation and social action, which is why he dramatizes Nigeria as an abiku nation. Azaro keeps flowing in

---

[55] Wright, "Whither Nigerian Fiction?", 331.

[56] Bardolph, "Azaro, Saleem and Askar", 46.

[57] Andrew Smith, "Ben Okri and the Freedom Whose Walls Are Closing in", *Race and Class*, XLVII/1 (July 2005), 10.

[58] *Ibid.*, 8.

people's dreams "of a dying country that had not yet been born, a nation born and dying from a lack of vision ... generations trying to give birth to itself, to its own destiny" (91).[59]

Given that dreaming and imagination are connected to the notions of vision and hope, the imaginary transformation of postcolonial nightmares into spaces of possibility seems for Azaro and Dad the first step in their revolutionary movement. Azaro wants to become a "new illumination, shedding light and seeing by it" (116). He seems to experience this transformation:

> ... out of the centre of my forehead, an eye opened, and I saw this light to be the brightest, most beautiful thing in the world. It was terribly hot, but it did not burn. It was fearfully radiant, but it did not blind .... The light went into my new eye and into my brain and roved around my spirit and moved in my veins and circulated in my blood and lodged itself in my heart. And my heart burned with a searing agony, as if it were being burnt to ashes within me. As I began to scream the pain reached its climax and a cool feeling of divine dew spread through me ... the feeling of a kiss forever imprinted, a mystery and a riddle that not even the dead can answer. (266-67)

Earlier, Azaro was taught to believe that existence is a mystery only the dead (ancestors) can convey to their progeny. Azaro's illuminated third eye deprives the dead of the final say. Although

---

[59] Although the materialist critique has valid points, it mostly repeats the argument that certain literary works are too culturalist and negligent of material factors of existence and resistant to pragmatic solutions to national problems. No critic meets this requirement either. In reply, Soyinka argued: "The 'causal-historical and socio-economic network of society' sought in every work of art by this particular school of criticism is, let it be understood clearly, only a further attempt to protect the hegemony of appropriation by the intellectual critic class *especially*, and this is especially true when such criticism chooses to ignore the *received* function as manifested in effect. Liberation is one of the functions of the theatre, and liberation involves strategies of reduction to the status and stature of the power wielding class in public consciousness, exposing and demystifying its machinery of oppression.... The mastering of reality and its transformation requires the liberation of the mind from the superstition of power, which cripples the will, obscures self-apprehension, and facilitates surrender to the alienating processes ranged against every form of human productivity. DEFLATING THE BOGEY – this is also socially valid and progressive art. It becomes seriously flawed ... only when it attempts to pander to socio-historical causes, thereby explaining away oppressors in rational (including economic) terms" (cited in Maja-Pearce, 100-101, emphases in the original).

Azaro has refuted the essentialist sense of selfhood, he still uses a rather poetic and essentialist sounding idea of one's immutable star (559). The reason for this, as Lim points out, is that modern cynicism towards anything that evokes inspiration, dreaming, or vision has become too naturalized.[60] Yet, as Wright argues, Azaro "never reaches a permanent halt along the circuit of this cycle and never settles into any of his options, whether of willed progress or powerless recurrence, of self-determining humanism of cosmic fatalism".[61] He becomes an entirely new riddle that neither living nor dead ideologues can grasp and control.

The decade before Okri's success, as Wright explains, revolutionaries called upon writers to create a general morality and become cultural managers as well as political activists. Okri's prose too is a response to this call. However, Okri is at the same time too aware of the failures of previous generations and their proletarian social realism to reduce his project to that which Smith asks for.[62] Okri emphasizes dreaming and imagination to compensate for the poignancy of the sheer force of hunger, which he never stops describing, and whose energy is one of the fundaments of his prose. "Famished" as a word in the title points out the complex workings of both bodily and existential hunger. In fact, Okri gives so much space to dramatization of hunger and communal violence, suffering and sickness that a reader cannot but be overwhelmed, and indeed feel benumbed and quite powerless. This excess produces the sense of life as a quagmire, which Okri tries to break by occasionally foregrounding the need for dreaming. His novel shows the double edge of imagination. While this faculty has value as a strong destructive and creative force, the novel seems to distinguish between fancy escapades into imaginary realms that produce some inner peace in the characters, but which in the end prove to be appropriated by society as a means of control of social action. The task of imagination,

---

[60] David C.L. Lim, "Redreaming the World: Multidimensional Reality in the Selected Novels of Ben Okri", *Southeast Asian Review of English*, XXXIV-XXXV (December 1997), 85-107.

[61] Wright, "Pre- and Post-Modernity in Recent West African Fiction", 14.

[62] Okri positions himself as the reluctant heir to the previous generations of Nigerian writers. As Wright suggests, he refutes any "consolidation of traditionalist models of identity around notions of authentic precolonial sensibility", as a "limited historical response to the political debacle of the first post-independence decade" (Wright, "Pre- and Post-Modernity in Recent West African Fiction", 10).

as Rushdie has argued, is to break through "conventional habit-dulled certainties about what the world is and has to be. Unreality is the only weapon with which reality can be smashed, so it may be subsequently reconstructed."[63] Okri is not unfamiliar with Rushdie's remark that India is a dream people agreed to dream, but he gives it another interpretation. As Appiah suggests, it does not mean such dreamed or imagined communities are unreal. Indeed, "nothing could be more powerful than the human imagination".[64]

Okri never envisions a futuristic history of Nigeria in which his ideas have born fruit. This might be the reason why Bardolph suggests that the book's otherwise open and fluid ending seems "static, repetitive, shapeless" and with "the lack of inspiration, a loss of narrative intensity and sense of direction".[65] She draws a direct parallel to the ending of *Midnight's Children*, to emphasize the authors' failure to inspire, to invest the readers with dreams. However, the novel does not seem to aim for any specific vision. Okri has argued with Wilkinson, "One has to know about the very hard facts of the world and one has to know how deadly and powerful they are before one can begin to think or dream oneself into positions out of which hope and then possibilities can come".[66] To redream the world is not have a dream and a hope for another world, but rather, to use Nancy's words, the idea that "it is ineluctable to invent a world instead of being subjected to one, or dreaming of another. Invention is always instead without model and without warranty", and it "implies facing up to turmoil, anxiety, even disarray. Where certainties come

---

[63] Rushdie, *Imaginary Homelands*, 122.

[64] Appiah, *The Ethics of Identity*, 242. Appadurai draws attention to *imagined worlds* as "constituted by the historically situated imaginations of persons and groups", which serve "to contest and sometimes even subvert the imagined worlds of the official mind and of the entrepreneurial mentality that surround them" (Appadurai, *Modernity at Large*, 33). Imagination is not "opium for the masses whose real work is elsewhere" or "elite pastime". Rather "the imagination has become an organized field of social practices ... and a form of negotiation between the sites of agency (individuals) and globally defined fields of possibility" (*ibid.*, 31). This view is close to Sartre's claim that "the imagination, which has become a psychological and empirical function, is the necessary condition for the freedom of empirical man in the midst of the world" (Jean-Paul Sartre, *The Psychology of Imagination*, tr. Bernard Frechtman, New York: Washington Square Press, 1966, 243).

[65] Bardolph, "Azaro, Saleem and Askar", 46.

[66] Wilkinson, *Talking with African Writers*, 38.

apart, there too gathers the strength that no certainty can match."[67] Okri's catharsis dreaming is not about an envisioned utopia but rather seriousness of "The Way of freedom and power and imaginative life".[68]

---

[67] Nancy, *Retreating the Political*, 158.
[68] Okri, *Songs of Enchantment*, 160.

CHAPTER 9

FROM COMMUNALISM TO THE COMIC ABSURD IN *MIDNIGHT'S CHILDREN*

The narrative of *Midnight's Children* is driven by Saleem's desire for meaning or purpose:

> I, alone in the universe, had no idea what I should be, or how I should behave. Purpose: it crept up behind me … I was nearlynine … a very early age at which to be perplexed by meaning. (194)

As noted previously, the historical crises of the postcolonial Indian nation in part make Saleem anguished, fearing "above all things … absurdity" (7). As a way of coping with his *angst*, he recounts over sixty years of family and national history as if the redeemed past will heal his shattered sense of purpose. He tries to historicize himself, to interpret himself in terms of the social and historical conditions that have contributed to the making of his identity. At the same time, he is struggling to articulate and communicate instances of freedom and action. Saleem's anxious ploughing through history is bifurcated. First, he seeks historical validation of his meaning as the allegory of India. Second, the fact that he is writing in retrospect with an ironic sting seems to suggest to his intended readers (his son Aadam, Padma, and indeed the entire India) that no such validation is possible, and that he is trying to articulate a more authentic meaning.

Meaning seems to be a goal that can be acquired and possessed as the essential core of his personality. However, since Saleem understands meaning as purpose, he calls attention to acting: "From ayah to Widow, I've been the sort of person *to whom things have been done*, but Saleem Sinai, perennial victim, persists in seeing himself as protagonist" (301, emphasis in the original). The question is not simply what he "is", but primarily "how" he acts. While the notion of a "protagonist" predicates Saleem on a literary discourse, that is, it points out that he is a character in a story, in the context of the narrative, "protagonist" appears to mean someone who is the main player in his life, who is active and not merely reactive, a Pinocchio who has become aware of "the strings" (199), and whose meaning/purpose arises through his actions. Being-a-protagonist for Saleem entails an active-literal mode of being: "all actions of mine which directly – *literally* – affected, or altered the course of, seminal historical events" (302, emphasis in the original). Being thrown or fallen into the complex and chaotic historical circumstances of post-Independence India, Saleem and his midnight's children face all manner of demands that intersect at various points, and which are anchored in religious or secular heritage.

As a group, the children reflect the "conflict in socio-cultural heritages" (325) of India. When Saleem introduces them to the question of "purpose, and meaning" (289), he finds "there was nothing unusual about the children except for their gifts; their heads were full of all the usual things, fathers mothers money food land possessions fame power God" (290). Indeed, the children,

> ... however magical, are not immune to their parents; and as the prejudices and world-views of adults began to take over their minds, I found children from Maharashtra loathing Gujaratis, and fair-skinned northerners reviling Dravidian 'blackies'; there were religious rivalries; and class entered our councils .... In this way the Midnight Children's Conference fulfilled the prophecy of the Prime Minister and became, in truth, a mirror of the nation. (323)

Despite their extraordinary abilities, the children remain ingrained in bad faith: "urchins spoke like old men with beards ... yes, certainly ... because children are the vessels into which adults pour their poison" (325). The question is, why does not Saleem allow for their different identities as a part of his pluralist vision of a form that contains multitudes?

At this point it is useful to recall Bhabha's distinction between diversity and difference. What splits the children in the quote seems to be their diversity. Diversity is the term from the politics of multiculturalism that sees cultures and ethnicities as separate, homogenous and often in conflict with each other, but which can be contained by for instance a democratic state. What is lost is the factuality of differences, of ambiguities and instabilities of these ties.

Saleem seems to oppose the children's diversity because it prevents them from communing on the basis of their differences, their shared freakishness, so to speak.

Saleem structures his story in a certain way to show he can do something about what he has been made of. In the beginning of the narrative, he shows how he builds up his identity and personality by internalizing certain institutions and experiences (family, class, nation etc.). Then his self-definition continues to be under strong influence of these factors, until he comes to exteriorize and re-exteriorize[1] what has been put into him, until he bites the hands that have been spoon-feeding him and rewrites family history. The revision of family history is most important because biological ancestry is frequently also the metaphor for political oppression of the fathers/mothers of the nation. According to Kimmich, what Saleem challenges is not the existence of parents/authors/originators, but rather the "naturalized notion that meaning flows unidirectionally" from such authors.[2] Saleem challenges the idea that one is "authentic only due to purity of descent", and that "authenticity is … an inherent quality".[3]

Indeed, upon hearing that Saleem's mother is Hindu, and his father an Englishman, Padma bursts out,

> 'An Anglo? … What are you telling me? You are an Anglo-Indian? Your name is not your own?' 'I am Saleem Sinai,' I told her, 'Snotnose, Stainface, Sniffer, Baldy, Piece-of-the-Moon. Whatever do you mean – not my own?'

Rather than speaking of Methwold and Vanita, Padma immediately jumps to the abstract terms, evoking the conflict between the English and Hindu (symbolic of the withdrawn colonial authority and the exploited native land). She immediately sees Saleem as the traitor to his "true" filial ties:

> 'What thing are you that you don't even care to tell the truth about who your parents were? You don't care that your mother died giving you life? That your father is maybe still alive somewhere, penniless, poor? You are a monster or what?' (148)

---

[1] See Sartre's "Itinerary of a Thought" (51).
[2] Kimmich, *Offspring Fictions*, 11.
[3] *Ibid.*, 32.

Much later, Saleem reverses Padma's stance by claiming that he has had "more mothers than most mothers have children" and that "giving birth to parents has been one of my stranger talents – a form of reverse fertility beyond the control of contraception" (308). The plurality of mothers and fathers signals his aversion to filial ties, but also to other models of affiliation. Saleem is also fathered by national history. The nation replaces biological parents. According to Kimmich, affiliation is an alternate way of bonding that constitutes "a potential strategy of selfhood".[4] In *Midnight's Children* various forms of affiliation become just as naturalized and exclusive as filiations. To have many parents is not a matter of desiring extra attention, love and care, but rather experiencing more pressures and more conflicts, because all these different parents do not join in a stable synthesis. Saleem's talent that allows him plural filiation and affiliation is contrasted to Ahmed's invention of ancestry. While Saleem invests into the "original" rebel, Aadam (like the Biblical/Qur'anic Adam), his father Ahmed claims descent from the Mughals. The difference between their invented genealogies is that Ahmed legitimizes his identity in relation to Methwold's supremacist attitude, whereas Saleem evinces a creative mimicry/mockery of ancestral bonds. As Kortenaar argues, Ahmed's genealogy might be "harmful because it is nostalgic and self-glorifying and serves to 'obliterate all traces of reality'".[5] Saleem's genealogy too contorts reality, but it is seen as positive in that it opposes the legitimating of status through genealogy (as when he questions Padma's cultural logic, or produces the simulacra of blood).

Looking at his history, Saleem distinguishes between two possible courses, conformity and non-conformity. He clearly prefers the latter: "my new fellow citizens [in Karachi] exuded the flat boiled odours of acquiescence, which were depressing to a nose which had smelt ... the highly-spiced nonconformity of Bombay" (391). Saleem is mostly intent on qualifying different religious (and also to an extent secular) faiths in terms of conformity and bad faith, which is a way of living in an unreflective manner, doing things because one does so. As an infant, Saleem was unable to open and close his eyes instinctively, and had to be instructed by his "two-headed mother", Amina/Mary (158). Mary's words, "'He is a good obedient child and he will get the hang

---

[4] *Ibid.*, 22.
[5] Kortenaar, *Self, Nation, Text*, 110.

of it for sure'" became "the first lesson of my life: nobody can face the world with his eyes open all the time" (159). Saleem's bizarre image foregrounds the idea of embodied meaning. He keeps his eyes open because he is supposed to consume the world (India) indiscriminately.[6]

Since he understands his allegoricity as his purpose, he is intent on the ways he embodies India, and not only symbolizes it. His mother Amina understands her son's meaning as merely political rhetoric: "It's just a way of putting things, Mary; it doesn't really mean what it says" (155), but Saleem's stress on bodily fluids (spit, blood) and anatomy (nose, cracking skin) is a way of asserting that his role is concrete, rather than merely symbolic. Since he is well acquainted with different religions, he knows that symbolic things have great practical purpose. Focusing on his own purpose, he seems to endorse embodiment and practice as the ground for his selfhood.

To conform or not to conform, that is the question

By pitting the acquiescence of the Karachi population against the non-conformity of Bombay, Saleem foregrounds his conflict with the need that Rushdie himself calls "communalism",[7] which arose, as Griffiths explains, in response to the colonizers' dominance.[8] Ashcroft *et al.* have argued that communalism or nativism employed "the rhetoric of authenticity" to give substance to its "politics of resistance in the process of decolonization".[9] As a strategy of resistance, nativism indeed seems to be a gesture of non-conformity, but speaking from a postcolonial context Saleem objects to the authoritative qualification of this authenticity, which strongly informs other politicized ideas

---

[6] This image seems to echo Rousseau's discourse on totalitarianism: "When an infant first opens his eyes he ought to see the fatherland, and up to the day of his death he should see nothing else. Every true republican has drunk in love of the country – that is to say, love of law and liberty – along with his mother's milk. This love is his whole existence .... When he is solitary, he is nothing; when he has ceased to have a fatherland, he no longer exists; and if he isn't dead, he's worse than dead" (Jean-Jacques Rousseau, *The Government of Poland*, tr. Willmoore Kendall, Indianapolis, IN: Hackett, 1985, 966).

[7] Rushdie, *Imaginary Homelands*, 27.

[8] Gareth Griffiths, "The Myth of Authenticity: Representation, Discourse, and Social Practice", in *De-scribing Empire: Post-colonialism and Textuality*, eds Chris Tiffin and Alan Lawson, London: Routledge, 1994.

[9] Bill Ashcroft, Gareth Griffiths and Helen Tiffin, *The Empire Writes Back: Theory and Practice in Post-Colonial Literatures*, London: Routledge, 1989, 63.

such as race, ethnicity, culture, religion, nation and class. While postcolonial nativism can be understood as a re-assertion of non-Western meanings, values and cultural practices as the means of decolonization, in the novel there is a deviation from the colonizer/colonized binary, and a focus on variegated nativist formations that introduce divisions and conflicts. Communalist essentialism is a political product without a real communal consensus. It is advocated as being imminent or intrinsic to the given community, but it is also imposed from above, just as Saleem's individual meaning is determined by political and religious figures:

> Soothsayers have prophesied me, newspapers celebrated my arrival, politicos ratified my authenticity. I was left entirely without say in the matter. (7)

It is for this reason that Saleem claims to love Bombay's ever-hybridizing crowd. [10] Saleem comes to live with people whose identities are not strictly tied to their religion, ethnicity and language, and who have lived with their differences, bartering both beliefs and practices of everyday life.

In *Midnight's Children*, the partition between Pakistan and India was produced by communalist desires, and which eventually resulted in escalated enmities and violence that caused innumerable deaths and displacements of several social groups and ethnicities. Saleem comes to describe a number of characters not as individuals but rather as stereotypes and metonyms of their particular communities, which do not share any common substance that can be the ground of the new nation. In a sense, as Kortenaar proposes, India defined as plurality incarnate resembles the impossible nation from the Orientalist vision of Sir John Strachey. [11]

Saleem articulates a desire for freedom, which he understands as non-conformity, with respect to a number of emblematic conflicts such as those between Tai and Aadam, Reverend Mother and Aadam, Bulbul-e-Din and Brass Monkey, Karachi and Bombay. Saleem's grandfather Aziz initially comes across as a non-conformist rebel against his Islamic faith. Upon his return to Kashmir from his medical studies in Germany, he tried to shed his European influences and re-

---

[10] This can be said about Rushdie himself. See Rushdie, *Imaginary Homelands*, 32.
[11] Kortenaar, *Self, Nation, Text*, 147.

embrace Islamic practices. Yet, during a prayer, the faces and voices of his anarchist friends "invaded his head", mocking his attempt "to reunite with an earlier self which ignored their influence". Aadam's friends obviously perceived themselves as modern rational individuals. They demanded that he abandon his faith, or at least stop maintaining it uncritically. His love interest Ingrid called his prayer "Mecca-turned parroting" (10). Failing to perform the prayer, Aadam breaks his big nose as a symbol of breaking his childhood bond with Islam, and is "knocked forever into that middle ground" (12) of existential confusion. Once he breaks with his religion and thus also with the core of his community, Aadam never really recovers. To dwell forever in a middle ground might at first sight seem to suggest that he only ever makes compromises, but the middle ground is that which for Rushdie himself is like a simultaneous straddling of two stools and falling between them. This condition results in "deep, permanent, operatic anguish".[12]

Two generations after Aadam's fall, Saleem repeatedly describes things such as "the long accusing shadow of the minaret of the local mosque" (391) to signal his aversion to Islam as the national religion of Pakistan, which he describes as the stereotype of conformity. Although Aadam later becomes a nationalist, it is his initial refusal to align along religious lines that elevates him in Saleem's eyes. This is why Saleem has an anxiety attack when his sister, Brass Monkey, starts "learning prayers in Arabic and saying them at prescribed times" and when her most exquisite singing heightens the spiritual sentiments of the Pakistani nation (371). She becomes a "public property", "'Pakistan's Angel', 'The Voice of the Nation', the 'Bulbul-e-Din' or nightingale-of-the-faith ... the whole country's favourite daughter" (398).

Although the conformist/non-conformist opposition is kept throughout the novel, the specific places of Bombay and Karachi do not correspond to them. While Bombay is presented as a plural place, it harbours a number of ethnic conflicts between Muslims and Hindus, between secular and religious factions of these ethnicities, between

---

[12] Rushdie, *Imaginary Homelands*, 32. Similarly, in *The Moor's Last Sigh*, Moraes' mother "no longer had a sense of an 'authentic' identity ... and this existential confusion had began to spread beyond the borders of her own self and to infect, like a disease, all those with whom she came into contact" (Salman Rushdie, *The Moor's Last Sigh*, London: Jonathan Cape, 1995, 266).

variegated political parties and their supporters. Eventually, its "spiciness" is threatened by the "civic beautification programme", during the state of Emergency:

> Sanjay volunteers, doing their bit for society ... but then I realized no, not volunteers, because all the men had the same curly hair and lips-like-women's-labia, and the elegant ladies were all identical, too, their features corresponding precisely to those of Sanjay's Menaka ... the ruling dynasty of India had learned how to replicate itself. (546)

The cloning of bodies is suggestive of an embodiment of ideology. It is like a modern version of incarnation only each soul is the same, or rather, there is none.

Since Saleem is the allegory of this conflict-ridden India, and since his parents expect this to show in his life in form of greatness, he cannot but wonder what exactly he is supposed to do. He sees their expectations in terms of capitalist production and exchange of value:

> ... our family believed implicitly in good business principles; they expected a handsome return for their investment in me .... I longed to give them what they wanted, what soothsayers and framed letters had promised them; I simply did not know how. Where did greatness come from? (198-99)

The problem is, the form of greatness is not specified, and the expected return is not necessarily pecuniary, but could also be symbolic. What, Saleem asks insistently, "can a baby do except swallow all of it and hope to make sense of it later? Patiently, dry-eyed, I imbibed Nehru-letter and Winkie's prophecy" (165). Nehru's letter creates in Saleem a sense of historical significance, and Winkie's prophecy adds a supernatural sense. Nehru comes across as something of a Big Brother, "we shall be watching over your life with the closest attention; it will be, in a sense, the mirror of our own" (155). Saleem's ayah, Mary, voices alarm:

> 'The Government, Madam? It will be keeping an eye on the boy? ... What's wrong with him?'

As if fearing he really is being observed, Saleem endeavours to reflect the nation's history:

> I am the sum total of everything that went before me of all I have been seen done, of anything done-to-me. I am anything that happens after I've gone which would not have happened if I had not come. I am everyone everything whose being-in-the-world affected was affected by mine. (488)

He seems desperate to conform, and yet he keeps failing. This failure elicits irony so that the political powers, if they are monitoring Saleem's conformity, can never be sure about his honesty. Saleem's failure is also a release. His best insight is that the greatest meaning turns out to be generally available:

> Nor am I particularly exceptional in this matter; each 'I', every one of the now-six-hundred-million-plus of us, contains a similar multitude. (488)

To be the representative of the nation is to be everyone and no one. Saleem and India engage in what Kortenaar terms "double mirroring".[13] Saleem is not unaware of this crux and the anxiety it produces in him. But there is more to it. Saleem's argument resembles Sartre's claim, "a man is nothing but a series of enterprises, and … the sum, organization, and aggregate of the relations that constitute such enterprises".[14] In Sartre's discourse, an individual takes on a universal responsibility and singular actions "commit all mankind".[15] For Sartre, particular actions, whether authentic or made in bad faith, create values that have a universal dimension. There is a universality that is expressed in particular forms.

In *Midnight's Children*, Saleem assumes an incredible responsibility, so much that he wants to be held accountable for everything. After a certain point, this position becomes a mockery in itself, because he cannot possibly be responsible on such a large scale. He sees the borders of his choices and thus also his responsibilities. His position remains Sartrean, only scaled down. A good example is found in the scene where Saleem stumbles into language marchers and provides them "with their battle cry" (302). This scene is indeed comic because Saleem does not intentionally or deliberately invent

---

[13] Kortenaar, *Self, Nation, Text*, 32.
[14] Sartre, *Existentialism Is a Humanism*, 38.
[15] *Ibid.*, 24.

this battle cry and give it to the marchers out of his specific political persuasion. He seems to lack agency and his action is more chancy than authentic. Saleem is not simply mocking the notion that everyone is ultimately free. Rather, he seems to construct a variation on this theme. Sartre claimed that "cast into the world, he is responsible for everything he does".[16] It is only in retrospect that Saleem realizes his stumbling among the marchers has affected history though not the way he wanted. The awareness of this impossible responsibility puts him on his toes so next time he does something he tries to be more aware of his choices, the fact that he is free and that he did not have to say anything to the marchers even to save his skin.

Saleem posits a singular universal relationship, but the universal is automatically narrowed down to the political history of the six-hundred-million people, which is a renunciation of a pure, and even metaphysical universal inclusion. Saleem seems to show that the singular-universal argument can be seen both in terms of nationalist essentialism, and a kind of existentialism. It is as if the mimicry of the singular-universal points out the essentialism at the heart of Sartrean existentialism, and even the opposite.

Given that Saleem foregrounds the body, the blurring of individual identities in the mob is not simply on the level of inner selves, but rather embodied existence. The self is foregrounded as something quite physical that can be literally crushed. While Saleem feels alienated from this mob, Aadam "penetrates the heart of the crowd" after the Brigadier Dyer massacre, and, as Kortenaar puts it, finds his nationalist self in it, even though it crushes him.[17] For Kortenaar, Saleem fears the mob because it denies the self, but he supports the crowd (of the nation) in which the self finds its proper subordination. Kortenaar further interprets national hybridity as a collection of internally homogenous blocks.[18] However, Saleem fears that in the multicultural nation there is no space for barter, but a drive to insulate and homogenize communities, which are described as parts of a large body. To argue, as Kortenaar does, that Saleem is trying to save his impossible national dream of being a vessel that holds everything together is to miss the tongue-in-cheek aspect of the narrative. Saleem shows his resentment towards political borders when arguing that his

---

[16] *Ibid.*, 29.
[17] Kortenaar, *Self, Nation, Text*, 151.
[18] *Ibid.*, 152.

powers disappear at the Indian borders. In Pakistan, the national and communitarian politics work to stymie his way of being free. While Saleem seems to fear disintegration of his self and his body, which is also the dissolution of the nation, this disintegration is finally positive because the desire for wholeness, for all-inclusiveness of plural existence is also the desire for containment of that which should not be contained.

To be or to act, what is the difference?
Acting against her lover Joseph (the revolutionary), whose attitude is that an individual cannot make a change, Mary Pereira swaps the babies Saleem and Shiva. As if conducting a nature versus nurture experiment, this Catholic woman later sings to baby Saleem a peculiar nursery rhyme: "Anything you want to be, you can be: You can be just what-all you want" (160). Mary's rhyme offers Saleem a sense of infinite possibilities lying in store for him. To be anything here means to be able do anything. This prospect initially intimidates Saleem more than gives him a sense of freedom:

> … if everything is planned in advance, then we all have a meaning, and are spared the terror of knowing ourselves to be random, without a why; or else, of course, we might – as pessimists – give up right here and now, understanding the futility of thought decision action, since nothing we think makes any difference anyway; things will be as they will. Where, then, is optimism? In fate or in chaos? (97)

If optimism has to do with singular agency and freedom, then there is none in either fate or chaos. In the case of chaos, it is as if there is no distinction between the claim that meaning is not absolute and that there is no meaning at all. The arbitrariness of meaning as well as the lack of it (implied in chaos) gives the illusion that he is not responsible for the course of his existence, and that he can do as he wishes because nothing matters (Shiva's basic principle). Saleem wonders:

> Was genius something utterly unconnected with wanting, or learning how, or knowing about, or being able to? Something which at the appointed hour, would float down around my shoulders like an immaculate, delicately worked pashmina shawl? (199)

Saleem wants his genius to be an authentic achievement rather than a natural/divine gift. He exclaims from his deathbed:

> No choice? – None; when was there ever? There are imperatives, and logical-consequences, and inevitabilities, and recurrences ... when was there ever a choice? When options? When a decision freely-made, to be this or that or the other? (537)

Indeed, in the beginning, the philosophical conundrum of free-will paralyses Saleem's abilities to act because it introduces a gap. Omitting commas in his demand on free "thought decision action", he stresses his desire for an uninterrupted flow from free will to action. His "will for freedom" paralyses his capacity to be free because it envisions freedom as something that lies in the future. He seems to think that he needs to "be" in order to act, whereas a survey of his life shows that he "is" only through his actions, or rather that he is always in the process of becoming.

Saleem fears those who "possess a devastatingly clear sense of purpose" (194), as for instance the Pakistani martyrs (*shaheed*), who witness the truth of their beliefs through sacrifices, for which they are promised afterlife compensation:

> No wonder Lahore was defended; what did the Indians have to look forward to? Only reincarnation – as cockroaches, maybe, or scorpions, or green-medicine-wallahs – there's really no comparison. (431)

For a *shaheed*, being and acting are not stages or hierarchies.

The most important aspect that pertains to Saleem is his own being-allegory-of-India. In order to maintain this meaning as his existential matrix, he deploys all his energy to show material connections between his life and national history, his characteristics and those he believes pertain to India. Among other things, he claims: "I became directly responsible for triggering off the violence which ended with the partition of the state of Bombay" (244). His being is validated only in his acting out his purpose. The problem is, although Saleem did not choose his purpose it is supposed to govern his understanding of the world, his place in it, his everyday discrimination and action. His basic problem is his belief that he must find a fixed purpose or his true self that lies dormant and hidden somewhere inside, and then act as it dictates. He applies the same logic to the midnight's children: "we must be here for a *purpose* ... there has to be a *reason* ... we should try and work out what it is, and then, you know, sort of dedicate our lives to..." (280, emphases and ellipsis in the original). Their simultaneous births for him signal that they must have some meaning, which would point out for them a specific course of action. At this early stage, Saleem faces Shiva's bitter materialism:

> 'Rich kid,' Shiva yelled, 'you don't know one damn thing! What *purpose*, man? What thing in the whole sister-sleeping world got *reason*, yara? For what reason you're rich and I'm poor? Where's the reason in starving man? God knows how many millions of damn fools living in this country, man, and you think there's a purpose! Man, I'll tell you – you got to get what you can, do what you can with it, and then you got to die. That's reason, rich boy. Everything else is only mother-sleeping *wind*!' (280, emphases in the original)

Later, when Saleem asks about "free will...hope...the great soul, otherwise known as *mahatma*, of mankind...and what of poetry, and art", Shiva counters,

> '... there is only money-and-poverty .... All that importance-of-the-individual. All that possibility-of-humanity. Today, what people are is just another kind of thing.' (324)

It certainly appears as if Shiva has the upper hand in this telepathic fight. He sees the search for meaning as rich people's whim. Critics such as Kortenaar concur and even argue that Shiva replicates a form of Marxist critique of the bourgeoisie: "Saleem's concern with order and meaning is a luxury that he owes to the circumstances surrounding his birth, and therefore a mere emblem of class privilege."[19] However, Shiva's speech reveals a desire for ultimate

---

[19] Kortenaar, *Self, Nation, Text*, 145. From the early work of Brennan and the criticism he spawned (for instance from M. Keith Booker, Loretta M. Mijares, Kathryn Hume and Jean M. Kane), critics have tried to funnel the novel's themes into neo-Marxist critique of late capitalism, and focus on Rushdie's avoidance of solutions for national problems of post-independence. Berlatsky argues that the entire novel, through its various ironies, renders a materialist understanding of the world. However, Saleem is not particularly interested in critiquing Western bourgeois or late capitalism in the third world. To use Bhabha's words, there are various social stratifications in the city, which "no longer simply 'cluster around class antagonism, [but] break up

individualism: "there is only money-and-poverty, and have-and-lack, and right-and-left; there is only me-against-the-world" (324). There is quite a shift from a definition of the world in terms of left and right politics to Shiva's ultimate principle of standing alone against the world in its entirety. He becomes the chaos that treats everything and everyone with equal malice. However, already in the mocking denomination *Communist Magician*, Saleem suggests that their position is possible only with some magic, only not supernatural magic as that of Parvati, but rather the art of illusion: "Picture Singh and the magicians were people whose hold on reality was absolute; they gripped it so powerfully that they could bend it every which way in the service of their arts" (507). Saleem "could never fully enter the world-according-to-Picture-Singh" (526). Eventually the magicians forget their purpose and their grip on reality vanishes. Picture Singh becomes "adrift and incompetent in a world he did not understand" (571), a world that does not fit his picture.[20]

Shiva starts as an anarchist and seems to lead an extremely individualized life, doing as he pleases, killing whom he pleases, because nothing truly matters, neither morality nor meaning. Although Shiva seems to highlight the class problem that is overshadowed by Saleem's insistence on purpose, it is hard to see how Shiva evinces the Marxist stance. Unlike the Communist Magicians, he has no sense of community, the greater good, or solidarity. He forces poor people to vote against the communist opposition in the election. His materialism is in fact an extreme selfishness that renders everything but his personal gain completely immaterial. Yet, he shows that his class, his poverty, and his unequal birth do not stymie him. Shiva endorses chaos, which he believes allows him uninhibited action, whereas for Saleem chaos precludes action. In fact, Shiva appears more of an existentialist than Saleem, perhaps a perverse version of Nietzsche's

---

into widely scattered historical contingencies'" (Bhabha, *The Location of Culture*, 246).

[20] Žižek writes: "Real Socialism failed because it endeavoured to impose onto reality an illusory utopian vision of humanity, not taking into account the way real people are structured through the force of tradition." Socialism here stands for a new way of describing and even mythologizing the world. Furthermore, "while Lenin still remained faithful to the 'real of the (Communist) illusion,' to its emancipatory utopian potential, Stalin was a simple 'realist,' engaged in a ruthless power-struggle" (Slavoj Žižek, *On Belief*, London: Routledge, 2001, 81). In *Midnight's Children*, Shiva seems to have Stalinist characteristics.

Übermensch who is allegedly beyond both good and evil, beyond purpose. He seems to show the universality of choice, the importance of decision and action. He cuts himself loose from his circumstances of birth and becomes a feared soldier. He may renounce inherent and inherited meaning, which Saleem does as well, but he remains cocksure in his action. He seems to have a clearer sense of purpose than Saleem. Shiva knows what he wants to do, and does it. Saleem tries to explain Shiva's change from an anarchist to a supporter of the Widow's cleansing project as Shiva's cowardice in the face of the destruction of the midnight's children (547). At the same time, Shiva does not seem to fear anyone, and abides by no ideology, even though he has become the super soldier of the ruling class.

As for Saleem, life in wealth indeed gives him more opportunity to leisure and schooling. While he voices guilt over his social status, his material situation neither aggravates nor ameliorates his existential crisis. In fact, both Shiva and Saleem begin their lives with strong crises, full of anguish in the face of particular forms of oppression and suffering. While Ahmed becomes anguished only when his business is plummeting, Saleem is always concerned with his purpose. Since he never finds any purpose he can settle on, it would seem that Saleem's existence is purposeless. However, his history does not give such an impression. There is indeed no single purpose, but rather his purpose arises from his actions, and from his desire to find new ways of being free. It is only when he is engaged in the negotiation of his life, a struggle for his life, that there emerge rather heterogeneous purposes that are articulated in each specific situation. The important conclusion that Saleem draws from various conflicts is that being is acting. Shiva's only point that Saleem eventually accepts is that meaning and identity might not be divinely or naturally determined, even though Shiva becomes re-inscribed as "the god of destruction" (281) who has strewn "bastards across the map of India" (520), but which he seems to detest and chooses to sterilize himself. Shiva could be taken as an existentialist hero, who shows that even if choices are limited, there is still a universality of choice. Saleem learns a lesson already after their initial fight, if he has the freedom to do whatever he likes, everyone else does.[21]

---

[21] As Simone de Beauvoir put it, "To will oneself free is also to will others free" (Simone de Beauvoir, *Ethics of Ambiguity*, Sacaucus: Citadel Press, 2000, 73).

Assuming that Shiva is the authentic, existentialist hero who actually acts and changes the world he lives in, as Sartre would like to see it, we must pay attention to what he does. Whether or not he believes in its supremacy, Shiva does things for the government. He helps them develop a stronghold in India by eliminating all those deviant, marginal, hybrid elements who either directly oppose the power, or whose very existence is a threat. Shiva sees a small number of options, and opts for serving the ruling class. Although he knows what powers put him in his untoward situation in the first place, he still plays in their court. Saleem, on the other hand, produces fathers and mothers, he is affected by all of them and he affects them and changes them, and in the end he leaves them all. What seems to be an inability to commit to any political and religious paradigms is actually a refusal to opt for and fully commit to anything that has been offered to him. He stays with his family in Pakistan and has contact with Zia-u-Haqq, he lives with the Communists for a while, marries a witch, works as a dog during the war, and many other things, but he does not stick to any. He is always half in and half out, acknowledging all the given choices, but desiring a third option.

While Saleem often laments that he has no choice and freedom, he keeps confirming and articulating his freedom by moving between fathers and rulers, looking for a third pill, to use an image from *The Matrix*. Shiva, on the other hand, exercises his freedom by choosing between given alternatives, the blue or the red pill. When Shiva the Destroyer realizes he is also like the mythical Procreator, he sterilizes himself. Saleem definitely tries to fall into bad faith and deny his freedom and responsibility: "No choice? – None; when was there ever?" (537). By manically insisting on the plethora of incompatible determinisms (for instance fate versus history), he also shows that he cannot really refer to either fate, or biology, or social and historical factors as the ultimate excuse for his actions, not even the banal and amusing actions he values so much. While Saleem and Shiva argue for different positions, their actions speak for themselves.

As an afterthought, Saleem articulates an authentic life as something that arises in and through action. Since he seldom does anything that truly shapes grand historical movements, the question is what, if anything, constitutes his particularity, his specific way of being free? His basic action is reduced to his wielding of irony and mimicry, which produce comic absurdity that is supposed to work against conscious and unconscious conformity. The comic aspects of his self-reflexive narrative serve to heighten his and the readers' awareness of the mechanisms that conspire in the regulation of his life. This self-reflexivity seems to constitute the beginning of a search for authenticity.

Comic-absurdity as the opening to authentic action

Saleem begins to narrate his life from his deathbed. He sees himself as a failure, as someone who has come to a too late recognition that his purpose is not defined by a politician or a prophet, but by his choices. The only way of being free left for him is the act of writing, through which he calls attention to some mechanics of self-definition, identity formation and social oppression. Autobiographical writing is an exercise in self-reflexivity, which in turn seems always to be oriented towards self-formation.[22]

Saleem begins by delving deep into his past, looking for the roots of his current predicament. Jung Su calls Saleem's basic strategy "cultural eclecticism",[23] which is qualified as an intentional "mockery of the idea of authenticity".[24] An eclectic selects from the world-repository of culture whatever appears usable for the immediate gain, a gesture that Rushdie claims to be "a hallmark of the Indian tradition".[25] It is a form of picking and choosing in the process of self-making that somehow seems unrestrained. However, Saleem's is a far more ironic eclecticism, the collecting in order to refute and transform, rather than endorse and preserve. When he uses cultural references, and tries to fit modern individuals into mythical narratives, and creates ties to several political and religious movements, he makes an immense hodgepodge of everything without committing to anything. Saleem collects that which he does not endorse. He seems to behave like that which Kierkegaard calls a *"fuimus"*,[26] someone who

---

[22] Archer has aptly argued, "the gift of reflexivity, which finally creates enough of a self for its workings in the world to become independent, can only work in the kind of world which morally prevents its independence from breaching conventions" (Archer, *Being Human*, 110).

[23] Jung Su, "Saleem's Quest for Origin: Authenticity and Nation in *Midnight's Children*", *Proc. Natl. Sci. Counc. ROC(C)*, X/1 (January 2000), 65.

[24] *Ibid.*, 61.

[25] Rushdie, *Imaginary Homelands*, 68.

[26] Kierkegaard, *Sickness Unto Death*, 89.

looks back at the past as an old man lying about it or inventing it in order to overcome surging existential anguish.

Saleem wants to argue that he has indeed acted against all the forces that have claimed him. While there is seldom, if ever, a head-on struggle, Saleem expresses his freedom in exaggerated mimicry/mockery of different beliefs, filiations and political affiliations. Take his mind-reading for an example. Saleem talks about it as a matter of fact, but its provenances or causes are as varied as they are far-flung. He offers both scientific and religious paradigms to explain his abilities, and even ascribes them to chance (he hit his nose in the washing chest). He knows these explanations are mutually exclusive. The scientific explanation that his mind is a radio, which gathers voices into a kind of a democratic parliament, falls flat within a magical realist discourse in which the powers are the mysterious gift of the midnight hour. Even if understood as telepathy, it figures more in science fiction. Saleem offers an interpretation in terms of his Judeo-Christian-Islamic context. He suggests that he is a new prophet hearing angelic voices: "like Musa or Moses, like Muhammad the Penultimate, I heard voices on a hill" (207). Yet, the voices turn out to be more mundane. His mimicry of the religious discourse seems an act of conformity, but it turns to be more mockery than imitation. This mockery seems aimed at his parents' (and readers) assumed bad faith.

With respect to the radio metaphor, what Saleem lays bare for the readers is that in his historical situation radio and television have a specific function for the constitution of the nation. The nation is too large and too diverse to produce a kind of communion and intimacy of its members that we ascribe to smaller traditional communities. In a large nation state, radio seems to serve, as Adorno has pointed out, to "reach the people at large in such a way that they notice none of the innumerable technical intermediations; the voice that announces resounds in the home, as though he were present and knew each individual".[27] A national consciousness is a false consciousness. When Saleem claims he excels the "All-India Radio" in that he actually brings all the singular voices to presence for each other in a communion or at least a perfect parliament, he shows that the one who commands the space of the gathering is also the mediator. This mediation is even viler than the radio propaganda during the Indo-

---

[27] Adorno, *The Jargon of Authenticity*, 62.

Pakistani war, because the children are given the false impression that they are actually present rather than represented. In a sense, he qualifies his brain as the crystallized space of bad faith, but he breaks the illusion and reveals that he has been manipulating the mental forum to exclude Shiva, control dialogue and barter thought. He told them he wanted them to be free, but his liberalism turned out to be authoritative.

Theoretically speaking, although mimicry has been Bhabha's hallmark, it seems fruitful to begin with a parallel to Sartre's figure of a waiter who does everything too much in order to conform to a certain stereotype or a role.[28] Assuming that the waiter is aware he is acting in bad faith, then for Sartre he is even more inauthentic because he denies the facticity of his freedom. If he is not aware, if his intentions are sincere, by accentuating every gesture of waiter-ness, the man draws attention to this particular social behaviour. The exaggerated conformity breaks the transparency of this role. He is not just a waiter, but also someone who foregrounds his desire to be perfect in his role. This practice stands out and reveals its place in the social order of things. Sartre's image captures social action in bad faith, which is akin the behaviour of postcolonial subjects such as Saleem's family in their practice of English customs. Bhabha has provided an important insight into the element of indeterminacy as to the sincerity of the performance. Is mimicry honest conformity, or mockery? In *Midnight's Children*, it is especially the histrionic aspects of Saleem's mimicry that produce the ironic and mocking effect. Saleem's ironic mode serves to alert the readers that his mimicry is anything but serious conformity.

Indeed, as Bhabha has argued, any "desire to emerge as 'authentic' through mimicry – through a process of writing and repetition – is the final irony of partial representation".[29] Since "authentic" here has its essentialist valence, Bhabha means to say that the irony implied in mimicry shows two things: first, the imitation does not constitute authenticity, and second, it does not hide another true self that is only obscured by the mask of imitation. Indeed, such "'partial' representation rearticulates the whole notion of identity and alienates it from essence".[30] In order to better understand Saleem's mimicry, we

---

[28] Jean-Paul Sartre, *Essays in Existentialism*, Secaucus: Citadel Press, 1993, 167-69.
[29] Bhabha, *The Location of Culture*, 126.
[30] *Ibid.*, 127.

can compare it to colonial mimetic desire, the kind of imitation or copycatting that nationalism denies "in the name of authenticity", as Kortenaar puts it.[31] Understanding mimicry only with respect to the colonizer/colonized dichotomy, nationalists "urge the abandonment of false roles" and "a return to authenticity".[32] The implied paradox here is that the nation itself is a foreign model, always "imperso-nation", as Sumita S. Chakravarty has argued.[33] Saleem's family becomes ersatz Englishmen to the point that his father turns white. Just as for a nationalist such imitation entails a betrayal of the true self, existential authenticity too stands in conflict with role-playing and imitation, which is obvious from Saleem's aversion to Pakistani acquiescence and Sanjay clones.

In a sense, it would seem that mimicry stands in opposition to authenticity in any sense of the word. It seems valid to argue, as Kortenaar does, that Saleem shows how all identity is role-playing, mimicry, imitation, parroting (as in Aadam's Mecca-turned parroting, and Ahmed's substitute bulbul which is in fact a parrot). There are no true selves, but only performances: "In a world of mirrors and parrots, there is no way of establishing one's authenticity." Saleem seems to produce an "irreverent twist on Marx's bitter phrase from *The Eighteenth Brumaire* [that mimicry is the inevitable fate of the middle-classes]" in order to "deflate the vaunted power of the European original".[34] Indeed, Saleem says as a matter of course, "it would be fair to say that Europe repeats itself, in India, as farce" (235). The key to Saleem's stance is his awareness, his thematization of mimicry. The deliberate exaggerations allow "the mimic to stand outside his performance".[35] For Kortenaar this still entails an utter denial of authenticity. If we take his idea that everything is always already a performance, it is possible to understand performance as a creative and dynamic gesture, not merely copycatting.

Saleem's mimicry, as when he assumes different mythological meanings, is not only an act of *mimesis* that is ambiguous in itself, but rather *poiesis*, to use terminology from aesthetics. He claims to be

---

[31] Kortenaar, *Self, Nation, Text*, 167.

[32] *Ibid.*, 170.

[33] Sumita S. Chakravarty, *National Identity in Indian Popular Cinema 1947-1987*, Austin: University of Texas Press, 1993, 4.

[34] Kortenaar, *Self, Nation, Text*, 170.

[35] *Ibid.*, 171.

creative and not merely mocking. Such gestures, comparable to the famous scene from *The Satanic Verses* where Jibreel is not sure whether he is an angel or a devil, is practically a dramatization of Sartre's claim about the responsibility in singular choices: "If a voice speaks to me, it is always I who must decide whether or not this is the voice of an angel."[36] Although the voice of an angel or a god seems binding, it is still a matter of choice. The individual must take responsibility for his or her belief. The scene from *Midnight's Children* in which Saleem meets the angel of death with Indira Gandhi's face poignantly illustrates this problematic. We find an even fresher image of this idea in Saleem's hearing of millions of voices of the Indian population. Saleem does not want his voices to be devilish, but divine. Yet, they turn out to be mundane. Saleem's parents, meeting his preposterous claims that he is talking with divinity, become terrified in the face of their own choice, or rather the fact that they have never really chosen to believe in the originality of Moses' and Muhammad's voices, or even that Moses and Muhammad themselves initially showed profound insecurity in the provenance of their revelations, an insecurity that is contained in the inceptive gestures of certain monotheistic movements.

Saleem's claims disturb the family. Instead of proclaiming his ability as the proof of the much-desired greatness, his parents chide him because his new self exceeds their frames of reference. From Aadam's secular viewpoint, no such thing as a divine messenger is possible, whereas for Naseem there is no prophethood after Muhammad. Saleem's voices also might be aspects of his split personality, the voices from his subconscious, which is an explanation more likely to be accepted in the secularized age. Given that Saleem describes the entire event as characterized by both infantile innocence and the adult tongue-in-cheek, no final decision can be made about his powers, voices, etc. Deducing from his parent's reaction, Saleem suspects everyone is conspiring against him. In the beginning, Saleem sees signs of his importance and meaning everywhere, but he understands that if everything is a sign then nothing is:

> ... prophets and prime ministers had created around me a glowing and inescapable mist of expectancy .... Adrift in this haze of anticipation ... cursed by a multitude of hopes and nicknames ... I became afraid

---

[36] Sartre, *Existentialism Is a Humanism*, 26.

> that everyone was wrong – that my much-trumpeted existence might
> turn out to be utterly useless, void, and without the shred of purpose.
> And it was to escape from this beast that I took to hiding. (193-94)

There is certain comic absurdity in Saleem's self-reflective passage. He embodies the nation, and his body is cracking because of the excess of conflicting traditions. Meaning seems to implode in to what Bhabha terms postcolonial non-sense. Saleem pretends to be describing his pure childhood experience at the same time as he infuses it with adult tongue-in-cheek. By first identifying with the prophets of monotheism, then also Buddha and Vishnu, Saleem tries to show that true conformity to their teachings is impossible in principle. To conform to Moses' teachings and imitate his acts in a de-historicized manner is an example of bad faith. In Saleem's case, the theatricality of conformity serves to show that social roles are never fully scripted, that the past does not offer explanations and prescriptions for all exigencies, and that he is always responsible for his actions.

If Saleem first asks, "Who am I", by giving his parents the impossible answer, he tries to show them that the recognition they want to give him is not directed at the right object. False recognition is not recognition at all. Saleem's desire for authenticity entails a risk that his actions never be recognized, a risk he must take since the intended object of recognition is constantly warped. The question "Who am I" is reformulated as "Who do I want to be", or rather "How do I want to be?". His craving for recognition could be a foreboding of the gravest inauthenticity. As Ferrara explains, nothing is "more inauthentic than an identity constructed with a view to recognition".[37] Saleem seems to fall into this trap. Yet, if his desire for recognition is yet another histrionic and ironic gesture, then it is the by-product of his desire to communicate authenticity through his action.

Just as he mocks the great prophets and thinkers, Saleem treats with irony modern role models such as the explorer Raleigh, Gandhi, Nehru, Mian Abdullah and others. He practically writes Gandhi out of the Indian history, and reduces this man's historical impact to the events connected to *hartal* and Gandhi's death (for which he gives the wrong date). Since he grows up in an ex-colonial home, he appears to be particularly concerned with Millais' painting of the young Raleigh

---

[37] Ferrara, *Reflective Authenticity*, 16.

as someone whose greatness is meant to be copied. When the Sinais move into Buckingham Villa, Amina complains that the pictures of the English on the walls leave no space for her ancestors. She fears her family will internalize the ideologies embedded in the foreign paintings. Her fears are warranted. Although Methwold has departed, the new owners behave as under a spell, observing British social practices to the point of absurdity. Amina and Mary strategically place Saleem's cot under the painting of "an old, gnarled, net-mending sailor" whose "liquid tales rippled around the fascinated ears of Raleigh" (154). As a birthday gimmick, "a proud mother and an equally proud ayah dressed a child with a gargantuan nose in just such a collar, just such a tunic", inspiring a comment: "It's like he's just stepped out of the *picture*!" (154) The two mothers make him look like the model imperialist sailor whose actions affected the course of history, except for the nose that makes the imitation a mockery. Subscribing to certain colonial ideals, the mothers desire to inculcate Saleem with the inspiring heroic theme, just as Raleigh is inspired by the sailor. They project their desires and fantasies in him, which is in part why Saleem practically ends his narrative with a twist on Sartre, "Hell is other people's fantasies" (577). As Kortenaar explains, "Millais's painting *does not depict heroic deeds*". It rather suggests, "as do the clipping and the letter from Nehru, that greatness is already present inside the child and awaits only the fullness of time to be recognized .... Greatness is not a question of achievement but of the recognition by others of what was always present within."[38] The family (and even the community/nation) expects Saleem to become great as an affirmation of their ideas. They can only understand him within "culturally sanctioned images of the nation and of the hero".[39]

Saleem transforms the inspirational painting by playing with the metonymic language of the painting, by making metaphors literal and pushing them to the limits of signification. He steps out of the frame of their reference, so to speak, and interprets the fisherman's metaphoric finger as pointing to other frames on the blue wall (sea?). Then he literally follows the direction of the finger in the historically specific Bombay home, over the Prime Minister's letter and the newspaper clip "with its prophetic captions" (155), eventually moving outside the house to thc ghettos. This renders the finger "an accusing

---

[38] Kortenaar, *Self, Nation, Text*, 66 (emphasis in the original).
[39] *Ibid.*, 65.

[one] which obliged us to look at the city's dispossessed". Finally, the pointer draws "attention to itself", marking a certain socio-ideological function of art, and the way reality is mediated through art, stories etc. Irony just oozes when he asks, "How much of my future hung above my crib, just waiting for me to understand it" (156). Saleem identifies with the anonymous boy in the painting, who is, as Kortenaar puts it "almost but not quite Walter",[40] the one who failed to "understand" his future, and find his greatness. Furthermore, Raleigh worked under the aegis of the colonial power, with strong allegiances to his race, religion and nation. He has helped create the past, the present (all the dispossessed outside the window), and the future Saleem faces. It is no coincidence that Saleem tries to connect this inspirational painting of a discursive and symbolic moment and the reality of Indian poor, a bridge between story and history.

Saleem's creative re-readings basically reveal his attempts to open up his self through acting, even if this acting is enacting or performing. He configures this childhood moment, and all that went into its constitution, displacing everything within frames of reference as well as displacing those frames. Saleem empties his midnight birth of that great meaning invested in it by his predecessors, by claiming that his great powers are the result of his own agency combined with chance. As I have stated before, the problem is that these re-interpretations are made in retrospect. This is why the evocation of the alternative futures as hanging above the crib can also be a clever literary device that signals to the reader (or listener Padma) the upcoming narrative twists and turns. One could claim that he has done nothing but conformed. Saleem's ambiguity presents the reader with a choice rather than serving to a fixed moral lesson. The reader cannot be entirely sure, and therefore his or her judgment is partly suspended and undermined.

The comic aspects of Saleem's very character arise in part from his way of foregrounding naivety with tongue-in-cheek. He makes himself laughable and gives his audience the sense of always being a step ahead of him. Then, he strategically places a self-interpretation: "If I seem a little bizarre, remember the wild profusion of my inheritance ... perhaps if one wishes to remain an individual in the midst of the teeming multitudes, one must make oneself grotesque"

---

[40] *Ibid.*, 183.

(136). He also says, "in India, we've always been vulnerable to Europeans … Evie had only been with us a matter of weeks and already I was being sucked into a grotesque mimicry of European literature [referring to *Cyrano*]" (235). He highlights the comic absurdity of his life as a wink to the reader that he is aware of the terms of engagement, but also that he is not entirely able to articulate his authenticity. Absurdity as such does not suggest absolute meaninglessness. On the contrary, as David Campbell maintains, "saying that life is absurd implies that the question whether life has a meaning itself has meaning, and is therefore to be taken seriously after all".[41]

Su argues that Saleem makes deliberate comical mistakes to "split the continuity of the 'authentic history' with their ruptured contradiction", and also that "Saleem's mockery of the idea of authenticity" shows that "authenticity, thanks to its inner logical contradiction, can be at once nationalist discourse's *tour de force* and its own stumbling block".[42] Concerned with communalism, Su argues that the comic aspects of the novel have the effect of laughing at all one's divinities, which resembles Nietzsche's "the comedy of existence". What Saleem calls heritage seems to be the equivalent of Nietzsche's allegorical "ethical teacher" who in no way wants "us to *laugh* at existence, or at ourselves – or at him".[43] Saleem produces a concatenation of comic relief as an outlet for his existential anguish, without relieving it.[44]

Great comic absurdity is found in Saleem's purportedly scientific experiment with allegory. Saleem himself seems to devalue the importance of metaphor when he distinguishes between his passive-literal mode of being and the active-literal. At the same time, when he draws a parallel to Indira Gandhi's metonymic character "India is Indira, Indira is India" (which rivals his own being-allegory), he shows what powerful political weapon allegory can be in that it inculcates people in believing that there is an essential connection

---

[41] David Campbell, "Nietzsche, Heidegger, and Meaning", *Journal of Nietzsche Studies*, XXVI (Autumn 2003), 53.

[42] Su, "Saleem's Quest for Origin", 73.

[43] Nietzsche, *The Gay Science*, sec. 28 (emphasis in the original).

[44] In his study of tragedy, Eagleton suggests that absurdity is the necessary downside of freedom of choice (Terry Eagleton, *Sweet Violence: The Idea of the Tragic*, Oxford: Blackwell, 2003, 223).

between the leader and the nation, that they are tied by the same substance, which in turn justifies her actions, enables her to demand full obedience and devotion, and thus become a blueprint for tyranny. Saleem's own allegory does not produce such effects because it is not embedded in the political discourse. This does not make it passive *per se*. In fact, *Midnight's Children* has been attacked for it blasphemous metaphoricity, just as similar gestures in *The Satanic Verses* caused much uproar and the infamous fatwa. As Bhabha has argued, "Metaphor produces hybrid realities by yoking together unlikely traditions of thought".[45] Since metaphoric language is frequently used for political gain, Saleem tests it to emphasize its political potency as well as its inherent paradoxes. Allegory, as Saleem's own paradoxical *doxa*, implies that a part is ripped out of its organic context and posited as the metonym of the whole. The singular hero is posited as the universal metonym of everything, and eventually turned into an empty form, which can contain everything like the spittoon, but itself has no substance, just as the spittoon does not share organic aspects of the spit it collects. At the same time as it promises great meaning, allegory opens up the hero to potential meaninglessness.

As Lloyd Spencer puts it, allegories are "symptomatic of a significant loss of a sense of genuine, immediately accessible, imminent meaning. Allegories, even those which proclaim the stability and fullness of meaning in the (hierarchical) universe can thus be seen as deconstructing themselves."[46] That which gives him meaning is actually a supplement for the lack or what he calls a hole in the chest. Saleem begins with an abstract empty form as his meaning, which is absurd and comic. By being an allegory (or allegorical hero), Saleem also participates in the myth of the nation as the form that keeps diverse ethnicities and cultures at bay. Every myth, as Nancy explains, typically has a single hero, an allegorical personality who

> ... makes the community commune ... in the communication that he
> himself effects between existence and meaning, between the
> individual and the people: "The canonical form of mythic life is

---

[45] Bhabha, "Third Space: An Interview with Homi Bhabha", 212.
[46] Lloyd Spencer, "Allegory in the World of Commodity: The Importance of *Central Park*", *New German Critique*, XXXIV (Spring-Summer 1985), 63.

precisely that of the hero. In it the pragmatic is at the same time symbolic."[47]

Saleem's exaggerated endeavour to be the allegory interrupts and suspends the mythical constitution of all heroic figures, especially the modern leaders.

Saleem's histrionic gestures also produce the sense of irony. It is not subtle and dark, but theatrical and comic irony. We could argue that Saleem uses what D.C. Muecke calls general irony, which reveals the crux in "the desire to know everything and the impossibility of knowing everything".[48] This general irony does not make Saleem any less a victim of his predicaments, but it might "enable him in some degree to transcend them".[49] At the same time, Saleem's irony may be of the type that produces "a constant dialectic interplay of objectivity and subjectivity, freedom and necessity, the appearance of life and the reality of art, the author immanent in every part of his work as its creative vivifying principle and transcending his work as its objective 'presenter'".[50] In this sense, irony is a part of that which I discussed in terms of mimicry and mockery.

Assuming, as the point of departure, that Saleem's narrative is overtly ironic and comically absurd, it produces the following effects: first, irony seems to produce a distance between Saleem and that which he deals with: parents, nation, leaders, history, myth, and most importantly his *angst*. His wielding of irony – as for instance when he repeatedly brings up the issues of blood, bloodlines and blood ties – serves to sensitize his readers that he does not believe in the kind of legitimacy these give to individual and communal identities. He seems to handle his quarrel with ancestry with bravado. However, on a deeper reading, we can see that though Saleem's irony takes on such a histrionic character it does not remove his existential *angst*. He may try to laugh at all his divinities, but it is an anguished laughter. The comic irony foregrounds his profound *angst*.

Another effect of irony is the production of ambiguity. Ironic narrative introduces the sense of epistemological uncertainty. Saleem is exaggerating so much so that the reader is persistently forced to see

---

[47] Nancy, *The Inoperative Community*, 51.
[48] D.C. Muecke, *Irony*, London: Methuen, 1970, 76.
[49] *Ibid.*, 77.
[50] *Ibid.*, 78.

the narrative as ironic, as for instance when Saleem uses the name Communist Magicians. When he argues that they are the ones who have the best understanding of reality and that this enables them to shape it with their art, he seems directly ironic about the Communist claims that they truly know reality, whereas others, like his bourgeois family, live within false consciousness. At the same time, it is perfectly possible to argue that he is sincere, that he indeed believes they know reality, but that they are simply deceitful about it and cheat like all politicians. Then, in the next instance, he seems to truly lament the fact that they were deprived of power in the national elections. He would prefer to have Picture Singh as a leader. The effect of concatenated ironies is that we cannot be entirely sure as to what exactly he believes. It is hard to pass judgment on him. Whichever interpretation we choose, we become conscious of that interpretative choice. Saleem's irony and mocking-mimicry do not, in the final analysis, force us to assume this or that position.

The best example may be Aadam's fall. Everything about the grandfather's loss of faith is so theatrical and embedded in grand religious imagery and rhetoric that we cannot be sure which aspects of the entire event are ironic. Saleem seems ironic about both faith and its loss. While he seems to approve of Aadam's abandoning Islam, he also appears to judge the fact that this happened because of the direct influence of Aadam's anarchist friends. He both welcomes and judges the loss of faith. He is ironic towards the religious and towards the secular Aadam. Does this mean he has a third option in mind? The reader is not served a final answer but must choose. Kortenaar suggests that Saleem's irony makes readers aware of their own choices, which define them rather than the book. Although "the mere fact of choice is not truly action, the self-awareness induced by the recognition that one has, in fact, chosen, is the kind of experience which underpins action".[51] Such choice, as Campbell puts it, "is not voluntarist in the sense that flipping a coin decides an outcome without effort, but is made amid struggle and strife. *Twilight of Idols* (IX. 38), for instance, describes choice or 'freedom' as 'measured ... by the resistance which has to be overcome, by the effort it costs.'"[52] Irony highlights the possibility of choice, the possibility that one does not have to submit to a particular social practice and belief.

---

[51] Kortenaar, *Self, Nation, Text*, 45.
[52] Campbell, "Nietzsche, Heidegger, and Meaning", 31.

However, an important lesson of *Midnight's Children* is that while irony and mimicry seem to have a certain function in the foregrounding of freedom, choices and responsibilities, they can lead to a certain excess of self-reflection, which, as Golomb explains, can produce a "reflective regression *ad infinitum*, without repose or stable commitment, until it paralyses our will to live".[53] While wielding irony is a form of action, it can also stifle Saleem's "thought decision action" and aggravate his isolation and detachment. Since Saleem seldom acts, his accomplishments seem reducible to this self-reflective awareness of the possibility of individual choice. Yet, to turn it all around again, it is exactly this isolation that makes him realize the importance of action for authenticity.

Desire for community

Dramatizing the oppressive effects of local-communal and national life, *Midnight's Children* seems to endorse isolation and inwardness as the only thing left for individuals caught up in violent historical circumstances as Saleem is. Yet, the private/public split is gone: "it is the privilege and the curse of midnight's children to be both masters and victims of their times, to forsake privacy and be sucked into the annihilating whirlpool of multitudes, and to be unable to live or die in peace" (599). There seems to be a desire to preserve privacy as a privileged sphere of existence, and posit the public life in negative terms. At the same time as he seems to lament the loss of privacy, this loss is also a privilege.

After the exhaustion of paradigms of filiation, affiliation and isolation, Saleem's narrative pushes us into a rethinking of both individuality and community. There are at least three instances in which Saleem is strongly isolated and yet it is in these instances that foreground the importance of community. There is his solitary writing in the factory, his seclusion in the tower, and his amnesiac existence during the war.

To begin with, Saleem assumes the posture of a loner whose social ties have been severed and who confines himself to his writing. However, this space is intruded upon by his lover, Padma. Since he is writing his memoir, we would expect him to have control and authority over his discourse. However, he partly shares his authorship,

---

[53] Golomb, *In Search of Authenticity*, 51.

which is also the authorship of his self, with the person who forms with him a community of two unorthodox lovers. The very writing process, as the articulation of his selfhood, becomes open to negotiation with this one-woman audience. Padma, as his primary audience, is not subordinated to him, but the essential interlocutor. She joins in, as Kimmich has argued, "the creation of meaning, becoming a co-author ... of Saleem himself".[54] She leaks into him, penetrates his self, which is strengthened by the fact that he is incapable of doing the same on the sexual level. Saleem tells his life in dialogue with Padma, not just in a fight "against absurdity but against isolation".[55] It is Padma who breaks his artistic illusions of grandeur and brings him down to earth, to the facticity of life. He is exposed to her. Even when she is not present, he is in some sort of communication with her.

There is strong emphasis on both the negativity of communalism and the necessity of community in Saleem's ironic treatment of Buddha-hood in the passages about his amnesia:

> I am stripped of past present memory time and love ... I am empty and free, because all the Saleems go pouring out of me, from the baby who appeared in jumbo-sized front-page baby-snaps to the eighteen-year-old with his filthy dirty love ... free now, beyond caring, crashing on to tarmac, restored to innocence and purity by a tumbling piece of the moon, wiped clean as a wooden washing-chest, brained (just as prophesied) by my mother's silver spittoon. (436)

In his account, the point of Buddhist struggle is reduced to a quite de-spiritualized experience of worldlessness. While "free", "pure", and "innocent" seem to point towards some form of Romantic shedding of social skins, the problem is that in this mode zero Saleem is not quite free, or pure, or innocent. He becomes a dehumanized being, a dog that lends his nose to the service of the army. He is "a *brinjal* ... a vegetable" (446), isolated from the human discourse. If the isolation in the tower is supposed to be the result of a willed severing of the family ties, in the army he is totally cut from his past history, and his heritage can give him no status. If this is an extreme purity then it deprives him of both personality and community. The amnesia is

---

[54] Kimmich, *Offspring Fictions*, 82.
[55] *Ibid.*, 83.

devastating for his sense of self and his purpose. The constant slippage between "I" and "he" shows his trouble with placing himself in the world:

> I, he, had begun again; that after years of yearning for importance, he (or I) had been cleansed of the whole business ... I, or he, accepted the fate ... emptied of history, the buddha learned the arts of submission, and did only what was required of him. To sum up: I became a citizen of Pakistan. (445)

As I stressed earlier, a model citizen of Pakistan is for him someone who acts in bad faith. In this case, even the ultra-obedient soldiers find him extreme. The freedom from everything that served to harm his selfhood leads him to absolute submission. While the army were "dedicated to 'rooting out'" the "rejection of past-and-family", which was "subversive behaviour" (447), Saleem's detachment from past-and-family is not subversive at all. They rename him "buddha" (Urdu for old man). He does not even resemble Buddha, "he-who-achieved-enlightenment-under-the-bodhi-tree", and was capable of "not-living-in-the-world as well as living in it" (445). Buddha's act of being-dead-to-the-world could be an example of authentic action that shaped history, whereas Saleem is a victim of an accident (a stereotyped, melodramatic gimmick from Bombay talkies). Eventually, snakebite cures Saleem's amnesia, "reclaiming everything, all of it, all lost histories, all the myriad complex processes that go to make a man" (464). Then, he says, "my old life was waiting to reclaim me .... What you were is forever who you are" (468). This pessimistic statement sounds like he is giving in to the enormous pressure of his complex past. He sings Mary's song to little Aadam, this time with a slight alteration: "Anything you want to be, you kin be, You kin be just what-all you want" (487). Heritage asserts itself again when Mary's dialect transforms the word "can" into "kin". Yet, while this burden is not desirable, the total opposite is even less so, because he loses all sense of being, freedom, action and articulation. (In contrast, Shiva's cut from the family and the ghetto community leads him to an excess of "will").

As a child, Saleem withdraws to the privacy in the womblike space of a washing-chest, where he is "concealed from the demands of parents and history" (198). When he enters his clock tower, and later on when he returns from Pakistan to Bombay, he indeed seems to become what Rege sees as a modernist hero, alone, ostracized, and alienated, seeking to escape from the mediations of family, immediate community and the nation. At the same time, since he reflects the nation – which is in the process of being-imagined – he needs seclusion for participating in that imaginary act, which Saleem calls the "dream we all agreed to dream ... a collective fiction in which anything was possible, a fable rivalled only by the two other mighty fantasies: money and God" (140). Unlike smaller immanent communities, the nation itself turns its citizens into the individual atoms of which it is made. Since a total cut from the world does not elicit authenticity, such an isolated character, as Blanchot puts it, "is the individual, and the individual is only an abstraction, existence as it is represented by the weak minded conception of everyday liberalism".[56]

However, such isolation is an important step in the process of reworking selfhood. Saleem needs to experience inwardness in order to know what it entails. It is in the tower that Saleem enters the minds of all Indians and finally also meets the other children, the other freaks. The movement inward becomes an ecstasy of his self. His communication with the midnight's children gives him a sense of sharing and bonding. Their dispersion and vast variety of abnormalities (or maybe supra-normality) make him start thinking about a new kind of community. While Kortenaar tends to see Saleem's voices as different aspects of his self and personality, Saleem's introduction of the children shows how he stretches beyond introspection and into the communal space. This is why he tries to pull together the M.C.C., wondering whether "collectivity [is] opposed to singularity?" (325). He sees their different powers as the abnormal ground for their community, which differs from bonding in terms of race, ethnicity or class. He envisions a "sort of loose federation of equals, all points of view given free expression" (280), and everyone is allowed his or her abnormality.

Saleem sees the M.C.C. as the potential third principle that is supposed to stand against all the ideological principles:

> Do not let this happen! Do not permit the endless duality of masses-and-classes, capital-and-labour, them-and-us to come between us! We ... must be a third principle, we must be the force which drives

---

[56] Blanchot, *The Unavowable Community*, 18.

between the horns of the dilemma, for only by being other, by being new, can we fulfil the promise of our birth. (323)

This speech indeed echoes Nehru's "Speech to Bandung Conference Political Committee" from 1955, in which the Prime Minister refuses alignment with the First and the Second worlds' political and economic blocs, which in a sense defined the Third World: "We do not agree with the communist teachings, we do not agree with the anti-communist teachings, because they are both based on wrong principles."[57] Besides the immediate connection, Saleem comes to desire the third principle, but not in terms of national alliances. Instead, he seems to seek a principle that is also not a principle. The "loose federation" of M.C.C. shows that he is thinking against the idea that a community must formulate a fixed set of principles that will keep its borders well defined, and be the glue to its unity not just in the present but also in the future, the glue that will hold together people synchronically and diachronically.[58]

Critics such as Kortenaar seem justified in arguing that such a community is idealistic even in the novel in that it is never truly realized. However, Kimmich has a point when he claims that this community only starts to "fall apart when Saleem denies Shiva a voice" and thus "silences an unwanted, uncomfortable, potentially disruptive voice and enforces a certain hierarchy".[59] Not only does Saleem assume a self-appointed leadership, he starts disregarding the children's differences and wants to find their common essence, their common being.

No matter how much Saleem fears and struggles against communal dogmas and restrictions, he always seeks community. Whatever authenticity or freedom there is, he seems to understand, is found in communal existence. The M.C.C. project is the experiment of his precocious mind, the third principle that does not merely synthesize different social oppositions and hierarchies, but offers something new. Since the M.C.C. fails, it seems as if the novel suggests that

---

[57] Jawaharlal Nehru, "Speech to Bandung Conference Political Committee, 1955": http://www.fordham.edu/halsall/mod/1955nehru-bandung2.html.

[58] Rushdie quotes Robi Chatterjee as saying, "We don't need glue … India isn't going to fall apart. All that Balkanization stuff. I reject it completely …. It is this nationalism business that is the danger" (Rushdie, *Imaginary Homelands*, 32).

[59] Kimmich, *Offspring Fictions*, 53.

individuality and community are opposed in principle and that
something like an authentic community is an oxymoron. While the
novel does not flesh out all the characteristics of an authentic
community, the very failure of M.C.C. basically serves to draw
attention to the ways in which older understandings of both
individuality and community contribute to this dissolution. When
Saleem starts talking about their community, his own understanding is
itself under the influence of older conceptions. To begin with, he is
interested in some kind of essentialism, the desire for an inherent
purpose or meaning for the children. His understanding of community
is based on both local communitarian models and the new national
ideals with a prominent allegorical leader at the top. The moment he
assumes leadership and introduces a hierarchical structure, he starts
censoring dialogue between the children and regulating their own
development. The M.C.C. dissolves.

The implied tragedy in this both amusing and serious drama is that
the third principle, which is strategically located in childhood, before
identities have become sedimented under the influence of "long
trousers" (324), "dies; or rather, it is murdered" (325). The visionary
childhood is nipped in the bud, and Saleem becomes a constant
migrant or immigrant, looking for community but not being able to
attach himself to any given social formation, especially not the nation,
which is envisioned as a community of all communities, the way a
galaxy is a system of star systems. Another problem may be, to use
Blanchot's argument, "theoretically and historically there are only
communities of small numbers".[60] Small communities seem to imply
communion and even the fusion of the individuals into "a supra-
individuality".[61] It becomes hard to conceive of a community without
the immanence of its members to each other. Nation practically
implies the lack of such immanence of equal and connected minds.
The midnight's children can have that through Saleem's own mind,
the parliament of his brain, but they remain disembodied. Saleem's
brain becomes a mere abstract space. Also, while it may make sense
that the one whose mind is the space of the new community is also the
one who shapes it, Saleem feels anxious about this role because it
immediately leads him away from genuine sharing, caring and
responsibility. The children are reduced to minds without materiality.

---

[60] Blanchot, *The Unavowable Community*, 6.
[61] *Ibid.*, 7.

In a sense, the communion of the children in Saleem's mind disbands immanence and calls for sharing of the impossible principle.

Indeed, as Blanchot has put it, even "the community of equals, which puts its members to the test of an unknown inequality, is such that it does not subordinate the one to the other, but makes them accessible to what is inaccessible in this new relationship of responsibility".[62] This equality, as an aspect of community, is not here a matter of social law, a constitution. It is not merely the equality in the distribution of wealth, rights and obligations, but an equal taking of responsibility for the inequality that may be the other face of equality itself and of freedom.

As long as it reflects the nation, the M.C.C. cannot become the kind of loose community in which their singularities can thrive. Saleem states:

> I am not speaking metaphorically .... Reality can have metaphorical content; that does not make it less real .... Midnight's Children can be made to represent many things, according to your point of view: they can be seen as the last throw of everything antiquated and retrogressive in our myth-ridden nation, whose defeat was entirely desirable in the context of a modernizing, twentieth century economy; or as the true hope of freedom, which is now forever extinguished; but what they must not become is the bizarre creation of a rambling, diseased mind. (255)

Saleem wanders between all kinds of communities, from the family, over Islamic Pakistan, to the communist gatherings in Indian slums. By entering and leaving several already defined communities Saleem tries to bond and share concerns but binds himself to none and nothing. He seems to propose the possibility of bonding and sharing across any number of lines, the possibility of coming together on several plains, of intersecting communities that are articulated through migration. Indeed, he takes the assumed negativity (of abnormality) and finds in it an opening towards something new, an articulation of his freedom.

Saleem also notices that many communities, especially the nation, have some sense of the work projected into the future and waiting to be realized. I argued earlier that in Okri's novel the work in question

---

[62] *Ibid.*, 17.

is a liberated, independent Nigeria. In a sense, the same is true for
Saleem's India. The difference is that Saleem explicitly thematizes the
creation of the work, which in his case is both singular and double. It
is double in that his life (and his autobiography) is a work, an *oeuvre*,
which is then juxtaposed to the national history, the national *oeuvre*.
The individual and the national community are detached and yet they
are supposed to be subsumed to the same working. Yet, for Saleem,
they are almost but not quite one and the same. At the same time as
Saleem and the nation struggle to create this work, they are both
cracking. Neither can be contained in or as a form. Saleem's work
undermines the workability of his and the national *oeuvre*. He
undermines, to use Nancy's words, all attempts at objectifying and
producing a common being that can be traced in "sites, persons,
buildings, discourses, institutions, symbols; in short, in subjects".[63]
The way Saleem proposes his self and the nation as the work only
expose their inoperativeness, or rather a simultaneous working and
un-working, is in part Saleem's way of being free.

---

[63] Nancy, *The Inoperative Community*, 31.

Conclusion

Michael Ondaatje, Ben Okri and Salman Rushdie are three immigrant writers who have been praised for their use of imagination in their engagement with the mutual inter-affect of their different heritages. As authors who have left their countries of origin, but also taken their cultures with them, as Ondaatje argued, they have persistently faced the question of their ethnic and cultural authenticity. Their migration, as Rushdie has emphasized, not only brings about the sense of uprootedness, cultural estrangement and existential *angst*, but also the possibility to rework existential issues of meaning, individuality, community, and perhaps most importantly, freedom and authenticity. In their countries of origin, the search for authenticity arises from a desire for political freedom, a most pertinent issue for postcolonial subjects. At the same time, they have been exposed to the long tradition of thinking about and asserting individual freedom in their European contexts. Rather than simply choosing between the seemingly opposed alternatives of community and individuality, these authors use fictional spaces to experiment with news ways of being free, being singular and yet also part of a community.

Their novels *The English Patient, The Famished Road* and *Midnight's Children* portray the ways in which postcolonial history causes the central characters' existential *angst* and makes them socially estranged, isolated, solipsistic and individualistic. This condition becomes a step in a process of rethinking freedom, authenticity and community. In the political and cultural spaces they dramatize, freedom and authenticity are often appropriated within communalist and nationalist paradigms. Authenticity is then the question of social ties, shared myths, proper communal belonging, duties, patriotism, that is, different forms of heritage. Given that the novels often present heritage as burdensome, as a dead weight that hampers individual development, it is no surprise that they also thematize freedom as an unburdening from such weight. Freedom from "dead habits, dead ways of seeing, dead ways of living"[1] initially takes the direction of what I have called "individualism", the ideal of a self as a self-sufficient. At the same time, these narratives are imaginative experiments that bring to crisis these generally relevant issues and concepts. In many ways, the novels engage the political and philosophical traditions that have dealt with the issues of freedom, authenticity, selfhood, singularity and community. The most prominent source of influence seems to be European existentialism. As Rushdie argued in a recent radio interview with Jian Ghomeshi, the historical period of the 1960s left his generation with hope that change is possible and that singulars can contribute to the shaping of their world. To juxtapose the politically charged postcolonial contexts of these novels to the European heritage of existentialist thought on freedom yields a creative dialogue in which hardly any belief is left unchallenged. If critical thought, at least since Adorno, has been overtly negative towards the heritage generally labelled "existentialism", the literature I selected seems much more open both to influences from this rather heterogeneous legacy as much as any other and a creative reworking of it. The fictional space, with its characteristic plasticity, more easily accommodates as well as contrasts (and puts into conflict) several discourses, beliefs and ideologies. Since literature, as Okri has claimed, does not need to submit to the demands of an analytical (and maybe even hermeneutic) thought, since it does not need to deliver final conclusions and solutions to certain problems, it can bring out the aporias of thinking as well as it can articulate the paradoxes of living. It can provide more space for an exploration of how similar concerns can lead to different articulations.

There are two concerns that drive the narratives. The first is the question of singular freedom and authenticity (its articulations and limits). The second is the question of community in its relation to individuality. I have elaborated on both similarities and difference between the novels. I will now recapture some main points that seem to pertain to all of them and explore their further implications.

The novels describe the dissolution of traditional communities and a re-aggregating of community on a larger scale of the nation states. Instead of integrating in these imaginary communities, the characters

---

[1] Okri, *Songs of Enchantment*, 289.

become detached from the social life they find oppressing, ideologically shaped, and which stymies their singular development. They are the atoms (among other atoms) of a certain national body. Yet, there is no true communication between the national subjects, except in their supposed participation in the dream they all agreed to dream. We can see how Saleem attempts a telepathic creation of the communion of national subjects who participate in the nation, and yet they are actually detached from it. The individualism of some characters then does not simply result from a will to existential authenticity, but is rather a residue of this failure of community to commune or be realized through the immanence of its members. Such characters often turn on themselves in introspection and introversion. In the next instance, they come to grasp the importance of community for individual selfhood. Instead of adopting communalist ideals of immanence and the return to the original cultures, the characters explore community as a space of sharing and bonding that is not binding. There seems to be an attempt to overcome the opposition between the individual and communal as a way of articulating singular ways of being free.

I have argued that authentic selfhood in the novels is performative, that is, constituted through action. Authenticity denotes processes involving the struggles of single characters to articulate their ways of being free. In many instances these processes consist in the characters' resistance to their political climates, as we have seen in the cases of Kip and the English patient, Saleem's relation to the ruling dynasty, and Azaro and Dad's involvement in the liberation of marginal populations in Nigeria.

Authenticity is a process insofar as "process" gives the sense of a continuity of struggle, rather than a desire for a stable essence. At the same time, we can distinguish between two conflicting and overlapping understandings of "process", technological and existential. In the novels, the existential process of becoming is partly defined in relation to the technological understanding, which has a negative value. Generally speaking, technological processes are supposed to entail progress, change, human improvement and power to shape the world. The problem is that such an understanding, as the figure of Shiva shows, turns everything into just another product, including human beings themselves.

Given the negative characterization of technology, machines, production thinking, and a concomitant effect of the destruction of nature, it would appear that all three novels use a Romantic opposition between technology and nature, between machines and biological life. This is most prominent in *The Famished Road* where monstrous machines uproot thousand-year-old trees in order to build infrastructure for the new nation. Metaphorically, singular characters such as Azaro stand like weak trees on the modern highways, trying to fight everything that seeks to turn them into just another thing.

The Romantic opposition between nature and technology is used to show the characters' anguish about their personal development in contrast to mechanical behaviour, sterilization of life's richness, inauthenticity. However, we also notice in the novels that the original natural condition (of blissful coexistence) is a myth. There is little difference between the primordial giant of the road and the new metal giants that come in its stead in *The Famished Road*. In this text, old and new roads equally demand sacrifice and turn people into raw materials.

Most importantly, the novels show that the machine is an outgrowth of the tree. The inherent paradox of the technological age is that there is a proliferation of possibilities for self-development, and yet, the range of authentic self-development had come down to nothing. While the use of technology seems to foreground general human freedom from different form of determinism, as Heidegger has argued, man *sui generis* becomes the author/creator and everything else becomes his or her product. From the exalted "posture of lord of the earth" everything "man encounters exists only insofar as it is his construct. This illusion gives rise in turn to one final delusion: it seems as though man everywhere and always encounters only himself."[2] If this condition is considered an essential relation, as part of modern metaphysics, then existential processes too are influenced by thinking in terms of production. Self-becoming is then understood as self-fashioning, or the production of selfhood and identity out of the raw materials found in the world as it is. The crux is that at the same time as the subject is supposed to produce itself it is also supposed to shape the world in its own image.

---

[2] Heidegger, *The Question Concerning Technology*, 27.

This belief in man as the producer, and the world as the sum of raw materials he can eclectically pick and choose from, might be hard to shake. When critics as different as Appiah and Eagleton argue that one cannot make oneself from scratch, they are analysing self-making in terms of production. They argue that the self is a product of dialogical processes that entail biology, history, society and/or one's own will. Such thinking indeed departs from the essentialist understanding of selfhood, but in turn it conceives of selfhood primarily as identity, and authenticity in terms of production and operation or operative-ness. We find such an understanding in some characters in the novels, and we can see that this view still presupposes a self or subjective will that performs the shaping of identity, which is related to it but not the same. In a sense, the self or subject is still there in its basic shape, and what it produces is its own social role or identity. There is also a split between a self and the raw materials, an implied hierarchy. Although the phrase "self-making" seems to have a double meaning – a self that develops itself, and a self that is "not-yet" but has to be made – it is the first meaning that is dominant.

The basic point of departure we have seen in the novels is that there is a sense of selfhood already shaped in relation to a given social identity. Such selfhood is then brought into question. The characters evince a desire for self-fashioning, but the narratives show how the characters' selves are shaped while their very subject position is undermined. In the novels, there is a movement away from self-making understood in instrumental terms. Saleem presents himself as a victim who suffers all conceivable forms of determinism, both natural and social. He appears comically absurd when he simultaneously links his supposed lack of freedom to both fate and history, to both laws of physics and social regulations. In a sense, given that these often contradict each other, Saleem seems to mock them all, and by playing them against each other, traces his own freedom. Ultimately, he refutes both the idea that everything cancels out his freedom and that he is the absolutely free shaper of the world (with his mind). He does not everywhere encounter only himself, or his image of the world, nor does he show a total lack of freedom, imagination and creativity.

Freedom in the novels is not about a subject exercising total control, but always contains an element of surprise, something unplanned for, unaccountable and unrepresented. Existential freedom seems to arise from the very condition of being-thrown into the world. It is not about an absolute free will and agency of an omnipotent being such as God, which seems to be the case in Rousseau's thought: "one is sufficient unto oneself, like God."[3] On the contrary, authenticity turns out to be something of a surprise, something that singular beings do not simply will as subjects, but something that they also surprisingly receive. The characters in the novels are surprised by this reception that seems to come without a cause, and as if from nowhere, as in the scenes when Azaro struggles free from the many-headed ghosts and receives something akin to a third eye. There is an element of unknowing and indeterminacy in the process of authenticity. As Okri puts it:

> Many have fallen into the abyss because they were looking for solid ground, for certainties. Happy are those who are still, and to whom things come.[4]

The characters are open for the alterity of what may be thought of as "raw materials". Rushdie's Saleem indeed starts with an assumption that his is the role of the author of his life, or at least his autobiography. His desire is initially to shape history with an all-powerful mind that does what it pleases. At the same time, he cautions his readers that this is an impossible position to hold, and that one must not enter "the illusion of the artist", and think of "the multitudinous realities … as the raw unshaped material of [one's own] gifts".[5] While authenticity is a process, there is also a resistance to the technological understanding of processes. It is this resistance that gives rise to an exploration of community as the *a priori* of singularity, as the shared space both shaped by singular characters and the condition of their self-development.

The novels indeed describe a conflict between individuals and communities (at any scale). The latter are generally understood in terms of social structures, frameworks, power hierarchies and habitual behaviour that stifle personal potentiality and creativity. Saleem asks,

---

[3] Cited in Berman, *The Politics of Authenticity*, 305.
[4] Ben Okri, *Astonishing the Gods*, London: Phoenix, 1995, 104.
[5] Rushdie, *Midnights' Children*, 222.

is "collectivity opposed to singularity?"[6] When Hana in *The English Patient* stresses that the explosion of the A-bombs will forever pit individual against national interests, she prophesies the widening split between the personal and the social spheres, a conflict between the communal ethos and the ethics of self-construction. At this point Hana seems to have forgotten about her bonding with the other inhabitants of the villa and readopts the notion of an individual-communal conflict. Or rather, she could be suggesting that the events impose this opposition on her and everyone else. For a moment it seems as if she reverts to the introvert state of individuality in which Kip and Caravaggio found her. At the same time as Hana seems to revert to privacy and detachment, Kip evinces what appears to be a nativist attempt to return to his homeland and traditional ties. Both these different movements come as the reaction to the same event. Both reactions are ways of dealing with strong existential *angst*. Just as such anxious withdrawal is a reaction to a certain negativity ascribed to society in general, so are communalist desires in part reactions to individualism that arises from the dissolution of communal life. Nativism is about communal ties, whereas individualism focuses on the self that is always departing from a community, and has a vantage point of a disinterested observer of the everyday, in which he by implication does not fully participate. Although the central characters deem nativism reactionary, the overall dynamics in the novels expose it as a modern phenomenon that arises in response to the dissolution of traditional communities and an integration of disparate individuals into nation states. Indeed, as West argues, "stress, drugs, nostalgia for a simple life, conversion to 'born again' religions or fanatical cults, the resurgence of Islam in countries subjected to Westernization, all point to an insufficiency at the heart of individualism". [7] Communalism seeks to address this insufficiency, which is in the novels described more in terms of a wound or even a hole in the place where once heart (soul, spirit) used to be, as Rushdie describes in the case of Aadam Aziz. Communalism seeks to mend some historical wounds and refill the holes through a return to the original common being and communal immanence. In Aadam's case, once he fails to reconnect with his Islamic identity, he seeks cure in the imaginary community that is the nation.

---

[6] *Ibid.*, 325.
[7] West, *Authenticity and Empowerment*, 68.

Given that the desire for individual authenticity informs the many discourses of social life, rights, obligations, laws, and even sacrifice, there is a risky possibility that it remains a form of social estrangement characterized by *angst*, a form of an exile from the world. Such estrangement can lead to a misunderstanding of the fundamental ways of being-in-the-world and self-sufficiency. The ideology of individualism, even if understood as a relative form of self-sufficiency, is a denial of the fact that existence is a matter of sharing. It seems to cultivate such social detachment and becomes a form of bad faith. If we conceive of community as society, we still maintain the opposition between individuals and society, even though the latter is then considered the sum of the individuals that figure in its frameworks. Arguing against the notion of indivisible individual and community-as-society, I have adopted Nancy's concepts "inoperative community" and "singular being". The latter is not an indivisible atom but open to its plurality:

> An inconsequential atomism, individualism tends to forget that the atom is a world. This is why the question of community is so markedly absent from the metaphysics of the subject.[8]

Indeed, as noted in the beginning of Chapter 2, Heidegger and to an extent even Sartre fail to think community.

In the novels we find as much resistance to such atomism as to social orthodoxies. There is still a focus on singularity of characters, but this singularity is articulated through a sharing of finitude, through being-exposed to others, through communication and care. The self is here not the subject that positions itself always in relation to an object, but rather it becomes, as the narrator of *The English Patient* puts it, like echoing sound: *"exciting itself in hollow places."*[9] There seems to be an attempt to articulate singular authenticity by moving from the ideal of self-sustained subjects who act upon the world, even though this drive is present in the novels. Selfhood never stands apart from the world, but is articulated through practical action in the world. The characters' being-in-the-world is indeed coloured by oppressive ideological structures that sustain certain power relations, but it is also a space of freedom, as is most poignantly articulated in Azaro's

---

[8] Nancy, *The Inoperative Community*, 4.
[9] Ondaatje, *The English Patient*, 21 (emphasis in the original).

decision to remain human. This being-free is then dynamic and not a teleological directedness towards some formal freedom that awaits in the future.

While authenticity is about singularity, it is not about individuality that seeks to maintain or accomplish detachment as its necessary condition. Authenticity is about singularity insofar singularity is plural. Azaro's case best illustrates how we could understand this. In the limbo-like place, Azaro receives a third eye. He becomes enlightened. In a sense, it seems as if he finds his true self only in exile from the world, self-sufficient, indivisible and alone. However, he does not stay in this void. His enlightenment means nothing until he re-enters a relation with the human world. When he opts to go back to existence his choice is not guided by his light only. Rather this light also changes. His singularity shows itself only insofar as it becomes plural. There is no contradiction between the idea that beings become in community and that they engage in rethinking and reworking of community. Community is *a priori* insofar as the singulars can only refrain from the illusion of God-like self-sufficiency and the dream of immanence in relation to others through their being exposed.

When Azaro chooses his human parents over heavenly bliss, we could interpret this choice in the way Sartre approaches the example of the man who sees two possible roads, serving his country or returning to his mother.[10] Azaro too is presented with two major options that he feels strongly about. According to Sartre, the choice is singular. No inherited social values, orthodoxies or morals ultimately can or should affect his choice. Azaro's case shows that although the choice is singular it is also plural. The singular (Azaro) makes his choice but not only between the family and heaven. He also chooses against the limbo state of isolation. He makes the choice through openness to his own otherness and the alterity of his parents. What is most important is that the two options are not the same in the end as in the beginning. The parents too change in the process in relation to Azaro. He does not choose a father who beat him but the one who had been transformed into a kneeling man. While Azaro changes through his choice, while he articulates his way of being free through this particular action, his singularity does not remain untouched. It is not a matter of self-producing his individuality, but rather his singularity

---

[10] Sartre, *Existentialism Is a Humanism*, 72.

becomes what it is through his openness to his family. The same holds for their singularities. And yet, the entire process takes place in a shared communal space, through a formation of bonds that do not tie him socially and contractually (whereas the spirit forces him to honour the pacts of the abiku). To use Nancy's words, he "frees freedom for itself, for its finitude, for its sharing, for equality, for community, for fraternity, and for their justice singularity, singularly shared/divided, singularly withdrawn from the hatred of existence".[11]

The novels show us both how difficult it has become to think freedom except as the mode of a singular being, and how hard it is to think community beyond the myth, common being, common work, society and ideology. The most important question seems to be whether it is possible to think singularity in terms of community, and vice versa. Does an authentic community function only insofar each member accepts certain parameters such as "care" and working-for-each-other's-freedom? How does it discriminate against those whom Adorno called the inauthentics? Does communal existence always imply a risk that singular authenticity taken as a communal ideal turns into ideology itself? We have seen how these novels foreground such issues and how they bring to crisis the notions of freedom, authenticity, singularity and community.

One marker of an alternate community could be the lack of requirement from each member to elicit an average response given his or her social role. Another aspect would be that others are not considered a part of all raw materials available for self-making. A third would be to abandon the idea that "hell is other people", that is, the idea that freedom to reject is the only freedom. On a political level of the relationship between citizens and their government, as Berman suggests, there must not be unconditional obedience. One is never justified to give one's government a blank check. At the same time, rejection and negation are crucial for the expression of freedom, but not exclusively so, as we have seen for instance in the example of Kip and Hana, and the insistence on spirituality in Okri's work.

If taken as the opposite of individuality, community-as-society is often understood as tied to a common being, mind, race, motherland, nation or leader. While nation states rely on subjects with rights and obligations, existential freedom requires a much more active

---

[11] Nancy, *The Experience of Freedom*, 141.

participation in the negotiation of responsibility, which is not reduced to coercion and duty. When Okri calls for responsible heirs, he is pushing a view of responsibility that consists in approaching one's heritages creatively. Okri argues that when "a nation or an individual creates things so sublime ... they create always from the vast unknown places within them".[12] He departs from the nationalist discourse on the production of a national substance. In terms of building a work as the basis of community, we have seen Okri's critique in the story of the heavenly road builders, which could be read as a comment on Fanon's belief in the production of a national culture as one step in the liberation from colonialism, especially after the revolutionary struggle. While Okri does not entirely abandon this idea, he offers a cautionary tale in which this work is also a form of un-working, a creative destruction. This project or operation is also inoperative. As Nancy put it, to think or re-work community beyond communitarian models of essence is to thwart "the techno-economical organization or 'making operational' of our world".[13] If community is still "essentially a matter of work, of operation or operativity", then it becomes valuable to rework community in terms of its inoperative-ness, or un-working. The lack of work-in-common excludes communion and appropriation, but gives rise to communication and sharing of the space of community. In the space of community, then, every subject is also exposed to its alterity and its dislocation (rather than a proper place of appropriation).

Ondaatje's villa community evinces the possibility of bonding and sharing across any number of lines, the possibility of coming together on several planes, of intersecting bonds, articulated through migration. It is also an attempt to resist a "hypostasis of community", in that "incompletion is its 'principle,' taking the term 'incompletion' in an active sense, however, as designating not insufficiency or lack, but the activity of sharing".[14] The villa crew does not achieve a common work, a perfect little society (whose completion would also be its annihilation, which is indeed one of the implications from Okri's story about heavenly builders). The political passion in/of a community seems to arise from its opening to its alterity, and thus to freedom, which calls for a responsibility for new ways of bonding, always

---

[12] Okri, *Astonishing the Gods*, 152.
[13] Nancy, *The Inoperative Community*, 22-23.
[14] *Ibid.*, 35.

between the production of a particular work, *oeuvre*, and its unworking, *désoeuvrement*. Incompletion, which implies indeterminacy, does not produce indecision. On the contrary, indeterminacy ultimately calls for decision, choice, agency and a heightened awareness of singular responsibility for the particular actions.

The quick dissolutions of the new forms of community in the novels seem to suggest that communities shaped with singular authenticity in view cannot persist, because any struggle for communal or national life entails an inevitable loss of singularity. Alternate communities – based in a more dynamic, fluid, heterogeneous understanding – form and dissolve. Some even overlap. Each singular participates in, gives form and allegiances to several communities rather than reduce communal bonding to one race, nation, leader, bloodline or class. Participation in multiple communities can elicit growth of both responsibility and common good though neither of these becomes dogmatized within the parameters of traditional alignments. There is value in dissoluble communities. I do not mean unstable or fragmentary communities. To deem a certain community unstable is to pose it against supposedly stable traditional communities, which is an illusion in itself. It is for this reason that the adjective "inoperative" is more suitable to describe alternate ways of thinking community. It is not necessary to argue for some few types of community especially given historical changes that pertain to this social configuration. In the novels, communities are defined, developed and dissolved. Their dissolution is not necessarily negative. Communal bonding that rejects traditional models can indeed develop in ways hard to anticipate because the processes of becoming imply choices and creativity, and also because this creativity takes place in varied social contexts.

Community can be perceived as a resistance to the common substance and immanence, and towards the kind of sharing and caring that leaves community open to its alterity and plurality. Indeed, it is "the immanence of man to man, or it is *man*, taken absolutely, considered as the immanent being par excellence, that constitutes the stumbling block to a thinking of community".[15] The appropriation into communal essence is death. There must be community because, as

---

[15] *Ibid.*, 3 (emphasis in the original).

Nancy puts it, any "fully realized person of individualistic or communistic humanism is the dead person".[16] To be dead here is to be appropriated into the immanent life of the community-as-society, whereas the loss of such immanence and communion in/of death opens community to its alterity, to the impossibility to fully assimilate death. If community is perceived in terms of the will to communion through the power of myth, the interruption of this myth is in the first instance the interruption of community. The loss of communion in respect to a common being gives rise to relation, plural singularity, communication, and sharing.

To the extent that singular beings are always "*being-with*", and "*compearing*" (that is, co-appearing), community as such resists this immanence.[17] It is not something added onto beings, but rather beings become in it. Singularity is only insofar as it is plural. It is based in the sharing of in-essential existence, finitude of being and freedom that makes existence and thinking possible. Bonding is not binding. Habits and rituals are not necessarily inheritable, and the direction taken is always from habituation as the norm, as the process of making certain practices normal, fixed, etc. There is no leader figure, especially not an allegorical one who is supposed to capture in his person the essence of the community, as Saleem tried to do. Once community reiterates itself in terms of a single being, it loses, as Nancy argues, "the *in* of being-*in*-common".[18] In this sense, inoperative community is not the work or creation of "a subjectivity and freedom is not self-sufficiency".[19] It becomes important to stress the "*in*" of "being-*in*-common" as something that does not elicit a common, immanent identity, a union, but rather a shared "lack of identity", which "philosophy calls 'finitude'".[20] At the same time, the thinking of community in terms of common being or essence forecloses the political, which appears so important in Okri's novel. In community, the political does not have to arise from a will to essence or a common identity. Rather the political is the relation to the very lack of a being-in-common. For instance, the political passion in *The Famished Road* arises from that space/time in which community is negotiated.

---

[16] *Ibid.*, 13.

[17] *Ibid.*, 58 (Nancy's italics).

[18] *Ibid.*, xxxix (emphases in the original).

[19] *Ibid.*, 32.

[20] *Ibid.*, xxxviii.

We have seen in relation to *The English Patient* how finitude is shared, and how this sharing reveals that community is finite as well. It is not "a limited community as opposed to an infinite or absolute community, but a community *of* finitude, because finitude 'is' communitarian".[21] Although community is *a priori* to singularity, the point is that there is no hierarchy between singular beings and community. In communitarian models, community is that which is above, the ruling project and operation. In various individualist models, the opposite is held true. Once we no longer think about individuals as social atoms and unwork the operational model of community, we lose the hierarchies, the pure oppositions, we think both singular beings and community as inoperative and exposed like the blasted-open villa from *The English Patient*. The image of walls with holes illustrates, in a sense, an ecstasy of community, which is then defined and redefined in that it reaches out of itself, just as singular beings are defined in such opening of their selves. It is significant that one of the smallest communities, that of lovers, actually starts when Kip meets Hana through a hole in a blasted wall. This image of the damaged insulation shows how community too can potentially be defined in terms of reaching out.

To rethink or rework community does not only mean to refrain from the communalist models, the fascist dream of absolute communion, or even to abandon modern individualism. It is in part to see how community escapes becoming an object or even a subject, and how it tries out our thinking and acting.

---

[21] *Ibid.*, 26 (emphasis in the original).

BIBLIOGRAPHY

WORKS BY BEN OKRI, MICHAEL ONDAATJE AND SALMAN RUSHDIE

Okri, Ben, *An African Elegy*, London: Jonathan Cape, 1992.

—, *Astonishing the Gods*, London: Phoenix, 1995.

—, *The Famished Road* (1991), London: Vintage, 2003.

—, *Infinite Riches*, London: Phoenix, 1998.

—, *Mental Fight: An Anti-Spell for the 21st Century*, London: Phoenix House, 1999.

—, *Songs of Enchantment*, London: Vintage, 1993.

—, *Starbook*, London: Rider, 2007.

—, *A Way of Being Free*, London: Phoenix, 1997.

—, "Interview", International Writers Center, Washington University, St Louis, Missouri, February 1994.

Ondaatje, Michael, *The English Patient*, London: Picador, 1993.

Rushdie, Salman, *The Ground Beneath Her Feet*, London: Vintage, 2000.

—, *Imaginary Homelands*, London: Penguin Books, 1991.

—, *Midnight's Children* (1981), London: Everyman's Library, 1995.

—, *The Moor's Last Sigh*, London: Jonathan Cape, 1995.

—, *The Satanic Verses* (1988), London: Vintage, 1998.

OTHER PRIMARY TEXTS

Achebe, Chinua, *Morning yet on Creation Day: Essays*, London: Heinemann, 1975.

Barnes, Julian, *Flaubert's Parrot*, London: Pan Books, 1985.

Coetzee, J.M., *Disgrace*, London: Penguin Book, 1999.

Conrad, Joseph, *Heart of Darkness*, Boston: Bedford/St Martin's, 1996.

Rousseau, Jean-Jacques, *Emile*, tr. Barbara Foxley, London: Everyman, 1955.

Sartre, Jean-Paul, *Nausea*, tr. Lloyd Alexander, New York: New Directions Books, 2007.

Soyinka, Wole, *Idandre and Other Poems*, London: Methuen, 1967.

SECONDARY TEXTS

Adorno, Theodor W., *The Jargon of Authenticity*, London: Routledge Classics, 2003.

Agamben, Giorgio, *Language and Death: The Place of Negativity*, tr. Karen E. Pinkus and Michael Hardt, Minneapolis: University of Minnesota Press, 1991.

Aizenberg, Edna, "'I Walked with a Zombie': The Pleasures and Perils of Postcolonial Hybridity", *World Literature Today: A Literary Quarterly of the University of Oklahoma*, LXXIII/3 (Summer 1999), 461-66.

Ali, Tariq, "*Midnight's Children*", *New Left Review*, CXXXVI (November-December 1982), 87-95.

Anderson, Benedict, *Imagined Communities: Reflections on the Origin and Spread of Nationalism*, London: Verso, 1983.

Appadurai, Arjun, *Modernity at Large: Cultural Dimensions of Globalization*, Minneapolis: University of Minnesota Press, 1996.

Appiah, Kwame Anthony, *The Ethics of Identity*, Princeton, NJ: Princeton University Press, 2005.

Archer, Margaret S., *Being Human: The Problem of Agency*, Cambridge: Cambridge University Press, 2004.

Arendt, Hannah, *Between Past and Future*, London: Penguin Classics, 2006.

Ashcroft, Bill, Gareth Griffiths and Helen Tiffin, *The Empire Writes Back: Theory and Practice in Post-Colonial Literatures*, London: Routledge, 1989.

Barker, Stephen, ed., *Signs of Change: Premodern→Modern→ Postmodern*, New York: SUNY Press, 1996.

Bardolph, Jacqueline, "Azaro, Saleem and Askar: Brothers in Allegory", *Commonwealth Essays and Studies*, XV/1 (Winter 1993), 45-51.

Bekingsale, Peter, "Studio Ghibli": http://mangalocity.com/studio ghibliarticle.html.

Berlatsky, Erik L., *Fact, Fiction, and Fabrication: History, Narrative, and the Postmodern Real from Woolf to Rushdie*, diss, University of Maryland, 2003.

Berman, Marshall, *The Politics of Authenticity: Radical Individualism and the Emergence of Modern Society*, London: Allen and Unwin, 1971.

Best, Stephen and Douglas Kellner, *Postmodern Theory: Critical Interrogations*, London: Macmillan, 1991.

Bhabha, Homi K., *The Location of Culture*, London: Routledge Classics 2004.

—, "Foreword", in Frantz Fanon, *The Wretched of the Earth*, tr. Richard Philcox, New York: Grove Press, 2004.

—, "Third Space: An Interview with Homi Bhabha", in *Identity: Community, Culture, Difference*, ed. Jonathan Rutherford, London: Lawrence and Wishart, 1990, 207-11.

Blaise, Clark, "A Novel of India's Coming of Age", *New York Times Book Review*, 19 April 1981, 18-19.

Blanchot, Maurice, *The Unavowable Community*, Barrytown, NY: Station Hill Press, 1988.

Booker, M. Keith, ed., *Critical Essays on Salman Rushdie*, New York: G.K. Hall, 1999.

—, "*Midnight's Children*, History, and Complexity: Reading Rushdie after the Cold War", in *Critical Essays on Salman Rushdie*, ed. M. Keith Booker, New York: G.K. Hall, 1999, 283-314.

Brennan, Timothy, *Salman Rushdie and the Third World: Myths of the Nation*, London: Macmillan, 1989.

Brittan, Alice, "War and the Book: The Diarist, the Cryptographer, and *The English Patient*", *PMLA*, CXXI/1 (January 2006), 200-13.

Bush, Catherine, "Michael Ondaatje: An Interview", *Essays on Canadian Writing*, Toronto: ECW Press, 1994, 238-49.

Camus, Albert, *The Myth of Sisyphus*, tr. Justine O'Brien, London: Hamish Hamilton, 1955.

—, *The Outsider*, London: Penguin, 2000.

—, *Selected Essays and Notebooks*, tr. Philip Thody, Harmondsworth: Penguin, 1967.

Campbell, David, "Nietzsche, Heidegger, and Meaning", *Journal of Nietzsche Studies*, XXVI (Autumn 2003), 25-54.

Campbell-Hall, Devon, "Dangerous Artisans: Anarchic Labour in Michael Ondaatje's *The English Patient* and *Anil's Ghost* and Arundhati Roy's *The God of Small Things*", *World Literature Written in English*, XL/1 (Winter 2002-2003), 42-55.

Cezair-Thompson, Margaret, "Beyond the Postcolonial Novel: Ben Okri's *The Famished Road* and Its 'Abiku' Traveller", *The Journal of Commonwealth Literature*, XXXI/2 (January 1996), 33-45.

Chakrabarty, Dipesh, *Habitations of Modernity*, Chicago: The University of Chicago Press, 2002.

—, *Provincializing Europe: Postcolonial Thought and Historical Difference*, Princeton, NJ: Princeton University Press, 2000.

Chakravarty, Sumita S., *National Identity in Indian Popular Cinema 1947-1987*, Austin: University of Texas Press, 1993.

Cheetham, Mark A. and Elizabeth D. Harvey, "Obscure Imaginings: Visual Culture and the Anatomy of Caves", *Journal of Visual Culture*, I/1 (2002), 105-26.

Cheng, Vincent John, *Inauthentic: The Anxiety over Culture and Identity*, New Brunswick, NJ: Rutgers University Press, 2004.

Cook, Rufus, "Being and Representation in Michael Ondaatje's *The English Patient*", *ARIEL: A Review of International English Literature*, XXX/4 (October 1999), 35-49.

Cooper, Brenda, ed., *Magical Realism in West African Fiction: Seeing with a Third Eye*, London: Routledge, 1998.

—, "Out of the Centre of My Forehead, an Eye Opened: Ben Okri's *The Famished Road*", in *Magical Realism in West African Fiction: Seeing with a Third Eye*, ed. Brenda Cooper, London: Routledge, 1998, 67-114.

Corey, Anton, *Selfhood and Authenticity*, Albany, NY: SUNY, 2001.

Cronin, Richard, *Imagining India*, Basingstoke: Macmillan, 1989.

Crowe, Benjamin D., *Heidegger's Religious Origins: Destruction and Authenticity*, Bloomington: Indiana University Press, 2006.

Deandrea, Pietro, *Fertile Crossings: Metamorphoses of Genre in Anglophone West African Literature*, Amsterdam: Rodopi, 2002.

—, "An Interview with Ben Okri", *Africa, America, Asia, Australia*, XVI (1994), 55-82.

de Beauvoir, Simone, *Ethics of Ambiguity*, Sacaucus: Citadel Press, 2000.

de Bruijn, Esther, "Coming to Terms with New Ageist Contamination: Cosmopolitanism in Ben Okri's *The Famished Road*", *Research in African Literatures*, XXVIII/4 (Winter 2007), 170-86.

de Zepetnek, Steven Tötösy, ed., *Comparative Cultural Studies and Michael Ondaatje's Writing*, West Lafayette: Purdue University Press, 2005.

Desai, Anita, "Introduction", in *Midnight's Children*, London: Everyman's Library, 1995, vii-xxi.

Eagleton, Terry, *Ideology: An Introduction*, London: Verso, 1991.

—, *The Meaning of Life*, Oxford: Oxford University Press, 2007.

—, *Sweet Violence: The Idea of the Tragic*, Oxford: Blackwell, 2003.

Edgar, Iain R., *Dreamwork, Anthropology and the Caring Professions*, Aldershot: Avebury, 1995.

Ellis, Susan, "Trade and Power, Money and War: Rethinking Masculinity in Michael Ondaatje's *The English Patient*", *Studies in Canadian Literature/Etudes en littérature canadienne*, XXI/2 (Fall 1996), 22-36.

Fanon, Frantz, *Black Skin, White Masks*, tr. Richard Philcox, New York: Grove Press, 2008.

—, *The Wretched of the Earth*, tr. Richard Philcox, New York: Grove Press, 2004.

Faris, Wendy B., *Ordinary Enchantments: Magical Realism and the Remystification of Narrative*, Nashville: Vanderbilt University Press, 2004.

Ferrara, Alessandro, *Reflective Authenticity: Rethinking the Project of Modernity*, London: Routledge, 2002.

Fledderus, Bill, "'The English Patient Reposed in His Bed Like a [Fisher?] King': Elements of Grail Romance in Ondaatje's *The English Patient*", *Studies in Canadian Literature/Etudes en Littérature Canadienne*, XXII/1 (Spring 1997), 19-54.

Fraser, Robert, *Ben Okri: Towards an Invisible City*, Tavistock: Northcote House, 2002.

Fynsk, Christopher, "Foreword", in Jean-Luc Nancy, *Inoperative Community*, tr. Peter Connor, Minneapolis: University of Minnesota Press, 1991.

Garuba, Harry, "Explorations in Animist Materialism: Notes on Reading/Writing African Literature, Culture, and Society", *Public Culture*, XV/2 (Spring 2003), 261-85.

Gauthier, Tim S., *Narrative Desire and Historical Reparations: A.S. Byatt, Ian McEwan, Salman Rushdie*, London: Routledge, 2006.

Ghomeshi, Jian, *Sir Salman Rushdie on QTV*, 10 June 2008: http://www.cbc.ca/books/MT/2008/06/salman-rushdie-speaks-with-jian-ghomeshi-about-the-surprising-ways-west-mirrors-east-in-his-new-nove.html.

Goldman, Marlene, "'Powerful Joy': Michael Ondaatje's *The English Patient* and Walter Benjamin's Allegorical Way of Seeing", *University of Toronto Quarterly*, LXX/4 (Fall 2001), 902-22.

Golomb, Jacob J., *In Search of Authenticity: Existentialism from Kierkegaard to Camus*, Florence: Routledge, 1995.

Grene, Marjorie, *Dreadful Freedom: A Critique of Existentialism*, Chicago: University of Chicago Press, 1948.

Griffiths, Gareth, "The Myth of Authenticity: Representation, Discourse, and Social Practice", in *De-scribing Empire: Post-colonialism and Textuality*, eds Chris Tiffin and Alan Lawson, London: Routledge, 1994, 70-85.

Hawley, John C., "Ben Okri's Spirit Child: *Abiku* Migration and Post-modernity", *Research in African Literatures*, XXVI/1 (Spring 1995), 30-39.

Heidegger, Martin, *Being and Time – A Translation of Sein und Zeit*, tr. Joan Stambaugh, New York: SUNY Press, 1996.

—, *Pathmarks*, ed. William McNeill, Cambridge: Cambridge University Press, 1998.

—, *Poetry, Language, Thought*, tr. Albert Hofstadter, New York: Harper and Row, 1975.

—, *The Question Concerning Technology*, tr. William Lovitt, New York Harper and Row, 1993.

Hemminger, Bill, "The Way of the Spirit", *Research in African Literatures*, XXXII/1 (Spring 2001), 66-82.

Hilger, Stephanie M., "Ondaatje's *The English Patient* and Rewriting History", in *Comparative Cultural Studies and Michael Ondaatje's Writing*, ed. Steven Tötösy de Zepetnek, West Lafayette: Purdue University Press, 2005, 38-48.

Hillger, Annick, "'And this is the World of Nomads in any Case': The Odyssey as Intertext in Michael Ondaatje's *The English Patient*", *Journal of Commonwealth Literature*, XXXIII/1 (January 1998), 23-33.

Hsu, Hsuan L., "Post-Nationalism and the Cinematic Apparatus in Minghella's Adaptation of Ondaatje's *The English Patient*", in *Comparative Cultural Studies and Michael Ondaatje's Writing*, ed. Steven Tötösy de Zepetnek, West Lafayette, IN: Purdue University Press, 2005, 49-61.

Huggan, Graham, "The Postcolonial Exotic: Salman Rushdie and the Booker of Bookers", *Transition*, LXIV (Autumn 1994), 22-29.

Hume, Kathryn, "Taking a Stand While Lacking a Center: Rushdie's Postmodern Politics", *Philological Quarterly*, LXXIV/2 (Spring 1995), 209-30.

Ibarrola-Armendariz, Aitor, "Boundary Erasing: Postnational Characterization in Michael Ondaatje's *The English Patient*", in *Tricks with a Glass: Writing Ethnicity in Canada*, eds Rocío G. Davis and Rosalía Baena, Amsterdam: Rodopi, 2000.

Ireton, Sean, *An Ontological Study of Death: From Hegel to Heidegger*, Pittsburgh: Duquesne University Press, 2007.

Jackson, Michael, *Existential Anthropology: Events, Exigencies and Effects*, New York: Berghahn Books, 2005.

Jameson, Fredric, *The Political Unconscious: Narrative as a Socially Symbolic Act*, London: Routledge, 1989.

Jollimore, Troy and Sharon Barrios, "Beauty, Evil, and *The English Patient*", *Philosophy and Literature*, XXVIII/1 (April 2004), 23-40.

Jussawalla, Feroza F., *Interviews with Writers of the Post-colonial World*, Jackson: University Press of Mississippi, 1992.

Kane, Jean M., "The Migrant Intellectual and the Body of History: Salman Rushdie's *Midnight's Children*", *Contemporary Literature*, XXXVII/1 (Spring 1996), 94-118.

Kella, Elizabeth, *Beloved Communities: Solidarity and Difference in Fiction by Michael Ondaatje, Toni Morrison, and Joy Kogawa*, Acta Universitatis Upsaliensis, Studia Anglistica Upsaliensia, CX, Uppsala: Uppsala University, 2000.

Khair, Tabish, *Babu Fictions: Alienation in Contemporary Indian English Novels*, Oxford: Oxford University Press, 2001.

Kierkegaard, Søren, *The Concept of Anxiety*, tr. Reider Thomte, Princeton, NJ: Princeton University Press, 1980.

—, *Sickness Unto Death*, London: Penguin Books, 1989.

Kimmich, Matt, *Offspring Fictions: Salman Rushdie's Family Novels*, Amsterdam and New York: Rodopi, 2008.

Lakshmi, Vijay, "Rushdie's Fiction: The World Beyond the Looking Glass", in *Reworlding: The Literature of the Indian Diaspora, Contributions to the Study of World Literature*, 42, ed. Emmanuel S. Nelson, Westport, New York: Greenwood, 1992, 149-55.

Lim, David C.L., *The Infinite Longing for Home: Desire and the Nation in Selected Writings of Ben Okri and K.S. Maniam*, Amsterdam: Rodopi, 2005.

—, "Redreaming the World: Multidimensional Reality in the Selected Novels of Ben Okri", *Southeast Asian Review of English*, XXXIV-XXXV (December 1997), 85-107.

Maja-Pearce, Adewale, "Darkness Visible", in *A Mask Dancing: Nigerian Novelists of the Eighties*, ed. Adewale Maja-Pearce, London: Hans Zell Publishers, 1992, 83-103.

Mann, Michael, *The Sources of Social Power, Vol I*, Cambridge: Cambridge University Press, 1986.

Michau, Michael R., "Fanon and a Radical Phenomenology of Responsibility", in *Department of Philosophy Graduate Student Colloquium*, Purdue University, February 2003.

Mijares, Loretta M., "'You Are an Anglo-Indian?': Eurasians and Hybridity and Cosmopolitanism in Salman Rushdie's *Midnight's Children*", *Journal of Commonwealth Literature*, XXXVIII/2 (April 2003), 125-45.

Mooney, Bel, "Mixing It", *New Internationalist*, 370 (2004): http://www.newint.org/features/2004/08/01/devout-scepticism/.

Muecke, D.C., *Irony*, London: Methuen, 1970.

Mukherjee, Meenakshi, "The Home and the World: The Indian Novel in English in the Global Context", in *Anglistentag 1993 Eichstätt: Proceedings of the Conference of the German Association of University Teachers of English, XV*, eds Günther Blaicher and Brigitte Glaser, Tübingen: Niemeyer, 1994, 140-49.

Nabokov, Vladimir Vladimirovich, *Lectures on Literature*, Harcourt, CA: Brace Jovanovich, 1980.

Nancy, Jean-Luc, *The Creation of the World or Globalization*, tr. François Raffoul and David Pettigrew, New York: SUNY, 2007.

—, *The Experience of Freedom*, tr. Bridget McDonald, Stanford, CA: Stanford University Press, 1993.

—, *The Inoperative Community*, tr. Peter Connor, Minneapolis: University of Minnesota Press, 1991.

—, *Retreating the Political*, Florence: Routledge, 1997.

Nehru, Jawaharlal, "Speech to Bandung Conference Political Committee, 1955": http://www.fordham.edu/halsall/mod/1955 nehru-bandung2.html.

Newell, W.R., "Heidegger on Freedom and Community: Some Political Implications of His Early Thought", *The American Political Science Review*, LXXVIII/3 (September 1984), 775-84.

Nietzsche, Friedrich, *Collected Works: Vol II*, ed. Oscar Levy, London and Edinburgh: T.L. Foulis, 1911.

—, *The Gay Science*, tr. Josefine Nauckhoff and Adrian Del Caro, Cambridge: Cambridge University Press, 2001.

—, *Thus Spake Zarathustra*, tr. Thomas Common, Ware: Wordsworth Classics, 1997.

Novak, Amy, "Textual Hauntings: Narrating History, Memory, and Silence in *The English Patient*", *Studies in the Novel*, XXXVI/2 (Summer 2004), 206-31.

Ogunsanwo, Olatubosun, "Intertextuality and Post-Colonial Literature in Ben Okri's *The Famished Road*", *Research in African Literatures*, XXVI/1 (Spring, 1995), 40-52.

Oliva, Renato, "Re-Dreaming the World: Ben Okri's Shamanic Realism", in *Coterminous Worlds: Magical Realism and Contemporary Post-Colonial Literature in English,* eds Elsa Linguanti, Francesco Casotti and Carmen Concilio, Amsterdam: Rodopi, 1999, 171-96.

Oppenheimer, J. Robert, http://www.youtube.com/watch?v=n8H7Jibx -c0.

Papayanis, Marilyn Adler, *Writing in the Margins: The Ethics of Expatriation from Lawrence to Ondaatje*, Nashville: Vanderbilt University Press, 2005.

Pesch, Josef, "Post-Apocalyptical War Histories: Michael Ondaatje's *The English Patient*", *ARIEL: A Review of International English Literature*, XXVIII/2 (April 1997), 117-39.

Phillips, Maggie, "Ben Okri's River Narratives: *The Famished Road* and *Songs of Enchantment*", *Contemporary African Fiction, Bayreuth African Studies*, XLII, ed. Derek Wright, Bayreuth: Breitinger, 1997, 167-79.

Provencal, Vernon, "Sleeping with Herodotus in *The English Patient*", *Studies in Canadian Literature/Etudes en littérature canadienne*, XXVII/2 (Fall 2002), 140-59.

Quayson, Ato, *Strategic Transformations in Nigerian Writing: Rev Samuel Johnson, Amos Tutuola, Wole Soyinka, Ben Okri*, Bloomington: Indiana University Press, 1997.

—, "Esoteric Webworks as Nervous System: Reading the Fantastic in Ben Okri's Writing", in *Essays on African Writing 2: Contemporary Literature*, ed. Abdulrazak Gurnah, London: Heinemann, 1995, 144-58.

—, "Orality – (Theory) – Textuality: Tutuola, Okri and the Relationship of Literary Practice to Oral Traditions", in *The Pressures of the Text: Orality, Texts and Telling of Tales*, ed. Stuart Brown, Birmingham: University of Birmingham, 1995, 96-117.

—, "Protocols of Representation and the Problems of Constituting an African 'Gnosis': Achebe and Okri", in *Yearbook of English Studies*, 27 (1997), 137-49.

Rao, K.B., "Asia and the Pacific: *Midnight's Children*", in *World Literature Today*, LVI/1 (Winter 1982), 181.

Ricoeur, Paul, *Interpretation Theory: Discourse and the Surplus of Meaning*, Fort Worth: The Texas Christian University Press, 1976.

Rege, Josna E., "Victim into Protagonist? *Midnight's Children* and the Post-Rushdie National Narratives of the Eighties", in *Critical Essays on Salman Rushdie*, ed. M. Keith Booker, New York: G.K. Hall, 1999, 250-82.

Renger, Nicola, "Cartography, Historiography, and Identity in Michael Ondaatje's *The English Patient*", in *Being/s in Transit: Travelling, Migration, Dislocation,* ed. Liselotte Glage, Amsterdam: Rodopi, 2000, 111-24.

Ross, Jean, *Contemporary Authors Interview*, Vol. 138, Detroit: Gale Research, 1993, 337-41.

Rousseau, Jean-Jacques, *The Government of Poland*, tr. Willmoore Kendall, Indianapolis, IN: Hackett, 1985.

Roxborough, David, "The Gospel of Almásy: Christian Mythology in Michael Ondaatje's *The English Patient*", in *Essays on Canadian Writing*, LXVII (Spring 1999), 236-54.

Roy, Anjali, "Post-modern or Post-colonial? Magic Realism in Ben Okri's *The Famished Road*", in *The Post-Colonial Condition of African Literature,* eds Daniel Gover, John Conteh-Morgan and Jane Bryce, Trenton: Africa World Press, 2000, 23-39.

Rutherford, Jonathan, ed., *Identity: Community, Culture, Difference*, London: Lawrence and Wishart, 1990.

Sartre, Jean-Paul, *Being and Nothingness*, tr. Hazel E. Barnes, New York: Citadel Press, 2001.

—, *Critique of Dialectical Reason, I: Theory of Practical Ensembles*, tr. Irene Clephane, London: New Left Books, 1976.

—, *Essays in Existentialism*, Secaucus: Citadel Press, 1993.

—, *Existentialism and Human Emotions*, New York: Philosophical Library, 1957.

—, *Existentialism Is a Humanism*, tr. Carol Macomber, New Haven, CT: Yale University Press, 2007.

—, *The Psychology of Imagination*, tr. Bernard Frechtman, New York: Washington Square Press, 1966.

—, *What Is Literature?* tr. Bernard Frechtman, London: Methuen, 1950.

—, "Introduction", in Frantz Fanon, *The Wretched of the Earth*, tr. Richard Philcox, New York: Grove Press, 2004.

—, "Itinerary of a Thought", *New Left Review* (November-December 1969), 43-66.

Smith, Andrew, "Ben Okri and the Freedom Whose Walls Are Closing in", *Race and Class*, XLVII/1 (July 2005), 1-13.

Smith, Anna, "Dreams of Cultural Violence: Ben Okri and the Politics of the Imagination", *Journal of Postcolonial Writing*, XXXVIII/2 (Winter 2000), 44-54.

Smyrl, Shannon, "The Nation as 'International Bastard': Ethnicity and Language in Michael Ondaatje's *The English Patient*", *Studies in Canadian Literature/Etudes en littérature canadienne*, XXVIII/2 (Fall 2003), 9-38.

Simpson, Mark D., "Minefield Readings: The Postcolonial English Patient", *Essays on Canadian Writing*, LIII (Summer 1994), 216-37.

Spencer, Lloyd, "Allegory in the World of Commodity: The Importance of *Central Park*", *New German Critique*, XXXIV (Spring-Summer 1985), 59-77.

Srivastava, Aruna, "'The Empire Writes Back': Language and History in *Shame* and *Midnight's Children*", in *Past the Last Post: Theorizing Post-Colonialism and Post-Modernism*, eds Ian Adam and Helen Tiffin, Calgary: University of Calgary Press, 1990, 65-78.

Su, Jung, "Saleem's Quest for Origin: Authenticity and Nation in *Midnight's Children*", *Proc. Natl. Sci. Counc. ROC(C)*, X/1 (January 2000), 60-78.

Suri, Sanjay, "Rushdie Appears on British TV", *India Abroad*, 5 October 1990, 26.

Storm, Heter, T., *Sartre's Ethics of Engagement: Authenticity and Civic Virtue*, London: Continuum, 2006.

Taylor, Charles, *The Ethics of Authenticity*, Cambridge, MA: Harvard University Press, 1992.

West, David, *Authenticity and Empowerment: A Theory of Liberation*, London: Harvester Wheatsheaf, 1989.

Wright, Derek, ed., *Contemporary African Fiction, Bayreuth African Studies*, 42, Bayreuth: Breitinger, 1997,

—, "Pre- and Post-Modernity in Recent West African Fiction", *Commonwealth* XXI/2 (Spring 1999), 5-17.

—, "Whither Nigerian Fiction? Into the Nineties", *The Journal of Modern African Studies*, XXXIII/2 (June 1995), 315-332.

ten Kortenaar, Neil, *Self, Nation, Text in Salman Rushdie's* Midnight's Children, Montreal: McGill-Queen's University Press, 2004.

Tew, Philip and Rod Mengham, *British Fiction Today*, London: Continuum, 2006.

Ty, Eleanor, "The Other Questioned: Exoticism and Displacement in Michael Ondaatje's *The English Patient*", *International Fiction Review*, XXVII/1-2 (2000), 10-19.

Wilkinson, Jane, *Talking with African Writers: Interviews with African Poets, Playwrights and Novelists*, London: James Currey, 1992.

Young, Robert, *White Mythologies*, London and New York: Routledge, 2004.

Žižek, Slavoj, *On Belief*, London: Routledge, 2001.